RENEWALS 458-4574
DATE DUE

GAYLORD			PRINTED IN U.S.A.

SHAMANISM AND THE ORIGIN OF STATES
Spirit, Power, and Gender in East Asia

SARAH MILLEDGE NELSON

Left Coast
Press Inc.

Walnut Creek, California

LEFT COAST PRESS, INC.
1630 North Main Street, #400
Walnut Creek, CA 94596
http://www.LCoastPress.com

Copyright © 2008 by Left Coast Press, Inc.

ISBN 978-1-59874-132-2 hardcover
ISBN 978-1-59874-133-9 paperback

Library of Congress Cataloguing-in-Publication Data:

Nelson, Sarah M., 1931–
    Shamanism and the origin of states : spirit, power, and gender in East Asia / Sarah Milledge Nelson.
        p. cm.
    Includes bibliographical references and index.
    ISBN 978-1-59874-132-2 (hardback : alk. paper) —
    ISBN 978-1-59874-133-9 (pbk. : alk. paper)
    1. Shamanism—East Asia. 2. Mythology, Asian. 3. East Asia—Religious life and customs. 4. Religion and state—East Asia. 5. Sex role—East Asia. I. Title.
BL2370.S5N45 2008
201'.44095—dc22   2008019852

Printed in the United States of America

The paper used in this publication meets the minimum requirements of American National Standard for Information Sciences—Permanence of Paper for Printed Library Materials, ANSI/NISO Z39.48–1992.

08 09 10 11 12   5 4 3 2 1

For Hal, with love

CONTENTS

LIST OF FIGURES

PREFACE AND
ACKNOWLEDGMENTS

I
N A WAY, this book began in 1970 and 1971 when I lived in Korea to conduct research for my dissertation. Much help came from senior archaeologists Kim Won-yong and Sohn Pow-key, as well as Im Hyo-jai, Choe Mong-lyong, and many others. In addition to surveying for archaeological sites along the Han River with my Korean colleagues and many of my international friends, I taught at the University of Maryland, Far East Division. I was fascinated with the *mudangs,* the women shamans of Korea, who are more politely called *manshin,* meaning "ten thousand spirits." At least once a term, whenever I could justify it, I would take my classes on a shaman expedition.

The shrine for these shamans was just outside the city walls, in an area of traditional one-story houses with tiled roofs. The students and I had to scale the wall and pick our way through the narrow streets. The hilltop above the shrine is graced with an oddly shaped pair of boulders that resemble humans wrapped in cloaks. A bit below the eroded boulders, a flat slab of granite provided a place to sit with a view into the shrine—a perfect place for the class to watch the ritual taking place in the *manshins'* traditional house. Sometimes we would be invited in, and one of the students might even be commanded to wrap in a colorful robe and dance at the end of the ritual. One of the male students especially amused the *manshin* with his dancing. Thus my interest in East Asian shamans goes back more than thirty years. But at that time, I couldn't find a way to study shamans in the Neolithic past. My dissertation concerned subsistence and settlement.

I returned to Korea in 1978, when I was invited to be an Inter-port Lecturer for semester-at-sea; in 1983 for a month thanks to the Academy of Korean Studies; and in 1986, when I was funded by the Korean Cultural Society. I visited Korea again in 1987, when I attended the Pacific Science Congress; in 1989, to lead an Earthwatch Project in Korea; and in 1990, when I stopped in Seoul on my way to the Indo-Pacific Prehistory Association meeting in Indonesia, with funding from the University of Denver. On each trip, I collected material for *The Archaeology of Korea,* and pondered possible connections between the archaeological past and current shamanism. On these trips, I attended shamanic rituals, called *kut,* and especially noted their material culture. What would archaeologists find if shamanism existed in the Neolithic? In the Bronze Age?

The Korean archaeologists who offered their time and expertise to me are too many to name. In addition to those mentioned elsewhere in this preface, they include Lee In-sook, Choe Chong-pil, Kang Bong-won, Lee Yong-jo, Bae Ki-dong, Yi Sonbok, Gyoung-Ah Lee, and Martin Bale.

As I pursued the Neolithic in Korea, I continued to wonder if it held any suggestion of ancient shamans. There were a few signs—a shell mask, a tiny female torso, bone objects with designs on them. But these were hardly enough to write a paper about. Many years later, I wrote a novel, *Spirit Bird Journey,* about the Korean Neolithic, in which an adopted Korean learns about the archaeology and dreams the prehistoric past of the site she is digging. This novel was an exercise in imagining the past from the fragments left in several ancient sites, as well as the story of a woman leader and shaman.

I led student tours of archaeological sites in China in 1981, 1982, and 1985, but my research in northeastern China really began when the northeast provinces of China, called the Dongbei, had just been opened for tourism to Americans. These trips were interfingered with visits to Korea. I began with an exploratory trip to Liaoning, Jilin, and Heilongjiang provinces in the summer of 1987. The draw for me was that sites in this region are related to sites in Korea, and I wanted to know about the region in more detail. On this first exploration, I was accompanied by a graduate student, Ardith Hunter, and our skilled interpreter, Ming Ming Shan. Ming

Ming ultimately earned a masters' degree from the University of Denver, and became a lifelong friend. Sun Shuodao and Guo Dashun were our guides. Ardith and I were the first foreigners allowed to see the Goddess Temple site, which is part of Locality 1 at Niuheliang. The site amazed us with its unexpected riches—the life-sized statues including the face of the "goddess," the finely carved jades, the unusual decorated building. The large mounded tombs nearby were another major find.

In 1988 I was funded by the Committee on Scholarly Communication with the People's Republic of China to spend six weeks exploring archaeological sites in the Dongbei. This time Guo Dashun and other members of the Liaoning province Archaeological Research Institute took me back to Niuheliang and to other sites in Liaoning. One of the important Neolithic sites is Houwa, very close to North Korea. Houwa has two levels, both of which have strange small heads, perforated so they could be strung on a cord. These heads could be interpreted as fetishes related to shamanism. The Chahai site near Fuxin also has ritual features. Besides, the pottery from both sites and others that I visited belonged to the same general styles as Neolithic pottery from Korea. We stayed in Dandong long enough for me to watch some North Korean television, and I looked longingly at the bridge over the Yalu (Amnok) River, which I was not allowed to cross.

Jiang Peng from the Jilin Archaeological Research Institute accompanied me in Jilin province, with Ming Ming as an invaluable aid all the way. Getting to the sites was particularly adventuresome, as there was no provision for foreign travelers. Among other places, we went to Jian, a former capital of the Goguryeo kingdom; to Changbaishan, where once again we could see into North Korea across the Heavenly Lake of Chonji; and to Yanji, the capital of Yanbian, the Korean Autonomous Region. On this trip I realized how rich the archaeology of this region was, and how little it was known outside of China. I approached the archaeologists from the three provinces of the Dongbei about writing chapters for a book on Dongbei archaeology to be translated into English. They were pleased to do it. Translations were accomplished by students Ming Ming Shan, Ke Peng, and me.

Several more trips to China included important meetings, where I met scholars interested in the Dongbei from as far away as Novosibirsk, Russia, and parts of Japan. The Circum-Bohai conferences were particularly useful to me. I attended meetings in Dalian, Shijiazhuang, and Chifeng. Other meetings included one organized by Emma Bunker in Hohhot, Inner Mongolia. In 1994 I was funded to attend a conference in Vladivostok, and I was able to spend a couple of weeks visiting sites in Dongbei on the way. Inner

Mongolian archaeologists drove me by jeep down dry river beds all around the Chifeng region, as well as to the Lower Xiajiadian site of Dadianzi, and many museums. I briefly returned to Harbin, then flew to Khabarovsk on the Amur River. Transportation was difficult in Russia in those days, but I finally caught a plane to Vladivostok, where I made many Russian friends with similar interests, including Irina Zhuschchikovskaya, Yuri Vostretsov, David Brodianski, and Yaroslav Kuzmin.

About 1990, Geoffrey Read of the World Bank contacted me to inquire about archaeological sites in the Dongbei, which the Bank might consider to fund for stabilization in the context of cleaning up air and water pollution in Liaoning. I suggested some sites, including Niuheliang. The whole project, however, was given to a British company, which chose Gina Barnes to report on it for them. She became interested in the site. As a result, she and I proposed joint research at Niuheliang, along with Yangjin Pak. Although we both found funding, a permit to survey from the Chinese Academy of Social Sciences was not forthcoming, and Gina withdrew from the project. Yangjin and I decided to keep trying and, with the aid of Hungjen Niu, we finally received a permit in 2005—ironically just as our other funding ran out.

A meeting about archaeology of the Central Asian steppes, and especially horse domestication, allowed me to visit sites in Kazakhstan with a bevy of archaeologists, including some who had worked with Okladnikov in the Russian Far East. I thank David Anthony and Dory Brown for this opportunity. I attended several meetings on Eurasian archaeology, subsequently widening my understanding of East Asian archaeology and its connections with surrounding cultures.

In 1994, after I had made many trips to study Niuheliang, I wrote another novel, *Jade Dragon*, inviting Clara, my imaginary Korean adoptee, for an adventure in Chinese archaeology. This time Clara dreams the past of a shaman named Jade, who lives her life in the Hongshan culture and travels to other places in the four directions.

Archaeoastronomy is another exploration represented in *Jade Dragon*. This idea comes from Robert Stencel, a University of Denver astronomer who taught a class with me on this topic, and at his urging we used the Hongshan culture, specifically Niuheliang (NHL) for data for the students to process. With Chris Rock, who went with me on an expedition to NHL in 2000, we made a CD of the site, including maps and measurements of all sixteen of the localities. Bob Stencel and I used the CDs with subsequent honors classes. The last one we taught produced interesting data, and a paper authored by myself, Rachel Matson, Rachel Roberts, Chris Rock, and Robert Stencel is currently under review.

Anne Martin-Montgomery, a graduate student at the University of Pennsylvania, collected data on the NHL site as a ritual landscape in 2000. In 2002, Charlotte Bell, with the help of Tiffany Tchakarides, conducted a ground-penetrating radar survey at Locality 2. They found possible buildings in an open area above the Goddess Temple.

The last trip to NHL included (briefly) Gwen Bennett, Josh Wright, and Yangjin Pak. Sadly we planned more research that was never funded. Sara Gale, a graduate student from the University of Denver, accompanied me to Anyang, where we were hosted by Zhi-zheng Jing, as well as Niuheliang.

Over the years, many conversations with Guo Dashun at the site, as well as my co-workers Yangjin Pak and Hungjen Niu, ranged widely over possible interpretations of this site—it is obviously a ritual area, but it is not obvious what kind of rituals might have occurred. At the time I wrote the novels, it seemed impossible to write an academic book about either shamans or gender. Now, however, new ways of thinking about archaeology (and shamanism) have made this book possible. Gender is now taken seriously as a publishable topic, and ideology has also come out from under its cloud. The length of the bibliography gives some sense of how many ideas I borrowed for this book.

Seven trips to Japan allowed me to visit sites and museums from Kyushu to Hokkaido, although I never had the opportunity to dig these sites.

I had assistance in writing the book as well. I want to thank Allison Rexroth for reading my handwriting and entering many changes in the manuscript. Caitlin Lewis did a heroic job of organizing the figures as well as being my graduate teaching assistant. Students in my seminar "Shamans in East Asian Archaeology" at the University of Denver deserve my thanks for reading the almost-finished manuscript and offering candid suggestions for making it more student-friendly. I acknowledge with gratitude the critiques of Doug Baer, Whitney Fulton, Joy Klee, Liz Meals, Meghan O'Halloran, Jenae Pitts, Alec Ropes, and Qiyang Zhang. Scholars also read all or part of the manuscript when it was in the writing stage. My thanks to Fumiko Ikawa-Smith, Laurel Kendall, Katheryn Linduff, and Robert Stencel for saving me from errors, although I would not make them responsible for any that remain. Thanks to my husband Hal for being patient while I wrote the book, which took about a year longer than I planned, and for turning old slides into black-and-white figures.

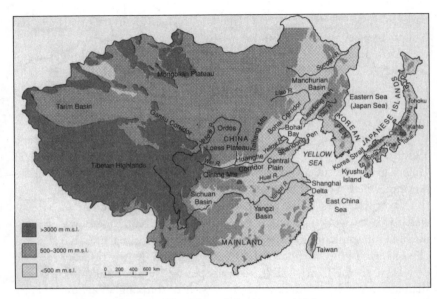

Figure 1.1 The geography of East Asia. After Barnes 1993

ONE

ORIENTATION TO SHAMANISM AND THE ORIGIN OF STATES
Spirit, Power, and Gender in East Asia

Shamanism is a traditional, religious phenomenon tied closely to nature and the surrounding world, in which a practitioner endowed with the special ability to enter a state of trance-possession can communicate with supernatural beings. This transcendental power allows the practitioner, the shaman, to satisfy human cravings for explanation, understanding, and prophecy.

—Tae-gon Kim 1998:19

THIS CHAPTER is called "orientation" as a play on words, but also to remind readers that the notion of a place called "the Orient" was a European concept that made exotic others of all people from the

Levant and Egypt to Japan (Said 1978). The concepts of "Near East," Middle East," and "Far East" are likewise European terms. Thus I use geographic terms in this book—"East Asia" describes the part of the continent of Asia that is on its easternmost side. This chapter is thus an orientation (a way to find one's place) to the topic of shamans in East Asia—China, Korea, Japan, and parts of the Russian Far East. As a region, East Asia is diverse, but coherent because of two powerful influences: the writing system of China (and the Confucian influence it carried) and the shamanism of the regions north of China.

In East Asia, ideology seems to have been particularly important in the formation of state-level polities. Several archaeologists who work in China have postulated that the early ideology/religion of East Asia was shamanism because various features of archaeological discoveries—especially burials and art objects—suggest shamanic rituals. Other archaeologists and historians are not convinced, seeing patrilineal clans and ancestor worship as creating the political and social ties that kept the state functioning. Among Korean archaeologists, the shamanic nature of early states is taken for granted. Likewise, in Japan figurines can be described as depicting shamans without fear of contradiction. Perhaps this difference stems from the fact that shamanism still exists in Korea and Japan (especially Okinawa), but other factors were at play, to be delved into in later chapters.

The topic of shamanism in early states provides an avenue into the larger question of the role of ideology as a factor in state formation. The nature of the patterns in the archaeological sites that are attributed to shamanism brings up other topics as well, which turn out to be inextricably interlinked. Since, in the present, most practicing shamans are women, the question of gender asserts itself. And because the shamanism of Korea and Japan is often linked to that of Siberia (through northeastern China), questions of continuity of practice as well as variations in practice require a close look at East Asia as a whole. When I began to think about organizing this topic, I kept visualizing the traditional decorative knots of Korea, called *maedup*. To understand its parts each strand has to be followed, but to understand the whole and appreciate the pattern, it must be knotted again.

To explore these interlinked problems, a broad swath through regions and times is the best approach to the question of shamanism and state formation. The questions of whether shamanism was prevalent at the formation of early states in East Asia, and if so, whether shamans became political as well as religious leaders, are only a beginning. In thinking about state origins we must consider *how* shamans might have become leaders, as well as *whether* they did.

The processes of state formation were not identical in the regions where the nation-states of China, Korea, and Japan are found. Related states formed in the Russian Far East (Table 1.1). Archaeological evidence forms the basis for this observation, but many relevant texts are also consulted in spite of disagreements among historians about when they were written and what axes their authors may have to grind. Art history, too, contributes to the understanding of states in East Asia, considering the meanings of prevalent symbols. Thus East Asian archaeology, mythology, ethnography, art, and texts provide a rich context to probe the notion of shamanism as contributing to state formation. Each of these approaches to the past has limitations, but adds a valuable dimension for the whole. Although archaeology is the emphasis in this book, more than mere description of sites and artifacts is needed, since relevant facts are subject to theoretical perspectives (Wylie 2002). The question of epistemology—how we know what we know—is never far from the foreground of this exploration.

Ideology as an explanatory factor in state formation has not been popular in wider archaeological circles for several reasons. For one, archaeologists have entertained a number of theories about the development of leadership and the purposes of leadership, and these theoretical positions do not necessarily leave room for shamanism. Another stumbling block may be that studies of current East Asian shamans show that they are preponderantly female. Just as shamanism has been proclaimed as incompatible with leadership in state level societies, so leadership is often said so be a male prerogative. Did shamans change genders, or could ancient leadership have been female?

What Is Shamanism?

The varieties of shamanism found in Siberia tend to be used as a touchstone for shamanism because of the emphasis in Eliade's (1964) *Shamanism, Archaic Techniques of Ecstasy*. However, shamans of ancient East Asia, as described in texts and interpreted in archaeological sites, are both like and unlike Siberian shamans of the past and present. Those who study shamanism in the present have documented the varied beliefs, rituals, and artifacts of shamanism according to time and place. Nicholas Thomas and Caroline Humphrey (1994:2) note that not all shamanisms are equal in terms of scholarship: "the

Table 1.1

BCE	China	Korea	Japan	Russian Far East
16,000	Late Paleolithic	Late Paleolithic	Incipient Jomon	Late Paleolithic
10,000	Early pottery	Mesolithic	Initial Jomon	Early Pottery
8,000	Xinglongwa, et al.	Early Chulmun	Earliest Jomon	
6,000	Yangshao, et al.	Middle Chulmun	Early Jomon	
4,000	Longshan, Honghsan et al.	Late Chulmun	Middle Jomon	Boismanskaya
2,000	Erlitou/ Xia Dynasty	Mumun	Late Jomon	Zaisanovskaya
1,500	Shang Dynasty	Early Bronze Age		
1,000	Zhou Dynasty		Early Yayoi/ Final Jomon	Yankovskaya
200	Han Dynasty	Lelang/ Samhan	Middle Yayoi	Ilou
CE				
100	Later Han	Iron Age Goguryeo	Late Yayoi	
300	Three kingdoms, Six dynasties	Silla, Kaya, Baekje (Paekche)	Kofun	
600	Tang	United Silla	Heian	

magnetism of shamanism ... has made some forms of shamanism peculiarly attractive as objects of scholarship, and has made others appear derivative, impure, or secondary." Everyone wants to study what they believe are the real, original shamans. But "pure" shamanism never existed. It is an anachronistic mistake to freeze an imagined shamanic past as "real" shamanism, and compare everything else to it. Scholars of current shamans often refer to shamanisms—plural.

But shamanisms must have shared elements to be able to discuss them at all. Current varieties of East Asian shamanism have in common the belief in spirits who are able to affect human lives, the ability of some special humans to reach the spirits, and, importantly, the belief that propitiating the spirits can change the course of events. The relationship between spirits and their human counterparts is the constant that underlies the considerable differences among forms of East Asian shamanism.

Who Were the *Wu*?

China scholars are mostly in agreement that practitioners called *wu* in ancient China are considered shamans, in the sense of dancing, trancing, divining, and presumably contacting spirits (Chang 1983, 1994a, 1994b, 2005; Childs-Johnson 1988, 1989, 1995, 1998; but see also Falkenhausen 1995 and Keightley 1998, who prefer to use the term "spirit medium" to translate *wu*). The character for *wu* is found on oracle bones of the Shang dynasty, about 1500 BCE, and the character was engraved on the hat of a figurine from Shandong (Liu 2003). Thus, *wu* is known to be an ancient concept, although shifts in precise meanings of the character *wu* surely occurred through time and within different regions (Tong 2002).

Wu could be applied to both male and female shamans, but sometimes a different term was used for male shamans, according to ancient Chinese texts. This suggests that the first shamans were women, since the unmarked member of the pair is female. However, the notion that leadership is gendered male is deeply entrenched in both Chinese and Western cultures, and this notion is not easily shaken (Nelson 2002b). I suspect that the gender balance of shamanism is another reason that shamanism has been seen as incompatible with leadership in state-level society. One may infer the dismissal of female leaders in archaeological discourse stems from the fact that the literature on state formation takes little notice of female leaders, although they widely existed (Arwill-Nordbladh 2003; Bell 2003; Davis-Kimball 2003; Gailey 1987; Linduff 2003; Linnekin 1990; McCafferty and McCafferty 2003; Muller 1987; Nelson 2003b; Piggott 1997, 1999; Silverblatt 1988; Trocolli 2002; Troy 2003; Vogel 2003).

Because the Chinese had a word for these practitioners—*wu*—and because the same word appears as a loanword in Korean (*mu* in modern Korean), I will sometimes use those specific terms to apply to the shamans of ancient China and Korea. Other designations used for shamans in East Asia are *miko* in Japanese, and *yuta* in Okinawan. The word shaman is often applied to these female practitioners but shamanisms in these regions are not identical—and the differences among them are instructive. They will be described later in the book.

State Formation

The hypothesis of this book is that the rituals and beliefs of shamans provided an important building block for the formation of states in ancient East Asia, and that shamans themselves could become leaders. Archaeological discoveries and texts provide evidence that shamans, both women and men, could be successful leaders of complex societies in East Asia. Their access to the spirit world provided the right to leadership. Their ability to lead, and the knowledge accrued as ritual leaders, led to the development of long-distance trade and craft specialization because the resulting artifacts were used in the service of evolving rituals.

While it would be difficult to deny altogether the presence of shamanism in East Asia, whether shamans themselves became leaders, or the elite used shamanism for their own ends, or whether shamans had any role in state formation are contested. Skepticism is difficult to confront because studies of state formation in ancient East Asia are not in agreement about how leaders arose or even how leaders led. However, widespread shamanism is seen in the fact that native words for shamans persist in each of the languages spoken in East Asia, in addition to Chinese loanwords that are used alongside native words in Japanese and Korean. The native words were present at least as far back as the time of state formation and are a reminder that shamans were active when secondary states arose in East Asia. Forms of both charismatic and institutionalized power were present in the Shang dynasty, as attested by oracle bone evidence and archaeology. Although not everyone agrees that rulers were shamans, there is no disagreement that the Shang people believed in a variety of spirits and powers (e.g., Keightley 2000). Some of the Warring States of the Eastern Zhou period almost a thousand years later are known for the prevalence of shamans. It is probably less known that shamanic beliefs helped to shape the state in Korea and Japan, and the details in those instances shed light on the general principles through which shamanism could generate state-level polities. In the peninsular and island societies, shamanism was either not gendered or gendered female, and it is possible to glimpse societies with gender parity and female rulers at the time of state formation (e.g., Nelson 1991b, 1993b, 2002b; Piggott 1997, 1999).

The first states in East Asia occurred in China, between 2000 and 1000 before the Common Era (BCE). The question of shamanism in the formation of the Shang state and its predecessors in the Neolithic has received attention from a number of archaeologists over the past few decades, both in the anthropological archaeology of Anglophone studies and the more historically and text-grounded archaeology largely practiced in East Asia. By gathering this data for students and the interested public, as well as archaeologists without access to primary East Asian sources, I apply the question of whether shamans became leaders to the whole gamut of the archaeology of East Asia. Even if shaman leaders were important, it is not likely that shamanism alone was sufficient to create complex societies. Rather, older forms of shamanism were adapted to fit new circumstances. One of the new circumstances was increasing population density filling in the East Asian landscape. Another was the presence of various ethnic groups in this increasingly crowded landscape, which created a cultural mosaic in which the hegemonic group varied through time. The ethnic groups bumped up against one another, both adopting and resisting parts of neighboring cultures. Developing elites may have intermarried, thus blurring ethnic divisions. These interactions surely refined the local versions of shamanisms and allowed them to develop wider constituencies and meld with other ideologies.

While some claims of shamanism in both texts and material culture are more reasonable than others, discovering which forms are "real" shamanism is not the aim. Whether or not some claims for shamanism in the ancient past may be overenthusiastic, there is no question that shamanisms have existed across East Asia—and still do exist in many regions. How and why shamans were able to gather the various resources necessary to form incipient states and to govern them effectively are the central questions. The ability to claim these resources was grounded in belief in differential access to spiritual power and, reciprocally, access to resources verified access to spiritual power.

This approach to shamanism in ancient East Asia brings two new dimensions to the discussion of shamanism and state formation. By including all of East Asia, the context of the debate about shamans in China is extended; and by expanding the time period under consideration to include the formation of states in Korea and Japan in the first centuries of the Common Era, the breadth and depth of shamanism and state formation in East Asia can be appreciated. In addition, using texts and archaeology together to analyze ancient shamanism, enriched by ethnographic descriptions of more recent shamanism, a convincing whole is created which allows appreciation of the broad picture without sacrificing the variability that characterizes East Asian shamanism.

Archaeology

Archaeological discoveries suggest that shamanism was an important force in early East Asia, perhaps as early as the Paleolithic, but certainly no later than Neolithic times. With so much archaeological activity in China in recent years, the Holocene archaeology with purported shamanistic activity and beliefs is more compelling and more varied in the (much larger) landmass that is now China than it is in Korea and Japan, but the excavations, while not uniform in either time or space, suggest widespread common beliefs and related rituals. These discoveries cannot be easily summarized—in fact, they contribute to the impression of a cultural mosaic, a mosaic made of repeating and similar hues. The metaphor of a decorative knot, like the Korean *maedup,* is also useful.

Although several archaeologists have suggested that the Shang state of ancient China was ruled by a shaman king, the Shang polity is not alone in having a ruler who is said to have been the chief shaman. Another notable example is the Silla state of the Korean Three Kingdoms period, situated on the southeastern part of the Korean peninsula (Kim Won-yong 1983, 1986; Nelson 1991b). The Yayoi period of southwestern Japan is similarly said to be shamanistic (Mizoguchi 2002), and ceremonies dating back at least to the Kofun period for the accession of Japanese kings have shamanic elements as well (Ellwood 1973). These assertions are based largely on texts, although figurines from archaeological sites provide visual evidence. An anthropological perspective is helpful to evaluate the claims for shamanism in early East Asia.

Dragons, jades, and altars to heaven and earth provide some of the data to be discussed in later chapters. Archaeology suggests some shamanistic interpretations, but the skeptical are rarely convinced because alternative explanations are almost always possible to entertain. Archaeological interpretations are usually underdetermined. However, the temporal and territorial distribution of shamanism in East Asia presses consideration of shamanism as a reasonable possibility. The persistence of shamanism beyond the formation of the states in the Korean peninsula and the Japanese islands is particularly relevant. By including early Korea and Japan in the discussion I show that leadership in state-level societies is compatible with East Asian shamanism and, further, that shamanism was instrumental in forming those states.

Texts

The major Chinese texts related to shamanism have been examined and discussed by those who command both the languages and the records of ancient East Asia. One of the clearest texts in regard to shamanism is a passage from the *Chu-yū*, which is quoted at the beginning of chapter 3. This passage from a document believed to date from the fourth century BCE is one foundation upon which the understanding of shamanism in ancient China is erected. Julia Ching (1997:14–15) and K. C. Chang (1983:44) both use this text to introduce their rather different discussions of ideology in early China. Chang believes that shamanism was the domain of the king in the Late Shang state. Ching refers to mysticism and kingship, looking for spirituality in general rather than the specificity of a shaman who brings down the spirits. The texts obviously allow for multiple interpretations. However, some particulars are not in dispute. The cited text clearly states that *wu* and *xi* were women and men, respectively, and that they had access to the spirits who dwelt above. The spirits would descend upon these persons because of their many virtues. Thus it is clear that women could be shamans as well as men, and women are widely known to be shamans in ethnographic contexts (Tedlock 2005).

Organization of the Book

Chapter 2, "Landscapes, Legends, and Skyscapes," begins with the environments in which the East Asian polities formed. Myths and legends figure in current discussions of the past and are needed to understand debates about interpretations of early prehistory/history. Earth and sky were equally important in early East Asia, and they were believed to interact. The landscape of East Asia is varied in elevation and climate, and the climate changed dramatically through time. East Asian cultural similarities and differences cannot be explained entirely by the landscape. The sky, on the other hand, was common to all. It is clear that the sky was closely studied as early as the third millennium BCE—and quite likely much earlier. The relationship between earth and sky is particularly important in early beliefs in East Asia. Not only could omens for humans be read in the movements of the sky, but events on earth were believed to influence the sky as well.

Chapter 3 explores the question, what is a shaman? Shamanism takes a variety of forms in East Asia, even into the present, but the fundamental concept of spirits who can influence earthly life and who can be contacted and even manipulated by chosen persons is ubiquitous. This concept formed a basis for shamans' claims to rulership. The ability of leaders to contact those spirits and influence them guaranteed the compliance of the populace.

Although the debate about exactly when and where shaman leaders in ancient East Asia arose depends on the interpretation of disputed archaeological and textual evidence. The negative side is strengthened by reigning archaeological theory. The very definition of state-level society has included religions dominated by priests and a written canon, suggesting that ecstatic practitioners who had direct access to the spirits belonged to "lower" levels of sociocultural evolution (Flannery 1972). In ethnology, too, shamanism is often seen as antithetical to the state, coexisting uneasily within state mechanisms, although the existence of shamans within current states is undeniable (Thomas and Humphrey 1994). When shamanism is seen as a characteristic of ancient and modern hunter-gatherers (Eliade 1964), shamanism and state leadership are constructed as a contradiction in terms. How could rulers of states be shamans?

Some of the disagreements about whether leaders were shamans in East Asian states may be resolved by considering ethnographic definitions of shamanism. It is pertinent to decide whether shamanism should be strictly defined by Siberian characteristics, or whether a looser definition, such as the presence of trance or ecstatic religion, is permissible. Still less stringent would be an interpretation of shamanism as a cultural belief in spirits and individuals within the culture with the rare ability to contact them. Thus, both ethnographic and archaeological uses of the term "shamanism" are explored in chapter 3, helping to chart a path through the textual and archaeological data.

The question of the development of leadership and the origin of states is taken up in chapter 4. Shamans are consistently described as leaders in less complex societies, and a common understanding is that they are "knowledgeable." The existence of leadership may be obvious, but the paths to leadership, and the ways that archaeology and texts can illuminate those paths, are not obvious and need to be teased out. The question becomes, do any manifestations of power make a compelling case for shamans as leaders and shamanic practices as a means to power? And were the shamans always male? Gender requires its own discussion in the context of leadership because of the subtle and not-so-subtle assumptions that have been made about the gender of shaman leaders.

While the Chinese word for shaman in general is the same as that for women shamans and a special word differentiates males, many Asian archaeologists see shamanism as a male preserve. I suggest that Confucian precepts—which insist that woman's place is secondary, not as a leader— have distorted the understanding of early East Asian cultures, and that we need to examine the archaeology and textual evidence without the weight of the opinions of later ages.

In chapter 5 the archaeological evidence for shamanism in the East Asian Neolithic is presented. The Neolithic in China is rich in burials and other archaeological data that suggest a belief in the existence of ancestral spirits and powers—and of leaders who were believed to be able to reach and influence these powers (Keightley 2000). To many Chinese archaeologists and some of their Western counterparts, the Neolithic data provide excellent reasons to believe that shamanism had a long history in China before the rise of the Shang kingdom. New discoveries have been advanced as examples of early shamanism, ranging from possible astronomical landscapes and a burial flanked by dragon and tiger mosaics to the use of drums, wine, and unusual clothing. These discoveries, individually and collectively, have suggested shamanism to a number of researchers of Neolithic China.

Shamanism in the Neolithic seems be less freighted with emotional baggage than discussions of shamanism and the state because it does not impinge on preconceived notions of what the Neolithic is about. Shamans belong in the Paleolithic and Neolithic by definition, while by the same evolutionary scheme, they do not belong in the state. Even with wider latitude for accepting Neolithic shamanism, multiple possible interpretations of the same evidence may be offered. For example, does feasting at a graveside point to ancestor worship—which is to be expected in China—or a belief in the power of spirits, also known in the Chinese context?

Chapter 6 turns to the Shang polity and its contemporaries and successors. Chang argues strongly that shamanism was the driving force in the Shang period, but Keightley (1982:299) explains in detail his skepticism on many points. Using both Chang and Keightley as guides, I confront Shang shamanism directly, discussing the evidence already gathered by scholars of the Shang.

It is possible to infer from Western Zhou documents that the *wu* were partly suppressed by turning them into bureaucrats and ritual performers soon after the Zhou conquest of the Shang. Although shaman leaders survived elsewhere in East Asia as leaders in a complex society, within China the *wu* were considered mere fortune-tellers or charlatans and gradually became despised. This degradation removed the *wu* from ruling roles. However, shamanism seems to have continued in its ecstatic form in the state of Chu, which is sometimes thought to be descended from Shang ancestors. In spite of the attempt to organize the *wu,* or even because of it, the activities of *wu* are specified in the *Chu-yū.* According to that document, the *wu* had both duties and talents. These included divination, knowledge of the proper way to perform sacrifices, knowledge of the movements of heavenly

bodies, curing, dancing to invoke the spirits (or send them away), and dancing for rain. This list of activities is helpful in specifying the kinds of archaeological remains that could result from shamanistic activities.

Secondary states in East Asia arrived at state-level society through the
medium of shamans, and those of the Korean peninsula are the topic of
chapter 7. Ancient histories describing the rise of states in the Korean
peninsula, and the archaeology of the period—although later than state formation in China—suggest that shamanism is implicated in the organization of Korean states. For example, excavations of royal tombs reveal that
the kings and queens of Old Silla (traditional dates 37 BCE to 668 CE)
were interred with shamanistic crowns bearing gold antlers and stylized trees
sprouting from a gold circlet as prominent symbols of royalty. Historic
sources indicate that state rituals of the Goguryeo (Koguryea) kingdom (traditional dates 57 BCE to 668 CE) did not merely tolerate shamans, but
required their services to mediate disastrous events. A portrait of a woman
shaman was painted on a Goguryeo tomb wall, even though Buddhist
motifs are more common in Goguryeo tombs.

Evidence from state formation in Japan and ethnography in Okinawa
relate to shamanism as well, as discussed in chapter 8. Regarding early societies in the Japanese islands, Chinese documents refer to *wu*, widely
regarded as shamans or spirit mediums, especially in a much chewed over
passage concerning Queen Himiko, a shaman in the Yayoi period. Archaeological artifacts and site plans tend to confirm the accuracy of some of these
semi-historical accounts. The early shamanic beginnings in Japan are echoed
even today in Shinto rites, as well as in the practices of the princesses of
Okinawa. The *yuta* and *miko*, who are local shamans in Okinawa, and the
rituals of the Ainu of northern Japan are also discussed in this chapter.

The concluding chapter wraps up the issues that appear throughout the
book. It is particularly useful to realize that China has been analyzed as if
it were a cultural entity, although in reality it was a mosaic of cultures. With
a perspective on contemporaneous cultural differences, the issues are easier
to grasp. Manchuria, the Korean peninsula, and the islands of Japan were
also cultural mosaics. Understanding this pattern unties the nationalist knots
and helps to conceptualize the varieties of shamanism, as well as connections among them over long distances.

Interleaved between the chapters are a series of case studies, each related
in some way to the chapter preceding it. The case studies show how archaeological data has led to the interpretation of shamans in each instance. They

also illuminate specific sites or time periods in more detail than can be covered in the theoretical chapters.

The study of shamanism and power in ancient East Asia thus has many strands. Each topic requires its own chapter, but in the end discussions of shamanism, power, leadership, and gender, using the varied archaeological discoveries and texts, can be shown to combine in a number of different ways in East Asia, producing different patterns, and knots made of similar but not identical strands.

NIUHELIANG, CHINA

The site of Niuheliang, near the city of Jianping, Liaoning province, China, is the earliest known example in China of an archaeological site that appears to be wholly dedicated to ritual (Barnes and Guo 1996; Guo 1995a, 1997; Guo and Ma 1985; Nelson 1991a; Sun 1986; Sun and Guo 1986a). The major features include fourteen identified groups of tombs, an artificial hill, and a structure that has been dubbed the Goddess Temple.

Locality 1 includes the Goddess Temple in addition to several other features (Fang and Wei 1986). The long narrow building (18.4 x 6.9 meters) has four lobes, three at the top and one at the foot (Figure A.1). Traces of interior decoration show geometric painted patterns as well as raised dots and indentations. Pieces of the building material imply wattle and daub construction, probably in the shape of a barrel arch. Within the floor outline of the structure were parts of unfired clay statues. The most spectacular statue fragment is a life-sized face with eyes of inset green jade, with cheeks painted pink and smiling lips (Figure A.2).

Additional fragments of statues include a breast and shoulder, thus it was concluded that the statues were female. Some statues represent animals—a pig jaw and trotters, and a large claw that could have been from a big bird or a dragon (Fang and Wei 1986). As soon as the face was unearthed, the Chinese team decided to cover the excavation and wait for the funding and expertise to excavate to learn the most from a thorough excavation.

Another section of Locality 1 is called the

Figure A.1 Goddess Temple from the air. After Guo 1995a

platform. It measures 175 x 179 meters and appears to have several areas edged with stones. Several piles of stones lie on various parts of the platform, which may be collapsed towers or other buildings. Several pits have been discovered in this locality. Broken pots are layered into one large pit, another contains sheep bones, and into yet another a painted jar with a lid was placed, apparently deliberately buried. The pits may all be the remnants of ritual events.

Another structure of interest at Niuheliang is an artificial hill at the entrance to the valley. It has been thoroughly searched for burials or other evidence of its use. On the ground level, the mound is encircled by a ring of neatly squared, white marble-like stones from a nearby quarry. Another ring of white stones is embedded in the middle of the height of the mound, and a third was placed near the top. The only artifacts found were near the top of the mound—crude clay crucibles, with traces of copper adhering to the interior. The top of a hill is a surprising place to melt copper, and thus it seems likely to represent a ritual event. The only other copper found at the site is a small copper earring with a piece of unpolished jade. A study of alignments from this hill found that burials on hills marked the north and south extremes of the moonrise in the east.

The largest group of tombs is labeled Locality 2 (Figure A.3). It includes four earthen mounds. One is roughly square, in the shape of stepped pyramid, with a central stone structure in the middle that must

Figure A.2 Face with inset jade eyes from the Goddess Temple. After Guo 1995a

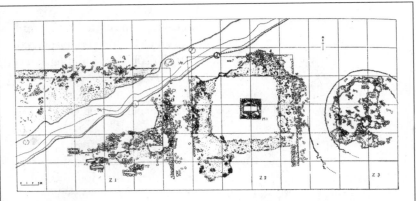

Figure A.3 Locality 2 burial mounds and altars. After Guo 1995a

have contained a burial. A round tomb contained fifteen burials, each enclosed in its own stone cist. Some of the skeletons were extended and some were bundle burials. Each grave contained only jades as grave goods. The jades included pendants lying on the chest, a hollow tube under the head, bracelets, and other jade objects (Figure A.4). No pottery or stone tools were placed in the graves with the dead. However, around the edges of the square tomb pottery cylinders had been arranged side-by-side. The best-preserved side included at least twenty-four of the cylinders, which were made of hard-fired red pottery with curvilinear designs painted in black (Figure A.5).

Other excavated tombs show some of the same elements, but they are not identical. Locality 5, for example, includes a single burial surrounded by a ring of stones. Instead of slabs of sandstone as walls for the grave, this tomb had a coffin made of small stones. Locality 16 produced some interesting burials, one with a raptor bird carved from jade beneath its head.

The jades are all small, designed for personal display. They include earrings, bracelets, pendants, and tubular objects that are interpreted as hair-dressing artifacts—perhaps to pull long hair through like a large ponytail. While each jade is unique, shapes follow particular patterns, especially the pendants that are usually found on the chest. They are described as clouds, combs, and dragons. Other shapes include rings, birds, turtles, insects, and fish. The "dragons" are so

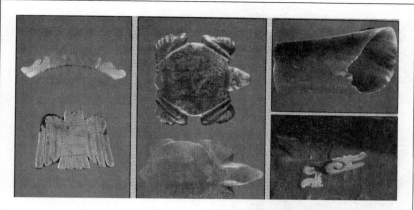

Figure A.4 Hongshan jades. After Sun and Gao 1986b

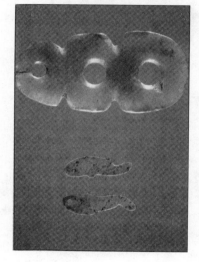

called because they resemble the earliest character translated as dragon. It is an open coil with an animal head on one end. Most chest ornaments are relatively flat and have "ox-nose" perforations on the back for attachment to clothing, but the dragons are rounded and have a hole for a cord. They come in two sizes, the smaller one with a pig-like head, the larger one thinner with a long head with a mane like a horse (Figure A.6).

Although it seems that rituals would have been performed here for the elite who occupied the grave mounds, the large area implies that audiences for the ritual would have encompassed all the villages of the Hongshan culture. Niuheliang is unquestionably a ritual area, but whether the ritual specialists were shamans or priests is not yet discernible.

Less than 40 kilometers, across the range that includes Pig Mountain, is a smaller ritual center called Dongshanzui. A layout of low walls and altars suggests the channeling of ritual activities into a pattern of

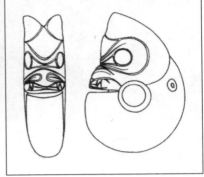

Figure A.5 Painted cylinder. After Sun and Gao 1986b

Figure A.6 Jade "pig-dragons." After Guo 1995a

movement. Clay figurines are smaller than those of the Goddess Temple. One figure holds something missing to her breast, and another is in the last stage of pregnancy. A piece of a statue that sat barefoot with crossed legs wears a rope belt that is probably significant.

A likely explanation for these two ritual centers is that Niuheliang centers upon rituals of death, and Dongshanzui upon rituals of life. Li (2003) explains them as ceremonial centers for the entire Hongshan culture, which developed from village altars and even earlier household goddesses. Some archaeologists have interpreted these sites as evidence of ancestor worship (Lei 1996), but an equally reasonable explanation is shamanism. In any case, the two interpretations are not mutually incompatible.

LANDSCAPES, LEGENDS, AND SKYSCAPES

The basic story of China is the four-thousand-year expansion of 'Han'
or 'Chinese' population, political powers, and culture from their birth-
place in the northwest and northeast, with secondary centers in the west
and center, into all the areas shown [on his map of China], *and*
indeed, beyond them.

—Elvin 2004:3

The Grand Historiographer said: Ever since the people have existed,
when have successive rulers not followed the movements of sun, moon,
stars, and asterisms?

—Shiji, Tianguo Shu, cited by Pankenier 1995:131

Landscapes

Ancient peoples attended to their environment in ways that we in the urban-
ized world largely have forgotten. They knew the hills and rivers, the animals and their habitats, the plants and their uses, where to find rare resources,

and what spirit dwelled within unusual formations of rocks. They knew what plants and animals to avoid. The environment was not looked upon as one merely of resources, as it might seem from some archaeological reports. It was familiar, it was home, and it was full of spirits. The sky was part of that environment, too. Without city lights, skies are brighter and more varied than electrified urban skies. Even during the Paleolithic, humans would have studied the sky and told stories about what they saw. Markings on Paleolithic bones have been interpreted as evidence of early attention to the skies (Marshack 1972). The sun and the moon were particularly important, marking day and night and the changing seasons. It is not surprising that many peoples personified these lights shining in the sky—and told stories about them.

The land mass of East Asia contains many different climates and topographies. Some regions are vast, like the grasslands of Inner Mongolia; others, like the swamps in the Shandong peninsula or lakes in the northern grasslands, have shrunk over the millennia, or even disappeared altogether. Humans have changed the landscapes—sometimes drastically—since they first arrived in East Asia with only stones, bones, bamboo, and shell as toolmaking materials, as well as fibers or skins to fashion carrying containers. Increasingly since Neolithic times, by clearing land and diverting water, humans have changed the shape of the land as well as the distribution of the flora and fauna (Elvin 2004). Thus it is not easy to summarize the varieties of landscape in East Asia; rather, summaries do not do justice to the variety of environments (both spatial and temporal) within East Asia. Later, I will emphasize East Asia as a cultural mosaic, but in this chapter I want to stress its mosaic of landscapes. Basic differences in the landscape affected what people could eat, the kinds of houses they built, and the types of clothes they wore. The topography of the land often channels routes of travel into valleys and mountain passes, and rivers may have been formidable barriers to cross or transportation routes. The sea was a source of food and a transportation route, as well, especially for coastal peoples. Early adaptations to the sea included boats, meaning that coastal peoples were probably in touch with each other, perhaps well back into the Pleistocene (Aikens and Zhuschchikovskaya in press).

Pleistocene Landscapes

I will not describe the landscapes of the first human inhabitants of East Asia—since little is known of their beliefs, they cannot contribute to the topic of shamans and leadership. *Homo erectus* fossils famously have been found in China, the best known being Peking Man. The Russian Far East may have been inhabited as early as the Middle Pleistocene (Derevianko and Tabarev 2006). The islands of Japan were first inhabited at least as early as the Late Pleistocene (Ikawa-Smith 2004). These sites are recognizable by their stone tools, but little that suggests ritual has been found. Such artifacts must have been perishable. A wooden plank with tool markings, which may be part of a boat, has been found. This plank is dated to more than 50,000 BCE, suggesting the elaboration of material culture already present at such an early date.

By the Late Paleolithic a glimmer of ancient beliefs begins to shine, although dimly. The Upper Cave at Zhoukoudian, outside Beijing, contains skeletons buried with ornaments, showing both an awareness of death and belief in an afterlife. People at this time, if not long before, decorated themselves for beauty, for ritual purposes, and/or to indicate personal qualities. Including such objects in burials suggests beliefs in spirits and an afterlife.

The climate of the Late Pleistocene was cold, and sea levels were up to 140 meters lower than at present at maximum glaciation. The coast was sometimes as much as 1,000 kilometers farther out than today, meaning that coasts and flatter lands from that era are now under the sea (Keightley 1999d), along with archaeological sites. Thus before sea level rose relatively abruptly, about ten thousand years ago, the Korean peninsula stood as mountain ranges beside a valley with a wide river running in what is now the basin of the Yellow Sea. The Liaodong and Shandong peninsulas were connected to the Korean peninsula, and the major islands of Japan were part of the landmass of greater East Asia. Kyushu was joined to Korea in the area that is now the Tsushima strait, and Hokkaido could be reached by land through the region that is now the coast of the Russian Far East (Figure 2.1). Fossils of ancient elephants and large extinct deer are found in Japan, showing that the land routes did not impede human or animal travel to this volcanic land (Huang 1984)

Inland sites required adaptations to long, cold winters. A sense of human adaptations to very cold winters is afforded by the site of Buret, Siberia. Some figurines made of mammoth ivory appear to wear furs, indicated by dots representing fur trousers and parka with hood. The nearby site of Mal'ta contained female figurines wearing only aprons hanging down front and back, suggesting clothing worn within dwellings. In addition to the figurines, other ritual is shown by a child burial that included an elaborate necklace. Carved plaques and flying birds may have had been used in rituals as well (Chard 1974).

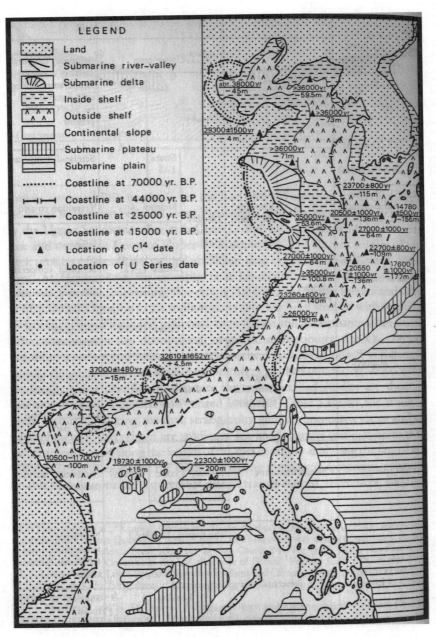

Figure 2.1 Estimated coastlines of East Asia at lowest sea level. After Huang 1984

A worldwide warming trend began about 10,000 BCE, which rapidly melted glaciers and caused sea level to rise even beyond the present stand, making the land that is now Japan into islands and creating peninsulas out of higher ground around the now-flooded Yellow Sea. During this time hunter-gatherers with microlithic tools gathered around lakes and other water sources fed by glaciers in regions that are now dry. Crude pottery is found mixed with microliths at some of these sites, from the Russian Far East to northern and southern China to Japan, to be described in chapter 5.

The first indications of East Asian shamanism are found in these landscapes. Although it is anachronistic to use the present countries of China, Korea, and Japan to describe the landscapes of the early Holocene, it is convenient to do so because it divides the region into continent (China), peninsula (Korea), and islands (Japan).

Continental Landscapes

The political boundaries of China today are not those of ancient China. Today China is immense compared to the small regions that were governed by the Sandai, the Three Dynasties of Xia, Shang, and Zhou. The polity of Chungguo—the Middle Kingdom—expanded little even up to the Warring States period of the Zhou dynasty. The larger China of today is useful only in terms of current archaeology and its interpretations. Ancient people knew different boundaries, or no boundaries at all, only areas where strangers lived.

The peoples of China probably spoke a variety of languages and certainly had different cultures. Some states in the Warring States period were considered non-Chinese by those who defined themselves as the Middle Kingdom. Keightley infers from the oracle bones that the Shang "state" did not include a solid contiguous territory, but surrounded barbarians, sometime enemies, in pockets within it (Keightley 1999d, 2000). Permanent capital cities did not exist in any of the Sandai. To imagine the world of East Asia, groups intermittently moving to a new region is an important concept. New capitals were marked by rituals and symbols (Price 1995).

The high Tibetan plateau is an area on the west of China that is poorly known archaeologically. It is nevertheless connected through valley routes to the Turfan depression, which although it is now a desert, in the early Holocene was still well watered with melt water from the Altai Mountains on the north. This region formed one branch of the renowned Silk Road.

It is the only area of East Asia below sea level. Another communication route through Central Asia went north of the Altai Mountains, to arrive in Inner Mongolia. This is sometimes called the Steppe Route (Wu 2004). Some ideas, artifacts, and even livestock reached East Asia through these routes, probably since the beginning of human treks across the landscape. Vast grasslands now included in Inner Mongolia connect with the steppes of Central Asia. In places the land is arable; in fact, some of the earliest millet and pig farming sites in China are found in Inner Mongolia.

China's major rivers arise in the Tibetan Plateau, coursing to the east in three winding but roughly parallel streams (Figure 2.2). The Yellow River runs through north China. It lies in the Temperate Zone and was once surrounded by thick forests. As it makes its way through lower but still hilly land, the river makes a sharp bend to the north and traverses what is now the Ordos Desert. Archaeological sites in this region show that the land was once full of lakes, where people lived on the shores, fishing and making beads from the eggs of ostrich-like birds that roamed the area. When the Yellow River bends south again, it runs along a valley west of the Taihang Mountains. Meeting major tributaries from the west, the river bends eastward again. From this point to the Shandong peninsula was the region that formed the heartland of China in the time of the Three Dynasties.

Figure 2.2 Karst hills along the Li River in southern China. Photo by H. S. Nelson

The Yellow River traverses the land of loess, a wind-blown soil that is fine and sometimes laid down in a layer hundreds of meters thick. The loess blew in from the edge of glaciers in the Pleistocene, and it continues to blow even today. The Shang dynasty kings divined incessantly about the wind. Beijing is known for its terrible dust storms—fine particles seem to find every crack in buildings and coat everything outside. The loess is fertile soil, but it erodes easily, and the Yellow River carries tons of "yellow earth" to the East China Sea every year. As it nears the Yellow Sea, the Yellow River, by periodically flooding its banks, has created a vast plain that spreads out on either side of the Shandong peninsula. At the highest stand of sea level, the mountains of Shandong rose above the sea as a large island. The flat land on both sides was deposited by the mighty river, which drastically has changed its course several times over the millennia.

But as different as the high plateau of the west is from the flat lands of the east, China's major division in both landscape and climate is between the north and the south. The southeast is warmer, wetter, and greener. Along the Changjiang, or Yangzi River, rice was first harvested and later domesticated. Millets were domesticated in the north, roughly between the Yellow River region and Liaoning province and Inner Mongolia, north of the Great Wall. The Great Wall is famously said to have been built to keep out marauding nomads, but in fact sites far north of the Great Wall show evidence of cultivated plants and domesticated animals as early as those of central China. Pigs are the most common domesticated animal in all of China, both in the south and north, including Manchuria, whose green valleys were part of the homeland of those who formed early Korean states.

The three provinces of the northeast, from south to north, are Liaoning, Jilin, and Heilongjiang. The Daling and Liao rivers run through Liaoning. This province shares many traits and site characteristics with Inner Mongolia. Jilin province contains many remains of the Goguryeo state, as well as earlier and later polities, most of which were only vaguely known to China even after the Qin and Han dynasties unified the Zhou states into an empire. Farthest north is Heilongjiang (Black Dragon River), which is the Chinese name for the Amur River. This is the homeland of the Manchu, a Tungus (Tunguz) people who ruled China as the Qing dynasty from 1645 to 1911. Earlier dynasties, such as the Wei, Jurchen, and Liao, also originated in this region. Fascination with the Mongols has obscured the fact that foreign conquests of China came mostly from Manchuria (Di Cosmo 1999).

The Yangzi River is China's longest, having carved out the beautiful, deep Three Gorges on its way from Tibet to the South China Sea near

Shanghai. The southern province of Yunnan is mountainous and was uncon-
quered by central Chinese states until after the Han dynasty. It is still inhabited by "national minorities," people with mountain adaptations and
non-Chinese languages. One of the shorter rivers of the south is the Li River,
which has created the karst hills that are familiar from Chinese paintings.
Although the paintings look artificial to Western eyes, these elephantine
shapes really exist, often covered with green vegetation clinging to the steep
sides. Most agricultural land lies in the lowlands, where rice padis shine green
or golden, depending on the proximity of harvest time, and water buffalo
swim in rivers when they are not being used for plowing or riding.

Peninsular Landscapes

The northern part of the Korean peninsula lies to the east of the Bay of
Bohai, with its west coast along the Yellow Sea. The east coast borders the
East Sea, called the Japan Sea on many maps. On the north, Korea bor-
ders the Russian Far East for a few kilometers, and the rest of its northern
border abuts Manchuria, the part of China which is called in Chinese
Dongbei—the Northeast. The North Korean border is mountainous for its
entire distance. The highest part of these ranges is called Paektusan
(Whitehead Mountain) in Korean, and Changbaishan, the Long White
Mountain in Chinese. A large lake called Chonji, Heavenly Lake, pic-
turesquely occupies a high caldera on the dividing line between North
Korea and China (Figure 2.3).

Figure 2.3 Chonji, the
Heavenly Lake in the
middle of Paektusan,
Korea. Photo by S. M.
Nelson

Three major rivers arise from the lake at Paektusan. The Tuman River makes a great bend to the north before arriving at Unggi Bay in the east. The largest part of the border between North Korea and China is a river called Yalu in English; Koreans know it as the Amnok River. The river meets the Liaodong peninsula at the Chinese city of Dandong. The Liaodong peninsula juts out to the south from there, with the Shandong peninsula almost enclosing Bohai Bay. The Ussuri River runs north through Jilin province in China, ending in Lake Khanka. The Russian Far East lies to the east at this point, forming part of the border between China and Russia. The Russian Far East—as far as Peter the Great Bay, Vladivostok, and beyond to the mouth of the Amur River, has many early sites that are part of the story of shamanism and the creation of states in East Asia. Some of this land is still very wild even along the coasts, with a large preserve for Siberian tigers, vanishing in the north for the same reasons that elephants and crocodiles are gone from the south—poachers and diminished habitat.

The Korean peninsula is essentially a block of ancient granite that has been tilted up on the east side to form the highest north-south trending mountains (Bartz 1972). The Taebaek range runs close to the east coast, which is relatively straight, with few bays or islands. The southern and western coasts of the block are drowned in the Yellow Sea and are full of islets with extremely irregular coastlines. Korea's major rivers rise in the eastern mountains and make their way to the Yellow Sea. Other than Paektusan, Korea has no peninsular volcanoes, although it is known for many hot springs, and ancient basalt outcrops occur in the center. The large island of Cheju Do off the south coast is volcanic, however, possibly created by the same forces that made the Japanese islands, part of the Pacific ring of fire.

Island Landscapes

The four major islands of Japan form an arc that almost touches the Russian Far East at Hokkaido and comes close to the Korean peninsula at Kyushu. The largest island of Honshu stretches between Hokkaido and Kyushu, with the smaller island of Shikoku on the Pacific side disconnected from Honshu by the Inland Sea. The Kuriles, an arc of islands to the north of Hokkaido, nearly connect to Kamchatka, and in the south the island arc of the Ryukyus reaches almost to Taiwan. Thus the islands were probably never isolated from the nearest island or from the peninsulas and the continent. The islands trend northeast-southwest, covering 20 degrees of latitude. The flora is correspondingly diverse.

The Japanese islands are mostly volcanic, with the famous perfect cone of Mount Fuji dominating some of the eastern scenery. Some Japanese volcanoes have produced vast eruptions, leaving ash layers that can be dated. Most of the major islands are in the Temperate Zone, but Kyushu is warmer and contains natural marshes well suited to early rice. Boats were clearly a necessity in this island region and probably were developed quite early. Ikawa-Smith (1986:203) infers that boats were constructed even before the beginning of the Holocene, and a recent discovery of a wooden plank with tool marks bears this out.

Built Landscapes

One of the characteristics of civilization listed by V. Gordon Childe (1942) is monumental architecture. The lack of monumental architecture in the Shang period seems to be an anomaly for early states. While Wu (1995) discusses monumentality in early Chinese art, he does not use the word monumentality as Childe did. Childe means stone pyramids, henges, and tells. China does not have large constructions commanding attention in the landscape as part of its formative period. The mounded tombs of Hongshan in the Late Neolithic may be the earliest large constructions, but even they are not as striking as stone monuments elsewhere. The largest Hongshan mounds were constructed in a valley in the Niuheliang district, and although they are partly built of stone, they may not have been very high (see Case Study A). Other Niuheliang mounds have more presence by their hilltop locations, their visual connections to each other and to the Goddess Temple, but they blend with the landscape rather than standing out from it. Baines and Yoffee (1998:14) point out that "However massive and durable a monument, it cannot be of the scale of the surrounding physical world, and this discrepancy cannot but draw attention to order's fragility and need of support." The ancient Chinese did not try to compete with the surrounding world, but utilized and incorporated it by means of sacred mountains. These mountains are covered with temples and shrines, making them part of the human world and co-opting the spirits of the mountains into the service of the rulers.

Early palaces must have been monumental in a sense. Palace foundations have been excavated even in some Neolithic sites, suggesting impressive size. Very likely they were ornamented with bright colors and complex designs. But China's palaces were made of wood and did not endure. In any case, they were not erected on the scale of the pyramids of Mesopotamia,

Egypt, or Mesoamerica. Ancient China rarely piled up earth or stone. Constructions such as the monumental stone works of the Inca and their predecessors—and the brick structure of the Indus civilization—have no counterparts in China. It can be argued that the kings' burials in the Shang required many hours of labor to dig so deeply (up to 10.5 meters), but no imposing superstructure dominating the landscape remained to remind people of the power of their kings. In the archaeology of memory, monuments are absent in China. Practices such as divination and sacrifices were clearly more important in the Shang period than the building of monuments, but they were ephemeral acts that needed to be repeated on a regular basis, rather than overweening evidence of state power. Nevertheless, it seems likely that places within the Shang state were inscribed with meaning. Even the hunting ground of the kings in a hilly area to the west of the capital was sacred. Hunting continued to be a royal sport some two thousand years later. A tomb of the Goguryeo state is decorated with a hunting mural that covers a wall, suggesting that the importance of the royal hunt continued beyond the Warring States period.

Burial grounds began to be separated from dwellings in the Early Neolithic. They seem to have been sacred space in which family ties were expressed. Although there are marked differences from one cemetery to another, they all demonstrate that the burial place was important, either by large communal graves or by secondary burial—or both. In the Japanese islands, too, the dead were treated with ceremony and the choice of burial place was significant (Figure 2.4). A few early burials in Korea also show

Figure 2.4 Seaside shrine in Japan. Photo by H. S. Nelson

respect for the dead, by arranging graves in rows, as at Nongpodong, or arranging polished jade axes on top of reburied bones. But for the most part, Neolithic burials have eluded the archaeologist's trowel.

The area containing palaces at Anyang was encircled by an inner wall, marking it as royal space, and perhaps sacred space as well. Temples were erected above ancestors' tombs to use for their continuous worship. But China used the natural landscape for its sacred monumentality. Many mountains were considered sacred, and one of them was specifically associated with shamans. On several levels, meanings related to spirits and powers were attached to both artificial and natural features of the landscape.

Beliefs about the interaction between the sky and the earth were present in China at least by the Early Neolithic. Some landscapes were sacred because of an association with the sky, especially mountains and hills. Textual references to mountain goddesses occur in regard to the noble ancestry of early queens in the Silla kingdom of the Korean peninsula. In China, the Sage Kings are said to have worshipped on particular mountains and used the tops of mountains for observations to rectify the calendar.

The Mongols carried on this same tradition. Tengri, as the personification of the sky, was worshipped in high places because they were closer to heaven. Cairns of stones were piled on mountain passes and other high places recognized for their supernatural power. Since rocks could be sacred as well as mountains, adding a pebble to the top of a mountain pass was a sacred ritual. But hills might have other functions as well. Sacred mountains were the home of mountain spirits and therefore an inevitable destination of shamans. Important ancestors were buried on the mountain slopes.

A Neolithic example of altering the landscape for purposes other than burial is a 30-meter-high artificial hill at Niuheliang in the Hongshan period. Archaeological explorations suggest that it was built for two purposes. One was related to the ability to melt copper ore, for crucibles containing traces of copper ore were found on top of the hill (Linduff et al. 2000). It is strange that copper would be melted in a high place. It must have been cumbersome to carry the ore, crucibles, firewood, and bellows to the top of the hill. Presumably, the event was held in this location in order to be attended by a large number of people gathered in the surrounding valley. Surely something spiritual or magical was implied by the ability to melt stone and turn it into shiny objects (Eliade 1964). Another use of the artificial hill was to sight over mound burials on eastern hills the risings of the moon at their farthest distance north and south (Nelson et al. 2005). It is impossible to know why the turning points of the moon were relevant; but the fact that the foresights are burial cairns suggests that keeping track of moon risings was ritually important—and that tracking the moon was ceremonial as well as calendrical.

Myths and Legends

Origin myths are different in the various East Asian regions, even though they were codified in protohistoric times. Stories about beginnings may be part remembered oral history and part new fabrication, but they contain kernels of history. It is useful to perceive differences as well as similarities among the myths of polities, because it suggests a variety of beliefs and rituals.

Ancient China

Reading legends of the past helps to understand the way that history and archaeology are intertwined in East Asia. Archaeological reports, especially in China, often use texts to illuminate archaeological discoveries. Western readers may be startled to find reference to the legendary Yellow Emperor, for example, in a discussion of archaeological discoveries of the Neolithic period (Guo 1999).

In spite of frequent references by archaeologists to myths and legends, these ancient stories were not codified into a single narrative in ancient China. There is no Chinese equivalent of Greek Homer, with his foundation tale of the Trojan War. Legends of early China are scattered in texts written in different times and places in the cultural mosaic that was (and is) China, even offering competing versions of the same tale (Allan 1991; Wu 1982). Although it is likely that the legends originated in a number of different cultures and societies within the territory that is now China, they have been summarized into a single time line that is systematized as including Three Primeval Emperors (Originators), Five Premier Emperors, and Three Dynasties (Wu 1982:37; Chang 1986b).

The Three Originators include more than three names, such as Fuxi (Animal Domesticator), Nuwa (Lady Divine Ruler), Shennong (Divine Farmer), Suiren (Fire Maker) and Youchao (Have Nest). Nuwa is the only female given the status of originator, and she is often described as Fuxi's wife or sister, perhaps to put her in her place within the patriarchy of later China. She is credited with the creation of music, as well as propping up the corner of the fallen sky with stones of five colors (Wu 1982). By the Warring States period, Nuwa and Fuxi were depicted with human heads and torsos ending in intertwined snake tails, implying that they were both powers and were of equal importance. In general, the period of the originators is perceived as too ancient to associate Nuwa and Fuxi with actual archaeological sites or cultures. They are worshipped in their own temples where local legends persist, although the actual temple buildings do not go back to ancient times (Da 1988).

The Five Emperors begin with Huang Di, the Yellow Emperor, whose feats were, of course, prodigious, including the creation of calendars, medicine, and writing. But the texts actually name nine "emperors" in this time period. Only those with heroic deeds attributed to them are included in the canonical five emperors, or Sage Kings. In the list of five, the second emperor was Shao Hao, followed by his nephew Zhuan Xu (Wu 1982:61), followed by Yao and Shun. Tong (2002) shows that each of these important legendary emperors was attributed with shaman-like traits. Whatever historical reality may lay behind the legends, like the patriarchs of the Bible, the Yellow Emperor and his successors are named and given reign lengths. Their time spans can be calculated in calendar years, although calculations differ. For example, K. C. Wu (1982) places the Yellow Emperor in the twenty-seventh century BCE, while Pankenier suggests the twenty-fourth century BCE. Often the Neolithic/Early Bronze Age Longshan culture is mentioned as the time of the Yellow Emperor, but the Hongshan culture is an equally likely candidate (Guo 1999), depending on the chronology selected.

The Three Dynasties are Xia, Shang, and Zhou. The Zhou Dynasty has always been considered fully historical because detailed records were kept and recopied through the millennia. Recently discovered bronzes with inscriptions corroborate much of the Zhou historic record, including names of nobles with their places and times. However, the Shang Dynasty was discounted by the generation of historians who doubted everything that could not be verified independently. In the 1890s surprising verification of the Shang period appeared in the form of writing on animal scapulae and turtle plastrons (Li 1977). The characters used for writing on the bones and shells are ancient forms of modern Chinese characters, and therefore most of the characters can be read by specialists (Keightley 1978). The objects are known in English as "oracle bones" because they are addressed to spirits and inquire about the future. Names of Shang kings recorded in the oracle bones confirm king lists that were copied down into Zhou histories. Intensive excavations at Anyang, the final capital of the Shang, have added to what is known of Shang times, both from writing on the oracle bones and the content and distribution of burials and buildings (Li 1977). The preceding Xia period, however, remained shadowy until excavations at Erlitou in Zhengzhou produced the earliest bronze vessels known in China. Although they were constructed by the remarkable technological advance of pouring molten metal into piece molds, the vessels are mostly undecorated. Nevertheless, the legend of nine bronze vessels created in Xia times adds luster to these first attempts at making bronze containers. Many archaeologists now consider Erlitou and related sites to be remains of the Xia dynasty not only because of the presence of bronze vessels but also extensive archaeological remains of palaces and bronze foundries (Liu 2004).

The Zhou period is divided into Western Zhou (1045–770 BCE) and Eastern Zhou. Eastern Zhou similarly is divided into two parts, called Spring and Autumn (770–450 BCE) and Warring States (450–221 BCE). Some states are better known than others, either because they are documented by their own texts or because important tombs, palaces, or cities have been unearthed by archaeologists. For example, the Zhongshan kingdom, with its capital near Shijiazhuang in Hebei, south of Beijing, was a small and relatively unimportant state in Zhou histories, but it is interesting because of the shamanic-looking symbols of royalty, including bronze mirrors, large bronze tridents, and animal-style art (Wu 1999). Another of the warring states was Chu, whose literature famously demonstrates that shamanism went on flourishing there (Cook and Major 1999) even after the unification of the Warring States by the short-lived Qin dynasty (the First Emperor, the megalomaniac of the famous pottery army) and the subsequent expansion of a centralized empire under the Han dynasty.

The Formation of States in the Korean Peninsula

The ancient history of Korea is also cobbled together from legends and myths. The extant histories were not compiled until the twelfth and thirteenth centuries (Ilyon 1972; Schulz 2004) from earlier records of the Three Kingdoms that have been lost (Gardiner 1969). Some descriptions of early polities in Korea are scattered in Chinese documents (Parker 1890; Seyock 2004), but contradictions abound and gaps are filled in intermittently with archaeology. Nevertheless, scraps of data relating to shamans can be gleaned.

Korean archaeology uses local terms to describe the Neolithic period. The earliest stage, when the first pottery appears, is called Chulmun (or Pissalmun, both meaning comb-marked), beginning about 6000 BCE. The time period is often described as based on hunting and gathering, although evidence of plant and animal domestication has been found at some sites. The following time period, beginning around 2000 BCE, has plain pottery (Mumun), and is agricultural without question, growing several kinds of domesticated plants. The latter half of this time period begins to include bronze (Rhee et al. 2007). The timing imputed to the first culture hero, Tangun, would locate him in the Mumun period.

The legend of Tangun, who was said to be the son of the high god and a bear-turned-into-a-woman, has been important in Korea for centuries, but the time of its first appearance is unknown. The story has been fanned in North Korea since the division of the peninsula by the reputed association of Tangun with the current leader, Kim Jong Il (Nelson 2006; Pai 2000:59). Kim was supposedly born where Tangun's spirit is believed to continue to dwell. The holy place is near Chonji, the Heavenly Lake in the crater of the sacred mountain Paektusan. The mountain range containing the lake straddles the border between North Korea and China. Virtually nothing that has been written about Tangun is reflected in archaeology, although an official announcement was made of the discovery of Tangun's tomb near Pyongyang in North Korea in 1993 (Pai 2000:60). A large tomb containing skeletons of a man and a woman was said to be that of Tangun and his wife. The bones are claimed to date to about 3000 BCE. The details of the tomb have not been published, so it is impossible for outsiders to evaluate its age, but the region where the burial was discovered is known for cemeteries with Goguryeo burials.

Tangun's polity was called Chosun (pronounced Chaoxian in Chinese), a name that is echoed in some place names of the Chinese northeast, such as the city of Chaoyang in Liaoning province. North Korea is known as Chaoxian to the Chinese, while South Korea (Taehan Minguk) is called Han Guo, the country of the Han (not the character of the Han dynasty, but of the Han River that flows through Seoul). Under the Japanese occupation (1910–1945) the peninsula was referred to as Chosen. Thus the name Chosun has been repeatedly applied to the Korean peninsula, as have variants of Korea (Goryeo, Goguryeo) and Han.

The second culture hero of Korea is a nobleman named Kija. The Korean legend of Kija is based on a few lines in a Zhou history regarding the overthrow of Shang by Zhou about 1050 BCE. Kija (Jizi in Chinese) was an agnate of the final Shang king, who was consulted as a shaman by the new Zhou king. Eventually he was allowed to take a large retinue to the northeast so that he could continue to worship the Shang ancestors (angry ancestors, especially ancestors of former enemies, need to be fed and pacified). Some Korean archaeologists believe Kija went northeast to the state of Yan, where bronzes are inscribed with the family name Ji (An 1974:20). However, Ji is also a family name of the Zhou dynasty, and thus when found on bronzes it is interpreted within China as belonging to the royal Zhou line rather than the Shang (Li 2006) Another complicating factor is that in some texts Kija is associated with the state of Song. Although his country in some texts was called Chaoxian, a name associated with the Korean peninsula, it is not known if any part of Chaoxian was located in the peninsula at that time.

In Korea, Kija's state is referred to as Ko Chosun (Old Chosun), to differentiate it from later polities by the same name. Some Korean historians would place Kija in Liaoning province of China (An 1974), but many insist on a location wholly within the Korean peninsula (Yi Ki-baek 1984; see Pai 2000:97–126 for an extended discussion). There is not a shred of archaeological evidence to substantiate the presence of Kija and his retinue in the Korean peninsula, however. One would expect to find a reasonably large population aggregate, having inscribed bronze vessels and other ritual paraphernalia for feeding, entertaining, and worshipping the Shang ancestors. Only a small amount of bronze has been found in northern Korea, at the earliest around 1050 BCE, and no bronze vessels. A few bronze buttons and ring-handled knives, both related to bronzes in the Northern Zone, north of the Great Wall of China, are the earliest bronze artifacts discovered so far (Kim Jong-hak 1978).

The first historic state in Korea is known as Wiman Chosun. Wiman is acknowledged in Chinese history as a renegade strongman from Liaodong who moved into the Korean peninsula in 194–195 BCE and conquered Kija's supposed descendant, Chun. When defeated by Wiman's forces, Chun is said to have fled by boat with his treasures and retinue to the southern part of the Korean peninsula to found the state of Chin. The state of Wiman Chosun prospered for two generations, but Wiman's grandson Ugo was attacked by forces of the Former Han. Ugo's state was strong enough to withstand a two-year siege of his capital by enormous Han Chinese armies who had arrived by land and sea, but ultimately succumbed in 108 BCE. The expanding Han dynasty established four commanderies in northern Korea and perhaps eastern Liaoning province, but the Han could not control such a large territory so far from their center. The commanderies dwindled to two and then to one. The lasting commandery is called Lelang in Chinese, Nangnang in Korean. The Han dynasty records, *Hanshu* and *Houhanshu*, include details about Lelang, including population sizes of various cities at two different time periods. Archaeology in northern Korea corroborates the existence of Nangnang (Kayamoto 1961; McCune 1962; NMK 2001). The Han presence is attested by burials containing artifacts manufactured as far away as Chu in the south of China, as well as seals and inscriptions naming Chinese officials. In spite of much evidence, North Korea officially denies the existence of Nangnang and claims the indigenous development of the Goguryeo state within the Korean peninsula (Nelson 2008; Pai 2000). A late commandery centered on the present city of Gaesong, just on the thirty-eighth parallel in North Korea. Although the southern part of the Korean peninsula was free from direct rule by Han China, it was nevertheless influenced by the proximity of the Nangnang colony. The *Weizhi* describes the inhabitants of the south and calls them Samhan—the Three Han: Mahan, Chinhan, and Pyonhan (see Seyock 2004 for a new and reliable translation of this document into German). These polities are described as federations of small walled towns, of which Mahan, the Horse Han, was the largest. Archaeology has confirmed the use of writing brushes at this time at the site of Dahori (Yi et al. 1989), as well as the local production of iron agricultural tools (Yoon 1984). The regions of Chinhan and Byeenban were rich in iron. Iron was an important trade item for the Han dynasty, which declared state monopolies on salt and iron (Gale 1931). The presence of iron may have been a contributory incentive for the conquest of northern Korea. (Nelson 1993a).

In the meantime, proto-Korean states were forming in Manchuria. These polities are described in Chinese historical records such as *Houhanshu*, *Hanshu*, and *Weizhi*. The state of Puyo existed entirely in Manchuria (Pak 1999) and perhaps was the predecessor of Goguryeo, which was one of the Three Kingdoms of early Korea: Silla, Goguryeo, and Baekje. A group of city-states along the Naktong River on the southern coast, collectively called Kaya, never coalesced into a united kingdom, and so it is not included among the early kingdoms of the peninsula. The Silla kingdom developed in the southeastern part of the peninsula, farthest from Chinese influence, as can be particularly appreciated from its archaeology. Silla legends of early kings associated with white horses and gold also indicate its non-Chinese origins (Nelson 2008). Legends of queens who were descended from mountain goddess mothers suggest animist/shamanist beliefs (Nelson 1995b).

Contemporaneous written material for the time period is scarce. A few stele, written in Chinese characters, have been discovered in both Silla and Goguryeo territories, and very rarely inscribed artifacts have been found in tombs (McCune 1962). Japanese histories refer to events in the peninsula, including claiming Gaya (called Mimana or Imna in Japanese) as part of their domain, but the claim is hotly contested in Korea (Hong 1994). However, both sides agree that Baekje had a strong influence on Yamato, and was the main source of the introduction of Buddhism and its arts to Japan. Archaeological discoveries in Japan demonstrate influence from the states on the Korean peninsula (Hong 1994; Nelson 1990; Seyock 2004), as do artistic treasures preserved in Buddhist and Shinto shrines (Covell and Covell 1984).

Legends in the Japanese Islands

Japanese legends begin with the Sun Goddess, Amaterasu, and her brother, reflecting the way that female and male pairs were often rulers in early Japan. A series a legendary rulers include a woman warrior named Jingu, who supposedly led conquering raids into the peninsula. New pottery types derived from Korea—as well as full-scale rice agriculture, bronze mirrors and weapons, and trade wares—mark the Yayoi period in Japan. While Yayoi is traditionally given dates of 300 BCE to 300 CE, new evidence of early rice causes some archaeologists to date the beginning of Yayoi much earlier: 1000 BCE to 300 CE (Ikawa-Smith 2000). It seems very likely that migrants brought the rice from Korea because many other traits, including pottery styles and burial customs, are the same or similar across the Tsushima Strait (Seyock 2004). Especially during the time of the Nangnang colony, China took an interest in the islands and made sea journeys to them—in their records using the character now pronounced *wa* to apply to the people who lived there (Hudson 1999; Imamura 1996; Mizoguchi 2002).

For example, *Weizhi* describes a journey in the third century to a polity called Yamatai, where a queen described as a shaman reigned. Artifacts, such as a Chinese seal inscribed for the "King of Wa," document the relationship of Japanese polities with Nangnang and Han China, and tradewares are found all along the route of the described journey across the Korea strait (Seyock 2004).

The Kofun (tumulus) period is roughly contemporaneous with the Three Kingdoms in Korea. Yamato became the preeminent region, with tombs contents that resemble those of Silla and Kaya. *Kojiki* and *Nihon Shoki* are histories written in the seventh and eighth centuries. These documents emphasize the dominance of the Yamato state, although other regions such as Kibi (Gorman 1999) and Izumo (Piggott 1989) produced contending states, where huge tombs can still be found, including the third largest in Japan in the Kibi region. The texts show that either a man or a woman could head the state and that sometimes a pair, such as sister and brother or husband and wife, ruled together. Evidence of shamanism is visible in the tomb figures, and shamans are mentioned in the Chinese texts.

Skyscapes

People who moved into these environments and settled down, as well as those who traveled in boats or on foot across other regions, must have been intimately knowledgeable about the sky. The light of a full moon would have guided night travel and provided light for social gathering and storytelling. The sky was full of information that was needed to journey in the landscape. The movements of the sun and moon must have been well known, even to the first inhabitants, as well as the wandering stars (planets) and the fixed stars. Lore about the seasons and their relation to the sky would have been elaborated and passed down from Paleolithic times. What is surprising is not that early people had knowledge of the sky, but that once in a while we have glimpses of the scope of that knowledge.

Powers of the Four Directions

The cardinal directions were so important in the Shang period that they were personified as powers (Keightley 2000). Even early cemeteries in China had a prevailing direction in which bodies were buried, often facing the east—the rising sun. Houses often faced south, especially in the northern latitudes to take advantage of the maximum warmth of the sun in winter. These directional tendencies lacked the precision one would expect if they knew how to find true north, so the practical considerations of directionality must have influenced the beginning of attention to the four directions, later to become powers.

The four directions are known to have become codified as each having a sacred animal and associated color, at least by the Han dynasty, when the directional animals are painted on the appropriate tomb walls, and even painted on a funeral chest. Groups of asterisms marked the directional animals in the sky. These included the blue dragon of the east, the red phoenix of the south, the white tiger of the west, and the black turtle and snake of the north. Each included six or seven star groups called *xiu*. Those for the dragon name the parts of the dragon, from horns to tail (Chatley 1938), suggesting detailed knowledge of the sky and an intense interest in dragons. A recently discovered star chart painted on the ceiling of a Han tomb near Xi'an, has the star named *xin* (heart) painted red, marking the heart of the dragon as central and particularly meaningful. This star is also called Huo, the Fire Star, and was used as a seasonal marker according to the *Yao-dian*. The shift in seasonal sky markers can be appreciated by the fact that the Bird Star heralded spring at the time of Yao. In Shang times, when Huo was visible in the east at dusk it marked the beginning of spring. On the basis of textual evidence, it has been argued that the emergence of the fire star at dusk and the rising of the dragon occurred in the middle of spring in the Shang period (Sun and Kistemaker 1997).

The earliest archaeological suggestion of sky lore in East Asia comes from a Neolithic burial in Xishuipo, Puyang, Henan (see Case Study B). This burial, with shell mosaics of a tiger on the west and a dragon on the east, suggests that by the fifth millennium BCE, some of the Neolithic inhabitants of northern China already had conceived of at least two of the four directions as being represented by a symbolic animal (Pankenier 2005:508). An adult male was the central inhabitant of the tomb, buried between the two animal mosaics, which demonstrate their importance by each taking up as much space as the central burial. These animals were placed at a slightly higher level than the burial itself, perhaps as guardians.

The animals guarding east and west are dangerous animals. The Chinese dragon is a water creature and may be a mythologized form of alligator (James 1993; Schafer 1973), although crocodile seems more likely for Asia. Bones of alligators (or crocodiles) are reported from Longshan sites, and crocodile skins were stretched on wooden frames to make Neolithic drums. Since Chinese dragons are associated with water, Yin, they are indirectly associated with women—although the five-toed dragon later became a symbol of the emperor, while the mythic bird, the phoenix, represented the empress.

Tigers were prevalent in both the north and the south, wherever the forests were dense enough to provide food and cover. Tigers were hunted by Shang kings, and Korean nobility were still hunting tigers more than a thousand years later. Tigers have vanished from the south, along with their habitat (Elvin 2004), but Siberian tigers still roam the forests of the Russian Far East, in spite of being endangered by poachers and shrinking habitat. Tigers still menaced Korean villages in the twentieth century (Zaichikov 1952), and folklore paintings illustrate many stories featuring tigers. Since the tigers were real, it seems likely that the dragons were also an earthly menace, becoming mythologized as they disappeared from the environment.

Paper (1995) finds evidence that the Vermillion Bird was recognized by Shang as both a directional marker and a power. He notes that the glyph for "bird" in oracle script wears a crest like the mythical phoenix. A jade from the tomb of Lady Hao (see Case Study D) has a crown-like crest and a long tail, like the fabled phoenix, although it is yellow instead of red. The importance of birds in several Neolithic cultures is detailed in chapter 6. The Bird Star is mentioned prominently in the *Yaodian* and Shang oracle bones.

The turtle and snake are also ancient symbols (Allan 1991). They appear in early folklore, but it is unknown when they became associated with the north. Cullen (1996:185) illustrates a mythic snake-like creature painted on a large bottle from 3000 BCE at Wushan, Gansu. Turtles are found in small jade carvings in Neolithic burials, and turtle plastrons were used for sacred writing.

Calendars

The influence was not all from the sky to the earth. Not only were the two realms believed to influence each other, but astronomy was closely linked to the calendar (Pankenier 2005:500–501). Certain constellations that marked the change of seasons were particularly important. Bright stars in Scorpio and Orion, on opposite sides of the sky, were the chief seasonal markers. The Big Dipper was important because it rotated around the North Star, which appears to be the center of the sky. By the Han dynasty, Polaris was associated with the emperor, seen to be the center of all things on earth.

The earliest textual material about the Chinese sky comes from a document called *Yaodian,* the Canon of Yao, which purports to have been written in the middle of the third millennium BCE in the Sage emperors period. The *Yaodian* tells of the making of calendars and the need to add extra days to keep the cycles of the sun and moon synchronized. Furthermore, Yao commanded his officers to "pay reverence to the grand celestial heavens, to delineate the regularities of the sun, the moon, stars, and constellations, and to relate respectfully to people the seasons for observance" (cited in Cullen 1996:174).

The time of the actual writing of *Yaodian* has been in dispute, but astronomers have not doubted its accuracy. As Chen (1996:113fn127) declares, "The crucial date is not the date when the document in its present form was complied, but the date when the astronomical knowledge contained in the document first emerged in history."

The requirement of changing the calendar suggests that some sort of calendar was even more ancient, since each "emperor" needed to rectify the calendar at the beginning of his reign. A luni-solar calendar is suggested, but one that had not yet been calculated to the exact length of years and months and lacked the refinements necessary to keep the seasons from slipping with the precession of the equinoxes. Based on the constellations that were said to pass through the meridian at the beginning of the four seasons, the date of Yao should be about 2400 BCE (Cullen 1996:171). The date is calculated by the backwards slippage over a 24,000-year period of the season in which each particular constellation rises (Cullen 1996).

Sky Lore

Some of the early myths of China also suggest that sky lore arose in the Neolithic. Guo (1999:46) relates that in the early period of Wu Di (Five Emperors), the emperor Zhuanxu ordered his minister Chongli to rearrange the cosmic order. A comparison of the constellations of that time and the myths about them as relating to the seasons suggests that "rearranging the cosmic order" had to do with the fact that the wrong asterisms were heralding the seasons.

Other sky lore presumably from the Neolithic or earlier is preserved in tales of creator gods. Nuwa, Changing Woman, propped up one corner of the sky with colored stones—possibly an explanation for the fact that at the latitude of China the sky rotates around a point in the northern sky, but seems to tilt.

The Shang period myth of ten suns is a strange and intriguing concept. The Shang week was ten days long. Three ten-day weeks approximate a month of twenty-nine days, in contrast to the four seven-day weeks in a month of the Western world, which also approximate a month. Neither pattern does the job perfectly, nor is it possible to do so with precision—the periodicity of days (rotation of the earth), months (the moon's travel around the earth), and years (circuits of the earth around the sun) are independent of each other and do not divide evenly. Although Western days of the week are named after ancient gods, there is no lore that associates each one with a different sun. But the Shang seem to have believed at some time in the distant past that in the beginning there were actually ten different suns. One sun rose each day from a mulberry tree in the east and set in the west in the Yellow Springs, whence it traveled back underground to the mulberry tree, awaiting its turn to cross the sky again. One terrible day, all ten suns rose at once, and Archer Yi had to shoot down nine of them (Allan 1991). It has been suggested that this myth could reflect a real event in which a comet or meteor gave unnatural illumination in the sky, but no specific event is mentioned. The sun was associated with a bird, perhaps because it flew across the sky. Thus a strong and skilled archer could shoot down a sun. Many birds appear in Neolithic art, either as realistic birds, as in the Hongshan culture, or associated with radiant circles probably representing suns, as in Hemudu and Liangzhu in southeastern China.

Other sky phenomena such as novae and comets were also observed and recorded. An oracle bone from the Shang dynasty tells of a "guest star," presumably a nova. It is the earliest known record of this kind of event. Such phenomena were usually considered good omens rather than evil portents (Feng 2001).

Interaction between Earth and Heaven

By the time extensive texts were written, the importance of watching the skies to keep track of the ways that objects moved in the sky is clear. Meanings were attached to particular configurations of stars or planets.

> The heavenly bodies loomed large in the lives of the ancient Chinese, and played a crucial role in China's political history, mythology, and religion. From the earliest written records down to China's first encounter with the West, comprehending the heavens was a primary goal. While departures from the heavenly norm were important (and almost always interpreted as omens), astronomers were also careful to observe the usual state of the heavens—the regular positions and motions of the stars (*hengxing*, or constant stars) and planets (*xingxing*, or moving stars). (Shaughnessy 2000:124)

The earliest Chinese conceptions of the heavens—traditionally attributed to the culture hero Fuxi—is called *gaitian* (covering heaven); a later and more sophisticated theory is known as *huntian* (englobing heaven). The *gaitian* theory, the more primitive of the two, depicts heaven as a hemisphere hovering over a square earth, and turning like a millstone (Sun 2000: 438–39). Divining boards from the Han dynasty were found in this shape (Major 1984) usually with the handle of the Big Dipper as a pointer. Such a board was unearthed in a Nangnang tomb, near Pyongyang, North Korea, indicating the distribution of this idea. To this day, many Korean shamans worship the seven stars of the Big Dipper, and a group of *menhirs* was arranged in this shape on the ground (Holt 1948).

The North Star was also a shamanic symbol in many places. Krupp (1983) relates that the Tungus cosmos is centered on the North Star as a symbol of constancy. "The sky just keeps turning, as it has always turned. In the minds of the Tungus, the universe has always existed, and the ever-spinning sky may have helped inspire this belief." This idea is very similar to that of the Chinese, who saw the Pole Star as the equivalent of the emperor, around whom everything else revolved. Tungus shamans also engaged in astral ritual, offering sacrifices and prayers to the stars of the Big Dipper, as the *mudangs* of Korea continue to do.

Massing of the Planets

"When the Five Planets appear in the east it is beneficial for China." This epigram was woven into the clothing of a Europoid man buried in a well preserved Eastern Han tomb in Xinjiang (Pankennier 2000:185). It is astonishing verification of the importance attached to this rare sky event—the conjunction of all five visible planets. Mars and Venus, being near the sun, are often seen together near the horizon. But Jupiter has a recurrence that places it in a group of five planets about every 520 years, so it can only join them (and Saturn and Mercury) rarely. The massing of the planets is said to have occurred when Shang overthrew Xia—and again when Zhou conquered Shang. The date of the beginning of the Zhou dynasty is calculated from the record of the five moving stars west of the constellation called the Vermillion Bird in China in 1059 BCE (Pankenier 1995:124). The beginning of the Shang should be about 520 years earlier. This suggests that records had been kept from the beginning of the Xia dynasty. King lists, recorded in the *Yaodian*, also suggest a written record more ancient than the oracle bones.

The exact dates of the earlier planet massings is debated, but the tradition that it occurred during the overthrow of Xia by Shang—and again when Zhou conquered Shang—was clearly important. Heaven's mandate was shining in the sky for all to see, validating these earthly events. Nivison and Pang note that an eclipse date of 1876 BCE was recorded in the Xia era. They calculate that the planets lined up "like pearls on a string" in late February 1953 BCE (Nivisson and Pang 1990:90) (Figure 2.5).

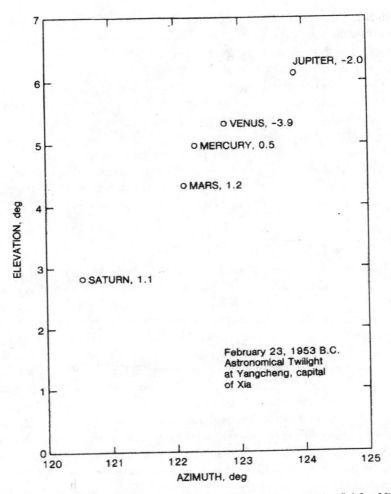

Figure 2.5 The five naked-eye planets lined up "like pearls on a string." After Nivison and Pang 1990

Sacrificing to Heaven and Earth

Sacrifices to heaven at a round altar at the time of the winter solstice and to earth at a square altar at the time of the summer solstice are described in the *Zhou Li*. K.C. Chang (2005:129) attributes such cosmological concepts to shamans. "The shamans and their cosmology were another important characteristic of ancient Chinese civilization. Shamanist practices played a major role in the acquisition of political power." Whether or not it was specifically a shamanistic rite in origin, the concreteness of offering to heaven and earth on altars at the solstices shows an ordered sense of the sky and its relationship to earth.

The Mandate of Heaven

Observations of the sky are important in China because they are linked to the ruler. "The ability to comprehend the celestial rhythms and to maintain conformity between their changes and human activity was a fundamental qualification of early Chinese kingship" (Pankenier 2005:122). Thus, the king had to be an astronomer (or employ astronomers) as well as a diviner. Since the heavens were believed to control human affairs, the shaman's contact with the spirits was political (Ching 1997:15). Just as important, the skies told the state of the earthly realm and predicted the future. Reading the movements of heavenly bodies was a necessity for leadership. Royal duties included checking on the movements of objects in the sky, performing sacrifices to the sky, and worshipping the ancestral tablets and the gods of mountains and rivers (Shaughnessy 2000:124).

Continuation of Sky Worship

Textual records of Manchurian sky worship indicate that the Puyo people of Manchuria celebrated an annual festival in which they sang and danced to honor the sun. Sun worship also extended to the Han people of southern Korea and to the early Japanese, who believed the islands were created by the Sun Goddess Amaterasu.

New archaeological work in Mongolia is beginning to confirm the ancient importance of the sky to the Mongols. Large stone conglomerations called *khirigsuurs* (Allard and Erdenbataar 2005) suggest not only ancient use but also continued horse sacrifices and other events that take place at these monuments. At least some of the experts believe they may have shamanistic contents. If "political power was actually conferred upon Genghis Khan by the sky through shamanic protocol" (Krupp 1997:191), then perhaps the ceremony occurred at a *khirigsuur* or similar monument.

The theme of rulers being related to the sky is important to understand East Asian rulership. It was not just the sun that mattered, nor the sun and the moon, but the actions of the stars and the planets, as well as changes through the seasons. The ruler was reflected in the sky, and the sky reflected landscapes on earth.

Conclusion

The landscapes, legends, and skyscapes are all part of the context of East Asian archaeology. Prehistoric and early historic peoples created their own stories from their surroundings and their own societies, thus they understood their world in specific ways. Some of this perspective can be gleaned from legends, history, and even from archaeological sites.

THE PUYANG BURIAL, CHINA

The most celebrated and complex of the Neolithic burials alleged to represent a shaman is the elaborate tomb complex M45 at Xishuipo, Puyang county, Henan province. It dates from about 4000 BCE. The burial is described as the earliest archaeological evidence of sky lore in East Asia (Figure B.1) (Zhang 2005:77). The burial complex includes four humans, two mosaic animals, and a smaller group of shells associated with two long bones. The central burial is a male, extended on his back with his head to the south. Three other

Figure B.1 Puyang burial. After Zhang 2005

bodies of young adults were ranged around him. They were placed at a slightly higher level than the burial itself, perhaps as guardians. Mosaics made of mussel shell were placed on each side of the central skeleton. The mosaic on the west side of the body is clearly a four-legged animal with a long tail, and it is reasonable to interpret this as a tiger. A saurian creature 1.78 meters long, glossed as a dragon, lies on the east. Both heads are pointed north. The shell animals are referred to as mosaics because a few shells of different colors are included—for example, the dragon's feet and teeth are made of white and gray shells, while the eyes are black and white, and the tongue is dark red. The body scales are made of arrow-shaped shells. The arrangement of shells and bones at the feet of the main burial is labeled "North Dipper" by the excavators. This construction was planned out in detail and clearly had a special meaning for those who participated in the burial ritual.

To many Chinese archaeologists this configuration suggests that by the fifth millennium BCE, some of the Neolithic inhabitants of northern China already had conceived of at least two of the four directions as being represented by symbolic animals (Pankenier 2005:508). The animal mosaics demonstrate their importance by each taking up as much space as the central burial. In fact, everything about the configuration looks like danger is expected from the north.

Other depictions made with shells belong to the same complex. To the north, more mollusk shells were laid on the ground, mosaic fashion. They seem to portray a creature with the body of a tiger and the head of a dragon. Nearby a deer and a spider are grouped together. It is likely that these animals illustrate lost myths or local stories. The third group is made up of a human riding a dragon, with a tiger, a bird, and two piles of shells nearby (Zhang 2005). It is interesting that the concept of a human riding a four-legged animal was present so early in the Neolithic. Perhaps ridden horses or reindeer had been seen, even if riding was not actually practiced. This complex is said to be the result of a ritual event—the burial of an important shaman. The tomb with its accompanying mosaic animal designs is unique in its details, although other examples of mosaic figures made from shells or stones are known, and other large dragons were sculpted from clay.

Although this grouping implies the eastern dragon and the western tiger, the belief in animals of the four directions is not attested in texts before the Han period. However, the size and placement of this tiger and dragon make a good case for the directional concept to have arisen at least by the Neolithic (e.g., Zhang 2005:77–78).

These mosaics were described as shamanistic because they imply a ritual practice, and the placement of dragon and tiger seem to relate to concepts of guardian animals in particular parts of the sky. Zhang specifically calls the complex a "sacrificial ritual performed by a shaman with the help of his three assistants" (Zhang 2005:78), but this description may be too specific. While this is a spectacular burial, it is not universally accepted as early evidence of the identification of asterisms in the east and west as dragon and tiger. Other archaeologists doubt that the three sections of shell mosaics were contemporaneous (Yang 2000:53).

Possibly relevant to interpreting the burial is the location: the Puyang site is near the Dragon Temple of Leize on the north bank of the Yellow River. This region was a marshland in ancient times and might actually have sheltered crocodiles. It is said that the culture hero Fuxi was conceived when a young woman stepped in the footprint of the God of Thunder. Thunder is associated with rain and dragons (Da Gen 1988).

THREE

WHAT IS A SHAMAN?

One thing about the shamans involving a condition alien to healthy individuals has always impressed observers: the incoherent exclamations and movements, the foaming at the mouth, vacant stare, and total loss of consciousness at one of the most critical moments of the ritual.

—Vladimir Basilov 1997:3

Anciently, human beings and spirits did not mix. But certain persons who were so perspicacious, single-minded, reverential, and correct that their intelligence could understand what lies above and below, their sagely wisdom could illumine what is distant and profound, their vision was bright and clear, and their hearing was penetrating. Therefore the spirits would descend upon them. The possessors of such powers were, if men, called xi *and if women,* wu. *They supervised the positions of the spirits at the ceremonies, took care of sacrificial victims and vessels as well as of the seasonal robes.*

—*Guo-yū, Chu-yū* part 2, 18:1a. Translated by Ching 1997:14–15.

51

THE TWO QUOTES above are entirely contradictory, describing two poles of opinions about shamans. The discrepancy causes me to wonder, what images of shamanism do archaeologists hold in their heads? Is a shaman some scruffy reindeer herder wearing a tattered costume, beating a homemade drum and pretending to contact spirits? A woman with wild hair and chains sewed to her coat, clanking as she dances? Or is the shaman a leader of the community, a respected person whose ability to contact spirits offers proof of the ability to lead while conferring the right to do so? These are not trivial questions. The mental image that the word "shaman" elicits is surely a factor in admiration or distaste for shamans in the past, which influences the willingness (or lack thereof) to consider shamans as leaders instrumental in state formation. Unfortunately, archaeologists and historians of China as a rule do not describe their perceptions of shamans, nor do they usually attempt to imagine (at least not in writing) the details of the rituals or other activities of the shamans whose existence they posit or deny. In the absence of such statements it is impossible to know, but it seems likely that competing versions of shamanism underlie the ongoing debate about shamans as early rulers in East Asia.

Although ethnographic writings on shamanism usually treat shamans with respect (occasionally mixed with skepticism about what "really" happens in shamanic events known as séances), the disheveled Siberian shaman is probably the image most archaeologists tend to visualize. It is the popular image, the one that is evoked by Eliade's (1964) influential *Shamanism: Archaic Techniques of Ecstasy*. The prevailing image is the shaman as psychopomp, not the shaman as knowledgeable community leader. Although many current scholars of shamanism find Eliade's work flawed (e.g., Howard 1998a; Kehoe 2000; Thomas and Humphrey 1994), his version of shamanism has held strong in popular culture. Furthermore, much that has been written about shamanism in the former Soviet Union was filtered through Soviet eyes, which, officially at least, considered shamanism to be a superstition needing to be stamped out, along with all other superstition and religion (Balzer 1997:xiii–xiv). Siberian shamanism, often taken to be the most ancient and definitive form, was distorted by the persecutions of the Stalin era. The resulting poverty and dislocation of many groups with shaman leaders often made the leaders less effective than they had been before Russian contact—and, what was more disruptive, séances either ceased altogether or were held in secret. For the most part, Siberian peoples with shamanistic beliefs and rituals were shamelessly abused (Reid 2002:157–66), and the remnant Siberian and Central Asia shamanism recorded today must be a shadow of its former self.

We cannot reclaim the earliest histories of Siberian shamanism beyond some stories and myths (Nowak and Durrant 1977; Van Deusen 2001, 2004), and some pre-Soviet records describing the earliest encounters with shamanistic séances (Balzer 1990; Glavetskaya 2001; Znamenski 2003). These snippets focus on séance events, rarely allowing a glimpse of the shaman's standing in the community. In considering the archaeological past, a broader understanding about what shamans did within the community is needed.

The archaeology of East Asia has produced many artifacts and sites that cannot be entirely explained in terms of economy and ecology. Some artifacts seem to have nothing to do with acquiring food, staying out of bad weather, or other practical concerns. These unusual objects or unexplained features in archaeological sites tend to be labeled as shamanistic, a trend that runs throughout East Asia. The largest numbers of sites believed to reflect shamanism in the Neolithic and Bronze Age are found in China, but China does not have a monopoly on apparent ritual. Many sites and artifacts in the rest of East Asia and contiguous regions are also designated as shamanistic. These sites present a variety of features. Rock art in the Russian Far East is said to portray shamanistic elements, including humans and animals with visible skeletons depicted inside the skin and sun-like faces surrounded by rays (Okladnikov 1981). Scenes with humans wearing flamboyant costumes in Siberia and Central Asia are believed to portray shamans (Devlet 2001). Just north of China, the ancient "deer stones" of Mongolia may be interpreted as shamanistic (Fitzhugh et al. 2005). Several protohistoric sites in Korea and Japan are believed to represent shamanic activities, ranging from shell masks in coastal Korean sites (Im and Kwon 1984) and *haniwa* tomb figures believed to represent shamans in Kofun period Japan (Kidder 1965), to bronze artifacts—especially mirrors and bells, which are often attributed to shamanistic rites in the early Bronze Age of both Korea and Japan (Won-Yong Kim 1986; Seyock 2004).

It is easy to understand why the attribution of ritual behavior to shamanism would be attractive in East Asia. The supposed homeland of shamanism is Siberia, a region which shares some archaeological attributes with East Asia in the Paleolithic and Neolithic and which is not so far away that it is unreasonable to posit connections between the regions either in the form of movements of people or the spread of ideas. But before examining the specifics of archaeological discoveries said to represent shamans, it will be useful to have a brief look how archaeologists interpret religion in general, and shamanism in particular.

The Archaeology of Religion, Magic, and Ritual

Very little that is analytical has been written about the archaeology of religion—and even less about shamanism in archaeology. Archaeologists are not uniform in their understanding of shamanism, or of religion, or even of ideology. More attention, however, is being paid to ritual in recent years.

Although explanations of archaeological sites and materials as related to ritual has been one of those perennial jokes in archaeology—"if you can't identify it, call it a ritual object"—the topic of religion is beginning to receive more serious consideration in mainstream archaeology. For example, Ralph Merrifield, differentiating religion from magic, defines religion as "the belief in supernatural or spiritual beings," and magic as "the use of practices intended to bring occult forces under control and so to influence events" (Merrifield 1987:6). These definitions separate ideology from activities, perhaps as a result of focusing on rituals more than on religion (Merrifield 1987:xiii). Rituals, in Merrifield's usage, are not necessarily religious, but are "prescribed or customary behaviors" that could be simply magical or might have social functions. The purpose of rituals is "to gain advantage or avert disaster by the manipulation of supernatural power." Shamanism falls within these broad parameters both as belief and as practice. Unfortunately for East Asianists, Merrifield's archaeological examples are largely drawn from Europe and tend toward intermittent events, such as depositing votive offerings in wells. Little help is available for recognizing shamanism in East Asia.

Although attention to religion as a phenomenon in the archaeological record is relatively new, even when religion is the topic of interest shamanism is not likely to be in the foreground. In a recent book on the archaeology of religion, Timothy Insoll (2004:43) allocates only a few paragraphs to shamanism, preferring to examine the more general question of religion and archaeology rather than any specific religious beliefs or practices. However, in his brief discussion of shamanism, Insoll makes an important point about archaeological attitudes toward shamanism, one which is directly relevant to East Asia. He notes that shamanism was seen as low on the evolutionary ladder by most writers about early religions, with shamanism falling between totemism and anthropomorphism (e.g., Tylor 1889). This evolutionary perspective may help explain why shamanism tends to be almost exclusively discussed in the company of other "primitive" religions, but it needs to be revisited.

Insoll does not attempt to define shamanism. He only suggests that shamanism can be better approached by archaeologists through context rather than definitions. That advice is well taken, because context—whether or not other evidence of shamanism is present—certainly provides the determining factor of whether a given site or object is reasonable to interpret as relating to a performance of a shamanistic ritual. Several items of material culture have been used as possible evidence of shamanism in archaeology. Since performance has received most of the attention in scholarly writing on shamanism, a context that suggests ritual performance can help differentiate among the possible uses of those artifacts.

Although often simply called shamans, there is disagreement about which word best conveys the essence of these early leaders. Tong (2002) feels more comfortable using the Chinese word *wu* to describe these practitioners in China rather than referring to them as shamans. He uses instead the concept of "wuism" (after DeGroot 1910) to emphasize the particulars of Chinese practices. In his discussion of wuism, Tong defines religion, simply, as relating to the supernatural world and the beliefs, duties, and practices that pertain to the interaction between the human world and that of the spirits. Tong cites thirty-six classical Chinese texts that pertain to wuism, and it is reasonable to assume that he found and assembled the majority of ancient Chinese references to the *wu* in the *Shanhaijing*, which is considered a manual for shamans. Such texts demonstrate that ancient people were well acquainted with *wu* and their practices. Tong observes that the meaning of the term *wu* changed through time, suggesting that the word was applied to shamanistic practitioners earlier, and "priestly" ones later.

Tong (2002:31) uses "magicians" as a larger category that includes shamans, but I am not comfortable with this taxonomy. Perhaps the Chinese word led Tong to this conclusion. *Wushu*, or the art of the *wu*, is translated into English as "magic." While some shamans may practice sleight of hand, ventriloquism, and other magic tricks in séances, magic is not the basis of wuism. In any case, Tong does not emphasize magic in his discussion of wuism. He defines shamans as "part-time religious practitioners, either male or female . . . [with] the ability to communicate with spirits through divination, sacrifice, exorcism, or spells." His emphasis is on communicating with spirits rather than the performance of magic. In late antiquity the *wu* were not primarily performers, but instead belonged to the intelligentsia. In this regard, Tong discusses the *wu* as possible originators of important facets of

Chinese culture, such as the Chinese script, astronomy, and music. These are salient characteristics, to be discussed in chapter 5 in the context of archaeology.

Archaeological attention to shamanism is beginning to affect mainstream archaeology somewhat, in spite of a slow start. A recent introductory archaeology text mentions shamanism several times in more than ten contexts. Shamans are defined as "men and women who serve as intermediaries between the living and supernatural worlds and are thought to have magical powers. . . . They are sometimes called *spirit mediums*" (Fagan 2007:460). Neil Price (2001) edited a volume specifically dedicated to describing shamanism in archaeological contexts. Regrettably, East Asia is not covered in these pages, although neighboring regions of Central Asia and Siberia are represented. Describing the archaeology of shamanism as being one of "altered states," Price discusses shamanism as a way to deal with a world full of spirits that must be placated.

European archaeological data that is believed to reflect shamanism is compiled in a volume that specifically seeks shamanism, not religion in general, through archaeology (Aldhouse-Green and Aldhouse-Green 2005). This book minimally defines shamanism as an ecstatic religion involving soul journeys of persons chosen by the spirits, thus following Eliade's overly specific and dated definition. Based on Eliade they likewise assert that shamans are able to induce the trance state in themselves in order to intercede with the supernatural world, thus promoting the prosperity and success of their group. The Aldhouse-Greens stress a worldview in which "souls may inhabit trees, rivers, mountains, and stones, where everything around them possessed (or was possessed by) a spirit force, whether sky, sun, river, mountain, rock outcrop, cave, house, or hunted creature" (10–11). Archaeological examples from Europe offered by the Aldhouse-Greens are ordered by time period. They include possible evidence of shamanistic beliefs—such as red ocher burials, rock art, megalithic monuments, bog bodies, and representations of humans wearing antlers—but they do not discuss what these might have meant to the overall culture, or to leadership.

Archaeologists thus use varying definitions of shamanism, including both beliefs and activities. Can archaeologists distinguish shamanism from other rituals or religious beliefs? For that matter, how do ethnographers draw the line between shamanism and other ways of dealing with an unseen world?

The generalizing of shamans through time and space can be laid at the door of Eliade (1964), who characterized shamanism as "archaic techniques of ecstasy." Emphasis on ecstasy remains the most central definition of shamanism for many archaeologists. Not only is the trance state perceived as a defining characteristic of shamanism, but so is "archaic," putting shamanism, as noted above, low on any religious evolutionary scale.

Because it is perceived as a primitive religion, many who study shamanism seek its origins (e.g., Tedlock 2005). Like Eliade, they find in the Paleolithic the source for all shamanism. However, for this exploration of shamanism in East Asia it is not necessary to seek either an original time and place of shamanism or a primal form of it in the ethnographic present. Changes are to be expected in cultural forms, and shamanism, even in its narrowest definitions, has changed through time and with different circumstances. To chase a "pure" shamanism of the distant past is to chase events as transient as a séance itself. It is more appropriate to allow for varieties of shamanism than to try to shoe-horn all shamanisms into one reindeer herder's boot. On the other hand, it is important to bear in mind that not all forms of "primitive" religion must be related to shamanism. For example, while animism and ancestor worship can exist without shamanism, the work of shamans can also partake of and enhance animism and ancestor worship. This topic is discussed further below.

Shamans in Ethnology

Definitions of Shamanism

In seeking a useful definition of shamanism for archaeological interpretations, problems arise if definitions are either too broad or too narrow. Broad uses of the term allow shamans to be identified in cultures worldwide (e.g., Eliade 1964), but narrow ones can hardly be applied outside their supposed homeland of Siberia. A middle ground is needed. While generally it is agreed that the word shaman comes from the language of the reindeer Tungus of Central Siberia (e.g., Price 2001:3), the concept has been applied to many peoples who are far from any reindeer. The prevailing tendency is for the term shamanism to be used broadly in many ethnographic accounts. Kehoe (2000:2) says that shamanism "is used so loosely and naively by anthropologists no less than the general public, that they convey confusion more than knowledge."

Defining shamanism is not only an archaeological problem. In a summary article about shamanism from an anthropological viewpoint, Atkinson (1992:308) voices skepticism. "Among cultural anthropologists there is widespread distrust of general theories of shamanism, which run aground in their efforts to generalize." If ethnographies fail archaeology as a source of usable definitions of shamanism, romanticizing of shamanism fails even more. "The magnetism of shamanism is not just a strand in pop religion or an aesthetic. . . . Shamanism is more of an exotic essence . . . than a scholarly category that can stand up to any sustained interrogation" (Thomas and Humphrey 1994:2).

Shamans are said to have many purposes. "Traditional shamans provided psychotherapy, cures, and leadership for their communities, along with poetry and entertainment" (Balzer 1997:xiv). Shamanisms have been identified on most continents (e.g., Tedlock 2005), but sometimes it is difficult to say exactly what it is they have in common. Laurel Kendall (1985:27–28) suggests that the term shamanism is often "sloppily applied," and others who discuss Korean shamanism agree (Howard 1998a).

Shamans vs. Priests

Shamans have been contrasted with priests in order to define both categories. Often shamans are said to be individual leaders with access to spirits, while priests are those with a written tradition and set rituals. For example, Takiguchi (2003:122) proposes that shamans are "inspirational individuals, and [priests] are institutional functionaries in some kind of religious hierarchy." However, not everyone uses these concepts in the same way. Sarah Allan (1991:85) considers the *wu* of the Shang dynasty, to be discussed in chapter 6, to have been "specialized priests who could call the souls of the dead." She does not use the term shaman; instead she considers the thinking of Shang to be "mythic."

Shamans as Spirit Contacts

Some scholars make a distinction between those who are believed to journey to the spirits and those in whom the spirits descend. The former are called shamans; the latter are spirit mediums. However, this is not always a useful distinction. For example, some Korean shamans call down the spirits and some Siberian shamans' souls journey to them, but otherwise they perform similar actions. In either case the shaman is personally in contact with spirits, and that is the characteristic that is important for Korean shamanism. Perhaps the simplest way to distinguish shamans from other religious practitioners is that the shaman's soul must contact spirits.

Shamans and Knowledge

Shamans are often described as knowledgeable people. Kehoe (2000) explains that the root "sa" as found in the original Tungusic word *saman* means "to know." "Knowledgeable" is a useful way to think about *wu* and *mu*, especially as they became leaders in increasingly complex societies. Hsu (1986) makes the same point about those who read the oracle bones in Shang China, noting that they were knowledgeable specialists. Of course being knowledgeable is not sufficient to define a shaman, for many people had various kinds of knowledge. Shamans, though, had specialist knowledge about spirits, presumably based on keen intelligence and observations of other people in the context of their lives.

While observations on shamans as leaders will be discussed further in the next chapter, emphasis on the shaman as a political actor as well as a religious practitioner is critical to the question of the shaman's sociopolitical position. The shaman as leader is particularly a propos for East Asia, for it has been argued based on both texts and archaeology that in the process of state formation "charismatic power may be appropriated and incorporated in the center" (Thomas and Humphrey 1994:4). Several archaeologists believe this appropriation describes the sequence in China.

Shamans as Healers

Treating illnesses is an important shamanistic activity often performed in the context of séance. For example, Balzer (1997) calls shamanism an "ancient medical system." She highlights the intention to cure as follows:

> Many writers would agree that shamans are medical and spiritual practitioners. The term "Medicine Men" applied to Native Americans, suggests the same combination of abilities and activities (and the usual gender mistake). Blessing, foretelling the future, and dancing for rain are among other specific activities that are connected with shamans, but they may also be seen as sorcerers, with the potential to do evil. But mostly they are intermediaries between two worlds: the spirits and humans. (Balzer 1997:xiii)

Balzer thus defines shamans as both healers and leaders. She discusses several debates about the nature of shamanism, including whether the healing is "real" (Balzer 1997:xvii). These debates center around the "political, mystical, and religious roles" played by shamans.

Ching (1997:13) also considers healing an important aspect of shamanism, defining the shaman thus: "He or she serves the community by divination and healing, although in China, praying for rain has been a principal responsibility." Indeed, as will be seen in the context of Shang and Chu shamanism, praying for rain looms large in texts as a shamanic activity.

The Shaman's Drum

Kehoe describes shamans as "religious leaders, men and women, who serve their communities by using hand-held drums to call spirit allies" (Kehoe 2000:15). The limited version of Siberian shamanism is too simple for exploring the varieties that became the Chinese *wu* and Korean *mu*, as well as many other East Asian traditions. While the statement about serving their communities is one that is important for East Asia, focusing on the hand-held drum is too specific. It omits much that is salient for shamanism as it is practiced in East Asia in the present. For example, drums are used in shamanistic séance almost everywhere in Asia, but they are not all hand-held drums, and even when drums are held, the shaman is not necessarily the one holding the drum. There are even shamanic traditions in which the primary instrument is not a drum at all. In Korea a member of the percussion band beats the two-sided large red drum, and others play smaller drums and cymbals as well, often in a trio sitting on a mat on the shaman's heated floor (Figure 3.1).

Drums found in archaeological contexts in East Asia are likewise of several kinds. Wooden drums stretched with crocodile hide were prominent in the Longshan Neolithic, and there are possible ceramic drums in Hongshan and Longshan. Red hourglass-shaped wooden drums with hide ends feature prominently in Korean rituals. The same red drums are used in recreation involving circle dancing. These drums are available to rent for a picnic with drinking and dancing on temple grounds in Korea. The huge decorated bronze drums in southern China and southeast Asia in the Bronze Age must have been used in ceremonies and rituals. Even allowing for the importance of percussive instruments, a problem for archaeologists may arise when hand-held skin drums stretched on a wooden frame left no traces, being made entirely of perishable materials. But even in cases where hand-held drums were not used, the *wu* and *mu* certainly had rhythmic ways to call up their spirit allies. Even hand claps can be used, as they are in some Buddhist temples. One must conclude that drums per se cannot be seen as the defining characteristic of East Asian shamanism, although at least some sort of rhythmic percussion does seem to be imperative for ritual dancing.

Figure 3.1 Shaman ritual near Seoul. Note the percussion band sitting on a mat on the left, and the altar on the right. Photo by H. S. Nelson

Shamans in History

Inner Asia

Excellent reviews and translations of writings about Siberia and Central Asian shamanism have been published in English (Balzer 1997; Knecht 2003; Znamenski 2003). This is not the place to detail the history of encounters with shamans, although the variability of shamanism is instructive. Reid (2002) effectively describes the terrible experiences of native groups in Siberia during the Stalinist era, and how shamanism was affected—as well as the dismal results for the careers and even lives of the ethnographers themselves. The point to be made here is that shamanism changes according to circumstances, as do the outsiders' responses to shamanism.

Chinese Wuism

If the word shaman can be used only to describe religious practitioners among the reindeer Tungus, then another concept is needed to apply within East Asia. This is probably the reason that the Chinese word *wu* is used for Chinese ecstatic religious practices and the neologism wuism, rather than shamanism, is preferred by some. However, not all scholars who use the word shaman to translate the character *wu* would agree that the *wu* mainly represent "archaic techniques of ecstasy."

Shuowen, an ancient Chinese dictionary, defines the character *wu* as follows: "*Wu* are Chu, female, capable of serving the formless [spirits] and dancing to bring down the spirits. [The character] is composed of a person extending the two sleeves in the act of dancing" (Ching 1997:20) (Figure 3.2). Chang has suggested that the oracle bone version of the character depicts an instrument used to draw circles and squares, which represent heaven and earth, respectively. He thus proposes that *wu* had access to earth and heaven by virtue of geometry, being able to draw circles and squares, which had magical meaning (Chang 2005). Fuxi and Nuwa, mythical founders of China noted in the previous chapter, are sometimes depicted holding the compass and square rule. "Thus, the shamans of the Shang and Zhou periods were mathematicians who understood the heaven and earth and were sages and wise men" (Tong 2002). Yet another suggestion regarding the character *wu* is that it represents yarrow (milfoil) sticks, which were thrown in ancient China for divinatory purposes. Keightley (1982:299) reports with skepticism that Akatsuka sees the graph for *wu* as "a picture of the altar stand possessed by the spirits summoned from the four quarters." The graph thus functions as a Rohrschach test for sinologists. So much has been seen in this simple character of six or seven strokes (the oracle bone version of the character differs slightly from the current character) that it seems wise to avoid interpreting the graph as an image, but consider it a concept.

Wu and *xi* also can be represented as "brilliant descendants of past sages" who have much occult knowledge. These descendants managed ancestral temples and knew the names of rivers and mountains. They could recite lineages leading back to distant ancestors, and their knowledge allowed proper ranking of generations. *Wu* were therefore historians, guardians of knowledge of the past (Wu 1982:12), even when it was remembered through oral history.

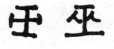

Figure 3.2 The character for *wu*, left, from oracle bone script, right, modern script. Calligraphy by S. M. Nelson

Other Beliefs and Rituals in East Asia

The problem of slippery definitions of shamanism in archaeology is even wider than the attribution of shamanisms to all manner of interesting discoveries. Other anthropological concepts—such as totemism, animism, and ancestor worship—are often evoked indiscriminately and likewise without definition. It is worth a brief look at these other religious concepts that become intertwined with shamanism to see to what extent they are useful or whether they contribute "noise."

Totemism

While totemism is not usually defined when evoked in East Asian archaeological contexts, the mere presence of animal depictions seems to be sufficient to call forth this response. Totemism is the belief that a particular group of people are related to a specific kind of animal and may include taboos related to that animal, whether it is a wolf, a kangaroo, or a worm. This is a group belief, not at all resembling the animal spirit helpers of some individual shamans. Often art historians and archaeologists use the word totemism without any explicit discussion about its relationship with shamanism. Since totemism as a useful concept has been discredited in anthropology (Atkinson 1992:308); its lack of definition when called upon in Asia need not give us further pause. It is not relevant to the question of shamanism in ancient East Asia and can be safely ignored.

Animism

Animism does relate to shamanism, although the presence of animism does not presuppose shamanism. Essentially, animism is a worldview that sees everything as alive in some sense, with an independent spirit. Rocks, trees, springs, rivers, mountains, and even diseases may thus have spirits, as well as buildings, birds, and hearths. Animism may underlie some shamanistic beliefs, such as the belief in spirits of mountains and rivers, wind, and rain, but without written documents it is impossible to recognize animism directly from archaeological discoveries.

Where archaeology fails, however, texts can be used with caution. Korean myths and legends, for example, strongly suggest early animism in the Korean peninsula (Nelson 1990). On the other hand, spirits can inhabit a stone or a tree without the stone or tree itself being a spirit. It is unlikely that archaeological materials will ever be able to make this subtle distinction, but it is important for understanding beliefs about spirits.

Myths that assert the prestigious ancestry of queens from goddesses of mountains are intended to establish the relationship of queens to mountain spirits anthropomorphized as females (Nelson 1990). Spirit shrines were (and are still) often erected on mountains, even if the mountain top also supports a military look-out post (Kendall 1998). A shrine can be as simple as a pile of stones—or a tree or rock with ribbons, paper, or straw attached. The marking of shrines can be too ephemeral to appear in archaeological contexts.

An example of a sacred place inhabited by spirits in ancient Korea is that sacred groves called *sodo* in southern Korea were marked by a tall pole, drums, and bells (Parker 1890). It is reasonable to suppose that these numinous places were inhabited by spirits who lived among the trees, although the text is not specific on this point. As recently as the mid-twentieth century, even after the Korean War and deforestation caused by poverty and limited access to fuel had destroyed most of Korea's forests, many Korean villages surrounded an old sacred tree that escaped the axes of villagers desperate for firewood. Some revered *mudangs* outside the walls of Seoul kept a large tree by their shrine to which strips of colorful cloth were tied (Figure 3.3). Old Korean villages had a pair of wooden guardian figures called *jangseung* on each road leading into the village. Inscriptions on the posts named them the

Figure 3.3 Sacred tree with ribbons. Photo by H. S. Nelson

Earth Grandmother and the Sky Grandfather (Figure 3.4). Since similar figures in Cheju Island and parts of the southern coast are made of stone, their ability to guard did not derive from the trees from which they were cut, but from rituals related to their manufacture and placement.

As for activities in sacred places, in texts written in the early centuries of the Common Era (Parker 1890), Korean rituals are said to have included singing, dancing, and drinking alcoholic beverages as ways to worship the gods. The place for such activities was specifically noted to be a cave in the case of Puyo—surely a place imbued with spirits. For that matter, many caves in China containing Paleolithic and Neolithic remains are called Xianren Dong, Spirit

Figure 3.4 *Miruk* from Puyo. Photo by H. S. Nelson

Cave, suggesting that these places were believed to harbor spirits related to ancient relics. Daoism in China preserves remnants of animism as well (Allan 1997). It seems that mountains, rocks, water, and trees are home to spirits throughout East Asia.

Ancestor Worship

Ancestor worship is yet another Chinese concept that sometimes has been alleged to be interpretable in prehistory and occasionally is conflated with shamanism. A belief in spirits of the dead who need to be fed and who can influence the living (Allan 1991) is connected to shamanism because some shamanistic spirits are ancestors. Ancestor veneration is probably the most accessible of these rituals to archaeologists, as well as being a known indigenous belief in East Asia. Neolithic evidence for ancestor worship is usually adduced from grave goods, which are interpreted as evidence of graveside feasting to appease the spirits of the recently dead (Fung 2000; Liu 2000; Nelson 2003a).

However, while feasting may involve intoxicants and riotous behavior, it is not the same as a séance. Ching (1997:25) notes that the graph *wu* appears in the context of sacrifices to nature powers, especially wind and rain, but not to ancestors. On the other hand, Keightley (1983:555) puts the emphasis on ancestor worship, not nature or the powers, as "the organizing metaphor of Shang life." Ancestor worship can exist without shamans, but the two may be intertwined. Spirits of the dead are among the pantheon of spirits called upon by shamans. Korean shamans to this day perform a separate *kut* for the dead, calling back their souls (Janelli and Janelli 1982).

Ancestor worship may have contributed to political consolidation. Tong (2002:43) specifically connects ancestor worship with the rise of the state: "In the course of state formation, if a clan or family became the ruling group of a polity, then its ancestors would become the gods of the whole polity." This apparently occurred in the case of the Shang kings. Tong points out that in the Zhou dynasty, "towns having an ancestral temple, with the spirit tablets of former rulers, were called capitals . . ." (Tong 2002:43). Having ancestral spirits thus *defines* a capital. Akatsuka further suggests that the town, the clan, and the ruler all had the same name (Keightley 1982). The identification of the elite and their ancestors with the religious ideology was thus complete.

It is clear that each of these belief systems—animism, ancestor veneration, and shamanism—is an independent variable. Each needs to be demonstrated separately; none implies any other. Animism, ancestor worship, and a belief that spirits of the dead exist and can interfere with the living are independent of shamanism, although they may coexist. It is inappropriate to use either animism or ancestor worship alone as evidence of shamanism in the past.

However totemism, animism, and ancestor worship are not the limits of concepts that have been related to shamanism in East Asia. Cosmological concepts are also implicated. Evidence for ancient astronomy is often tied into cosmological concepts of later East Asia (e.g., Nelson et al. 2005). Since the purpose of early Chinese astronomy was to discover the will of heaven (Pankenier 1995; Sun 2000), reading the sky is closely related to other kinds of divination.

Archaeologists have used Chinese cosmological concepts to interpret prehistoric sites. For some archaeological examples, the ancient Chinese belief that heaven is round and the earth is square has been used to explain several kinds of archaeological objects and features. Square and round constructions, especially flat-topped altars and rounded burial mounds, are said to be evidence for the antiquity of this cosmological belief (Sun and Guo 1986a). Round jade objects (*bi*) and square ones (*cong*) are likewise implicated as cosmological symbols.

These are all interesting ideas, and I am not suggesting that they are wrongly applied, only that the synergy between other religious concepts and shamanism needs to be queried in each instance, and the connection made explicit. In order to examine the question of shamans as leaders, it is necessary to ask what aspects of shamanism can be teased out of archaeological sites, what activities occurred, and how shamans brought about the desired effect.

Practices of Shamans

If ethnographers—with live people and events to observe and describe, and participants to question—cannot be specific about what is and is not shamanism, what hope is there for archaeological explanations, with our much more impoverished catalog of material objects and their relationships to describe and explore? We are warned that "shamanism should not be thought of as a single centrally organized religion, as there are many variations" (Stutley 2002:2), which is no doubt good advice for ethnographers, but difficult for archaeologists. For archaeological interpretation, it is important to focus on practices and the associated material culture used in shamanistic séance.

The literature of shamanism suggests that the major activity of shamans is staging dramatic events, which ethnographers often call séance. Balzer calls séance "the heart of shamanism." The activities of séance include music, dancing, trancing, and audience involvement, as well magic and special effects. Balzer's (1990:xvii) insistence on public performance is a key to interpreting archaeological sites. If there is no audience to see the séance, is it shamanism? For example, audience involvement is important in Korean shamanism, but not, as far as is known, in the oracle bone divinations of Shang China. Divination was not usually performed before an audience (Keightley 1982), but was there an implicit audience? And even if there was no audience for the act of divination, were there other public events? Were there announcements to the public that the ensuing sacrifice was to Ancestor X in order to cure the king's toothache? Who watched the sacrifices to the powers that were the subject of divination? These questions are not answerable with present data.

Still less is known about performances of Neolithic shamans. In contrast to activities of Siberian shamans and later shamans in East Asia, there is no written description of what alleged Neolithic shamans may have done. A catalogue of activities of the *wu* is found in an Early Zhou document (Falkenhausen 1995), which implies differences from Siberian practices, but continuity nevertheless from a time when séances were part of the repertoire of the *wu*. Activities listed include rain-making, star-gazing, medicine and healing, divination, music and dancing. In later times and in various places, as will be explored in more detail in chapter 8, these practices are sometimes divided among different kinds of practitioners. For example, in Korea fortune tellers, who use a number of devices including astrology, are not the same as those who dance to heal and to learn the reasons for ill fortune of other kinds. As a general rule, neither group includes rain-making in their repertoire.

Practices performed by shamans may be carried out by other ritualists as well, so that in many cases archaeologists may be able only to recognize ritual, but not specifically shamanism. Nevertheless, it is still helpful to consider shamanistic activities and the items of material culture that might indicate shamanism. While many take trancing (or ecstasy) as the essential element of shamanism, trance and dance leave few archaeological traces. What can an archaeologist hope to find to indicate shamanism?

Material Culture of Shamans

Archaeologists need guidance about the kinds of material culture to expect, dependent as we are upon the material manifestation of ephemeral events that relate to the question of performance. The objects said to represent shamanism in East Asia include a variety of artifacts. The underlying logic to the claims of shamanism in archaeological contexts relates to both practices and beliefs. The problem is that shamanistic artifacts often have no continuous thread. The dazzling gold crowns of the Silla kingdom of Korea seem to have little in common with the depictions of possible animal masks on Shang bronzes. While it is important to consider each within its own context, it would be reassuring to find repeated patterns.

As we have seen, Kehoe (2000) takes the shaman's drum as the central feature of shamanism. She likewise emphasizes the reindeer livelihood of those whose language gave us the word shaman. But—although I will argue for the importance of antlers as a shamanistic symbol—even reindeer symbolism cannot be depended upon as universal in the symbolic language of shamanism. Antlers do occur in possibly shamanistic contexts in East Asia, even away from reindeer territory. Antlers are obvious on Silla crowns in Korea, where reindeer did not roam, and antlers attached to noncervine creatures also appear in Chu statues of southern China, which was not reindeer country either (although the antlers may represent those of local deer, not reindeer). In any event, deer in Korea are symbols of long life, related to the supposed medicinal value of the antlers.

Shamans' clothing is usually intended to attract attention—not only the attention of the participants but of the spirits as well. Costumes may be colorful, fringed, or feathered—and likely to make noise as well. The shaman's hat may be intended to convey the spirit is being called down, or may simply be another focal point for the display of symbols. Shamans' clothing and symbols vary widely, even among Central Asian shamans, and should be expected to have different characteristics in different regions.

Paraphernalia of shamans used in séance can include masks for impersonating spirits, bells and rattles, flags, fans, or bowls of wine. Some events call for whole cooked pigs, or parts of them, and some use dried fish. Shamans may also have altars or shrines, with simple objects such as pebbles, or perishable materials like food, which the archaeologist may not discover at all or may find difficult to interpret.

Another problem for archaeologists is that few objects that are used by shamans are exclusively shamanistic. Drums can be used for communal dancing as well as séances. Fancy clothing may mark the elite. Food for the ancestors may be difficult to distinguish from feasts for the living. It is therefore necessary to argue from the total context, rather than having any single mark of a shaman that will appear in an archaeological site. However, once the archaeological hunt is on, the material accouterments of shamans are seen to be many, and involve most of the senses. For example, *wu* might have left evidence of sound-makers of various kinds. Rhythmic sound can be produced by drums, chimes, and bells, while haunting melodies can be played on flutes, not to mention other more complicated percussion and melodic instruments. Sound can also be produced by jingles and rattles attached to clothing, which are activated by the shaman's dance. The kinetic sense of course also would be represented by dance, which can be inferred not only from musical instruments but, some allege, by the early forms of some Chinese characters. The *wu* dance with long sleeves, arms extended, as shown in later paintings. The sense of smell might be activated by smoke from aromatic plants or incense and taste by wine and food.

Whether narcotics and/or stimulants might have been ingested by the participants and onlookers at rituals as well as the shamans is unknown. Hemp seeds and leaves were certainly available, although there is no evidence that any part of the plant was used to create euphoric visions. Some hemp seeds were found in a burial context in Siberia that suggest a final rite for the deceased that involved burnt hemp seeds (Gryaznov 1969:136). However, the drug of choice among the Shang and at least some of their Neolithic predecessors seems to have been wine. It is usually described as most probably made from fermented grain rather than fruits (Underhill 2002).

Visual effects would have been many, including colorful costumes. Parts of costumes that swirl, dangle, or glitter—and showy or sharp paraphernalia—are often part of the shamanistic show. Shamans have favored headgear that attracts attention: hats that are tall, or colorful, or include antlers or other animal representation suggesting spirit helpers.

Styles can alert the archaeologist to the possibility of shamanism as well. Depictions of birds or wild animals, drawings of the sun with rays, and the indication of bones inside the body of humans or animals are often seen as shamanistic traits (Okladnikov 1981). Transformations from one type of being to another, as well as composite animals, are also interpreted as indicating shamanism (Chang 1983, 1994b; Childs-Johnson 1995).

Archaeological features that can be examined for possible shamanic indications include extraordinary burials, rock art depicting shamanic symbols or activities, mural paintings in tombs, early writing or symbols on pottery, and the landscape (as its usage may reflect rituals). Artifacts and their contexts also are important, because objects with daily functions may take on shamanistic meaning in a ritual context, and in that context may be larger than their functional analogues and/or made of impractical materials.

Neolithic archaeology in China is vast and varied, including the contents and layout of burials—as well as ritual buildings and landscapes, statues and figurines, and carved jades with symbolic meanings from several regions. Altars and the placement and shapes of graves also help to understand Neolithic shamanism in East Asia. Shang shamanism is another possible touchstone, for it has been adduced from several different sources: writing on oracle bones (Keightley 1978), documents from the Zhou or later (Falkenhausen 1995; Pankenier 1995), symbolism depicted on bronzes (Chang 1983), and from other symbolism, especially on jades (Childs-Johnson 1995).

Current Shamanism in East Asia

There are several reasons for restricting this archaeological exploration of shamanism to East Asia. First, this is where shamans have been said to become leaders and rulers. Second, through time many elements can be found in common among the people of East Asia, although there are significant divergences. Third, I avoid implications of relationships with far-flung alleged shamanisms, for example in Europe (Aldhouse-Green and Aldhouse-Green 2005), South America (Tedlock 2005). Finally, the East Asian cultures have interacted with each other for millennia, making the differences among them of interest as well as their similarities.

But even limiting the discussion to East Asia, close to the possibly "original" shamanism of Siberia, the question of what is shamanism remains. In any case, while the scholarly concept of shamanism is based on Siberian data, the notion was that Siberian shamans were "living fossils" allow a glimpse into deep antiquity. When it comes to other current shamanism, the question of which groups are "really" shamans can become heated. Howard (1998a:12) suggests, "in Korea the brush we use to paint our descriptions of shamanism needs to be broad." If ethnographers studying living Korean practitioners who go into trances and call down spirits can't agree on whether or not they are shamans, what chance do archaeologists have of teasing out shamanism from scattered and impoverished bits of material culture? Although the difficulties are many, it is an effort worth making because of the light it may shed on paths to rulership and the rise of states.

While linguistically Chinese is unrelated to Siberian languages, the other East Asian languages spoken where shamanic rituals were practiced in state level societies, especially Korean and Japanese, are usually considered to be anciently related to Tungusic or Siberian/Manchurian languages (Miller 1971, 1980). There may be a more direct link between peninsular and island forms of shamanism with the northeast than between Siberia and China, but influence from China (as well as Buddhism and Christianity) is also part of the mix. "Religions" in Asia lack the exclusivity of the religions of the Bible lands.

Shamans, even those of Siberia, may be either born into a shamanic family or "called" to it later in life. In China, Wu even became a family name, and shamans with the surname Wu are mentioned in the Shang oracle bones. In Korea, two types of *mudangs* have been described—*kongsin*, who are called by the spirits, and *seseup mu*, who are born into shaman families (Seong-Nae Kim 1998:33–34). Another group of *mudang* live on Cheju

Island. Called *shiumbang*, they belong to *mudang* families but also use trance. The performances of these groups, however, are similar enough for all of these shamans to be called *mudang* by most Koreans.

In desiring to distinguish Korean *musok* from other forms of shamanism, Tae-gon Kim (1998:19) produced a definition of the general term, which was based on his observations of and participation in shamanic events from many part of Central and East Asia. This is a useful understanding for archaeologists to work with:

> Shamanism is a traditional, religious phenomenon tied closely to nature and the surrounding world, in which a practitioner endowed with the special ability to enter a state of trance-possession can communicate with supernatural beings. This transcendental power allows the practitioner, the shaman, to satisfy human cravings for explanation, understanding, and prophecy.

Variability of Shamanisms in Ancient East Asia

In accepting Kim's definition of shamanism, I should make it clear that I am not positing an ancient religion from which Chinese *wu*, Korean *mudang*, and others descend. Many scholars who investigate living shamanism today disagree with the approach of Eliade (1964), which suggests that shamanism is both primitive and timeless. Kehoe is among the scholars who warn against this approach. Shamanism should not be placed "in a time warp outside of history" (Kehoe 2000:39). It will be useful to keep in mind Kehoe's dictum that "ethnographic particularities are highly significant clues to societies' histories" (Kehoe 2000:15). It is necessary to recognize that the *wu* and *mu* were specific to times and places. Seeking their antecedents or successors is not meant to imply a lack of change throughout this spread of time.

Others have emphasized the situatedness of shamanism. Thomas and Humphrey (1996:2) find Eliade's work inadequate because to him shamanism reflects as "a romanticized inversion of Western rationalism." They hope to "recover and analyze the diversity that essentialism has masked." Kehoe (2000:4) makes the point that it is important to "historicize shamanic activities by understanding their particular manifestations as results of historical processes."

A characteristic of shamanism in northern Asia as well as East Asia is that the "concept of heaven or the sky as the all-encompassing principle of cosmic order and human destiny" that is held in ancient China is similar to that of Mongols and Manchus. Deities are sky deities, and the sky itself is a source of power (Humphrey and Onon 1996:197). This emphasis on the sky ties observations of the heavenly bodies closely to East Asian shamanism and the practices that became Daoism.

K. C. Chang suggests a similar definition, but he emphasizes a version of the world particular to China, in which heaven and earth are equal spheres. "In the context of ethnography, a shaman is defined as someone who can communicate with both heaven and earth, in other words, with both gods and humans, and this ability is considered to be inborn" (Chang 2005:129). However, in describing Shang kings as shamans, Chang does not emphasize trance or ecstasy, but foretelling the future, utilizing animal helpers, and communicating with spirits of the dead. It is not known whether these practices were performed in the context of trance, although reaching the spirits was the goal (Chang 1983, 1994a, 1999, 2005).

Ching is less interested in the ecstatic than she is in the mystical. The fact that "the human being is open to the divine and the spiritual . . . this was the primeval experience of the shaman" (Ching 1997:xi). Although she defines shamanism as relating to "the claim of spirit possession and the ensuing ecstatic experience" during which the "shaman controls the spirits" (Ching 1997:13–14), it is ultimately the way that shamans became rulers that is of interest to her. "Charisma associated with shamanic ecstasy created the aura for the office of kingship" (Ching 1997:xii). Shamanic figures—original, spontaneous, and charismatic religious individuals—were often, although not always, also the political leaders, or kings, assisted by other, lesser, shamans (Ching 1997:xiii). It is important that, focusing on the Chinese case, Ching also looks at divination and the knowledge of stars as an important element of shamanism in China. Both have left traces in Neolithic China.

Let me reiterate that in discussing shamanism in East Asia from the Neolithic to the present, I am not implying that shamanism remained unchanged though time and space. The point is only that shamans in this instance were able to claim exclusive ability to reach the spirits, and hence had the power, or even the mandate, to become secular as well as spiritual leaders in the community, as will be discussed more fully in chapter 4. The populace would have wanted to follow them to enjoy the benefits from the spirits and the protection from harm that the spirits could grant. It is an "ethnographic" approach, based primarily on archaeological, historical/textual and ethnographic data, and considering variations through time and space. What began with shamans as rulers became bureaucracy, with *wu* sometimes performing as priests. This occurs earlier in China, and later in Korea and Japan, under the influence of Chinese Confucianism. But shamanism stubbornly, and interestingly, survives alongside.

The Korean *mudang* were seen to be powerful because they could call down the spirits and control them (Hogarth 1998:47). But this power goes beyond the personal possession of spiritual power.

> If a *mudang* experiences ecstasy, a non-ordinary personal phenomenon, it is interpreted as evidence that he or she has spiritual power. However, this power stems not only from personal innate competence; it can also be understood as a cultural and social construction. It comes from the authority or prestige that believers and clients acknowledge in the *mudang*, authority or prestige which they assign for personal or collective interests. Both the belief system and the presence of this power in the ritual context—in keeping with the demands of the clients—are necessary ingredients for the comparison and judgment of spiritual efficacy. (Seong-Nae Kim 1998:41-42)

Conclusion

Ethnographies thus warn interpreters of archaeological sites that the phenomenon called shamanism in various places around the world has multiple beliefs and practices. It is a familiar term with too many meanings—or better, a potpourri of practices. This makes the archaeology of shamanism an even more slippery subject than "sloppily applied" ethnographic attributions may suggest. While for the purpose of this book it is important to delineate what a shaman is (and is not) to have a measuring stick to recognize shamanism in archaeological discoveries, probably more useful for the understanding of the past are the spin-off questions. What do shamans do? How can shamanistic practices be recognized in ancient sites, burials, and artifacts? When shamanism has been identified, what can be inferred about the society? What is the nature of shamanistic leadership, and it is different from other leadership?

The basic aim of this exploration is not to discover whether or not shamans were rife in ancient East Asia. It is ultimately to ask, why would it matter whether or not there were shamans? Shamanism is magical and mystical and mysterious. As such it is attractive to researchers as well as to the general public. Can we move beyond the mysteries of shamanism to inquire about leadership? What is the context in which shamans flourished (when they did), and how did shamanistic ideology affect the organization of society, economics, and politics? Were shamans leaders in East Asia? If so, what kind? Did shamans or shamanistic families become the elite, or did they stand in opposition to persons and families with budding economic and political clout? To begin to address these questions it is necessary to be more specific about what is being sought. In particular, we need to ask, can shamanistic power be instrumental in the formation of states?

YOSHINOGARI, JAPAN

The part of the Yoshinogari site that is open to the public occupies 22 hectares on a hill in Saga Prefecture, northern Kyushu, Japan. The discoveries include bronzes, swords, beads, urn burials, and pottery styles that are typical of the Yayoi period of Japanese prehistory. Although several time periods are represented at the site, the layer of interest dates to between 100 and 300 CE (Hudson and Barnes 1991). It is a large village surrounded by deep outer and inner moats, and guarded by high watch towers (Figure C.1). The towers were made of six posts up to 1.4 meters wide, which, based on their diameter, may have been as much as 10 meters high. Each tower covered about 4 by 5 meters. Both rectangular and round pit dwelling have been unearthed. More than eighteen raised storage pits were present, presumably for storing rice and other crops.

About two thousand burial urns have been found (Figure C.2). One very large mound at the northern edge of the site, from the Middle Yayoi period, is oval, measuring 40 meters long and 30 meters wide. It was constructed using a stamped earth technique in the first century BCE. Eight burials in double urns occupied the mound. The center of the mound contained the oldest urn, identified by the pottery type. This mound is believed to be the burial place of the high-

Figure C.1 Reconstructed watchtowers and granaries. After brochure from site

Figure C.2 Burial urn. After brochure from site

est ranking people in the society. The largest burial contains a bronze sword (Figure C.3). It is identified as male by five teeth. Another mound has attracted attention because of an unusual sword with a T-shaped hilt, like daggers from Liaoning province, China. There are also seventy-five blue glass beads of cylindrical shape (Figure C.4). These beads are thought to have been attached to a crown because they were found near the place where the head would have been. This is the only burial to contain blue beads. Finely woven hemp cloth was attached to the sword, along with several kinds of silk. A path leads to this tomb, strewn with ceremonial pottery.

Weizhi, a Chinese text written between 280 and 297 CE, records some practices of people referred to as Wa, which seem to have been based on eyewitness accounts (Seyock 2004). A number of "states" were part of a confederation ruled over by a queen of Wa named Himiko, who "occupied herself with magic and sorcery, bewitching the people" (Seyock 2004:50). She controlled more than twenty countries and lived in a palace with a tower surrounded by a fence. The burial ground of Queen Hamiko is described as a round mound and, converting the Chinese *pu* into meters, it measured 25 to 30 meters across. It is

Figure C.3 Bronze sword. After brochure from site

argued that Wa was situated in northern Kyushu because 80 percent of bronze mirrors and weapons from the Han dynasty of China have been found in Kyushu. Her country is called Yamatai (or Yamaichi) in the *Weizhi*, with specific directions about how to travel there by sea and land. The directions are problematic because, while in describing the areas of the Korean peninsula and the islands of the Korea Strait they are reasonable, after

Figure C.4 Blue cylindrical beads. After brochure from site

arriving in Kyushu one would end up far out in the Pacific Ocean following the further directions. There have been many learned papers placing Yamatai either in Kyushu (which archaeological description favors) or in Yamato because of the similarity of the name (Barnes 1988). The main point, however, is that a shaman leader was noted by the Chinese chronicler—a shaman queen, at that.

A burial in a large jar included tubular blue beads and a T-shaped dagger in the style of some daggers from Liaoning province in China. Both the dagger and the beads were imports. Similar blue beads were found at the site of Hapsongni in Korea (Seyock 2004). Excavation of the Yoshinogari site seemed to confirm the *Weizhi* description of Yamatai—a walled city where the queen lived behind a palisade and was rarely seen.

But according to the Chinese text, Himiko died after 247 CE. Yoshinogari is much earlier, from the first century (Hudson and Barnes 1991). Although Yoshinogari is the wrong timeframe for Himiko, the site is a very popular destination. Tourist items such as t-shirts and coffee mugs are emblazoned with Himiko's likeness, in which she carries the sword and wears the blue beads configured on her head like a crown.

Figure C.5 Raised granary. After brochure from site

POWER, LEADERSHIP, AND GENDER

In Tikopian eyes [the chief's] overlordship and control are not only jus-
tified but natural, since it is he who is responsible for the people's wel-
fare. He is their principle link with the ancestors and their only link with
the supreme gods. He alone can perform the basic kava ceremonies which
form the root of Tikopia religion.

—Raymond Firth 1967:56, cited in Thomas 1994:77

For despite the proof of language and artifacts, despite pictorial repre-
sentations, ethnographic narratives, and eyewitness accounts, the
importance—no, the primacy—of women in shamanic traditions has
been obscured and denied.

—Barbara Tedlock 2005:4

Shamanism and Power

The nature of power and the exercise of power in human societies are central questions in many archaeological inquiries about polities in the past.

81

The view of power as negotiated and contingent conforms to power as it has been studied in early states better than construing power as absolute. Power is not a single "thing" that can be "had," nor a preexisting condition that a leader can "come to," but a continuously negotiated process (O'Donovan 2002:14–16; Wylie 2002). Several kinds of power have been described (e.g., Wolf 1990), including power to make one's own decisions. In many versions of state formation, the definition of power is skewed toward political and economic power, while ideology has often been slighted as a source of power. Explanations of state formation tend to treat belief systems as less relevant, preferring instead economic, political, and social forces as explanatory mechanisms. The problem with this emphasis is that identities and agency are lost, and much that is relevant to the dynamics of state formation is omitted. The shift to considering order, legitimacy, and wealth is a reframing that moves toward restoring ideology as a player in state formation (Baines and Yoffee 1998).

Although shamanism has been seen as relying on individual characteristics and as disorderly by nature—hence at odds with leadership in state level societies—a case can be made for shamanism as an important source of state power in ancient East Asia. Two different kinds of public power, the first related to reaching nonhuman powers and the other based on force, were both grounded in shared beliefs about sources of power. The power of shamanism was obtained from unseen spirits and was used to convince others to conform on the basis of messages from these potentially dangerous spirits. Warfare and sacrifice were rife in the Shang period. They constitute the kind of terrorizing that is built on brute force—and the threat of force—even when it is sanctioned by the spirits. The powers and spirits can be bloodthirsty, not satisfied with only wine and meat, but demanding human lives as well. Both sides of the powers, beneficent and terrifying, were exploited by the Shang rulers. Later states in the Korean peninsula and the Japanese islands used a somewhat different approach, which included legitimization by spirits and descent from gods, but did not terrorize through human sacrifice.

Insistence on the political and economic realms as causative factors is insufficient to understand state formation in East Asia, in spite of the efforts of K. C. Chang (1983, 1989, 1994a, 1994b, 2005) to call attention to the importance of ideology in the Shang period. Chinese ancient states still are not as well known to archaeologists as other examples of "pristine" states. China is completely absent from an influential book about state formation (Feinman and Marcus 1998), and secondary states are still less known. East

Asia is poorly represented in introductory textbooks on world prehistory (e.g., Fagan 2007). This neglect occurs in spite of a rich new literature in English, published in accessible books and journals, especially for China (e.g., Liu 2004; Liu and Chen 2006; Underhill and Habu 2005) and Japan (e.g., Habu 2004; Hudson 1999; Imamura 1996; Mizoguchi 2002). Although neglected, East Asia is particularly important in comparative archaeology because the region suggests models of state formation different from other parts of the world, allowing for alternative visions of the human past. Ideology as a motive force in the formation of Chinese states has found several champions in spite of general neglect. Tong (2002:40) is explicit about the importance of ideology in China, noting that "some scholars have not fully appreciated the importance of ideology in bringing about this turning point [origin of civilization and the state] in the history of ancient society." Tong points to the construction of religious structures and the management of rituals as ways that the elite could gradually "organize and control the rest of the population." Inscriptions on oracle bones show that the inhabitants of the Shang state lived in a symbolic world (Keightley 2000:121–29). The Shang kings divined to the ancestors and nature powers for guidance in nearly everything they did. This rich source of written material about ideology directly from the Shang world is unparalleled in any other ancient state.

Under different circumstances, shamanism was important in ancient East Asia beyond early China. East Asian secondary states include those that formed in Manchuria, such as Puyo (Pak 1999), the Three Kingdoms of Korea (Nelson 1993a), and Yamato Japan (Barnes 2007; Holcombe 2001). None of these incipient states conform easily to models of state formation, which emphasize economics and political power to the detriment of ideological power. It is difficult to pinpoint why this is particularly obvious in East Asia. Maybe ideology simply was more important there than in other regions where early states and civilizations developed. Or perhaps the tools to perceive and understand ideology are unusually available in East Asia. Unlike Mesopotamia, for example, where the first written tablets relate to the distribution of food and agricultural supplies from the temple (Yoffee 2005), in China the earliest interpretable writing was directed to the realm of the spirits. While it is easy to imagine that in both cases other writing may have existed that would have revealed other facets of these polities, the fact remains that we have to use what was preserved from what was probably a much richer corpus.

While I do not mean to imply that physical coercion was less prevalent in East Asia than in other complex societies (indeed, as mentioned earlier, warfare and human sacrifice were rampant in the Shang dynasty), I do mean to foreground the *way* that belief systems helped to form not only China but other East Asian states, creating the rationale that supported authority of the state and allowed the state to function without interference. Belief systems in China even granted the right (or obligation) to sacrifice humans and animals on behalf of the ancestors and powers, and demanded warfare to protect the ancestors' temples and perhaps to enlarge their domains. The power of the state to control people's lives and possessions was grounded in beliefs about spirits and ritual control over spirits.

As Thomas and Humphrey (1994:11) forcefully note in their discussion of shamanism within states, we must be mindful of the fact that "political power, even in state systems, operates through ideas of fertility, blessing, ancestry, or knowledge of destiny, which are also the domains of inspirational agencies." Therefore, by focusing on leadership and shamanism, the ideology of state formation is highlighted, allowing some insights into differences in early East Asian states and the particularities of Asian paths to power.

Leadership Strategies

The question of the formation of complex societies is one that has occupied several generations of archaeologists (e.g., Feinman and Marcus 1998; Flannery 1972; Wright 1977; Yoffee 2005). However, most of these discussions tend to focus on a societal level rather than on leaders and their activities. An example of the depersonalization of leadership is Yoffee's (2005:11) statement that "states maintain the central symbols of society, and undertake its defense and expansion." It is a shift of emphasis to say that *leaders* rather than states are responsible for these activities. And yet history abounds with examples of bad leaders who were responsible for the downfall of the polity they ruled.

To consider whether shamans can become leaders of states requires attention to leadership strategies. Since shamanic performance and knowledge can serve as leadership strategies in simple societies, it is important to ask what processes in simple societies could aid shamans in becoming leaders and maintaining leadership of larger polities. We already have seen that shamans are "knowledgeable people," but can that knowledge, or the ability to reach the powers, transcend simple societies? Put simply, the question of this chapter is, if shamans did become leaders of states, how would that work?

Various perspectives on the issue of state formation are compatible with shamanism. Yoffee (2005:38) suggests that control of knowledge, ceremonies, and symbols is important for states to emerge. This means of control is typical of shamans. Along the same lines, Chang (1989) describes a trajectory to power in ancient China that includes shamanic control of knowledge, oracle bone divinations, and control of the symbols on bronzes to demonstrate that knowledge of the spirits belonged ultimately to the king. If this interpretation is correct, then the Shang king, as head of the state, was personally in control of ideology. Chang concludes that Shang kings ruled by virtue of their spiritual knowledge.

Although many argue that ideology was a driving force in the Shang state, it is not universally agreed that Shang kings were shamans. For example, Keightley (1998) finds it inappropriate to call the Late Shang kings shamans because divinations occurred (as far as can be deduced from the writing on oracle bones) without trance or séance. As has been described in previous chapters, shamanism is usually considered incompatible with states. Rebuttals to that notion focus on control of knowledge and symbols. It has been suggested that in some cases shaman-leaders may be able to reorganize shamanism and the society concurrently (Chang 1989; Tong 2002). A likely process by which alterations in shamanism might have been accomplished in East Asia is by adding other compatible elements such as animism and ancestor worship to shamanism. The strength of these beliefs and practices together might have provided the path to leadership of larger polities. Wealth rightly has been seen as both a source of power and a legitimization of power. In the Shang period, bronzes were wealth as well as connections to the spirits and powers. In the rest of East Asia, gold was more highly prized.

Theories of Leadership

The topic of shamans as rulers requires concentration on the leaders of complex societies, rather than the social and political organization as such. But what to call these leaders is a problem. Categories for rulers have been lacking beyond chief, king, and emperor, which are titles reflecting the supposed size of the polity—chiefdom, kingdom, empire. These words do not describe the activities of the leaders, only the size and nature of the polity they govern.

Because of this nomenclature problem, I avoid using chief and king as much as possible. In discussing ancient women leaders (queens), I have approached the topic without resorting to androcentric terms (Nelson 2003c). Unfortunately these words are so entrenched in archaeological thinking about leadership that they are difficult to avoid. In this book I use "leader" for someone who is recognized as having some power but whose power is limited. A "ruler," on the other hand, has considerable power, sometimes even that of life and death over his/her subjects. I have deliberately chosen gender-neutral words for this discussion (although for many readers even these neutral terms will still conjure up a male image) for reasons that will become clearer. But for the moment it is relevant to point out that ethnographically and historically many shaman leaders are women, and their participation in the paths to power should not be seen to be excluded a priori by using gender-specific terms.

The rise of leaders has been hypothesized to occur in several ways. One version favors feasting to obtain and maintain alliances (Bray 2003; Dietler and Hayden 2001), another suggests that the power of chiefs may accrue from economic or political prowess, including, of course, force in the form of warfare (Earle 1997). Earle (1997) acknowledges that ideology can be a source of power, but finds it weaker than economic or martial power and explains his lack of enthusiasm for ideology as explanatory with the observation that ideology is "difficult to monopolize" (Earle 1977:190). Shamans, however, may be able to monopolize access to the spirits, and to sustain that access with specialized knowledge of healing, of the sky, and of the future.

Claessen and Oosten (1996:385) focus on the person of the king in their discussion of ideology in early states, referring to a king as a "pivot of power," invoking sacred kingship. But sacred kingship involves the notion that the king himself embodies the gods. This is quite different from shamanism, in which the separation between the shaman and the spirits is clear and distinct. The shaman can reach the spirits but does not become sacred on that account—and does not become one of the powers.

Obtaining Power

Some of the theories about leadership in the ancient world focus on paths to power, others on the qualities of a leader, and yet others on reasons that the populace would accept leadership at all. These facets are, of course, related and even intertwined, but it is helpful at the beginning to analyze them as separate processes. The cultural sense of the way the world is constituted underlies the ways that leadership can be accepted.

Kinship

One of the paths to power that is often overlooked at the state level is kinship, due to the supposed shift from kinship to territory at the state level

(Morgan 1887). Morgan meant by this that citizens were included within the state because they lived within its boundaries, rather than being defined by kinship. In the case of East Asia, this is a major misapprehension, for kinship is clearly important in ancestor worship, seen as one foundation of the Chinese state. Chang (2005) believes that the lineage system, evident at least as early as Longshan as interpreted from the burial system, was the source of the Shang king's political power. Falkenhausen (2006) extends this concept to the Zhou period with archaeological examples.

But kinship by evolutionary definition belongs to chiefdoms, not states. This problem is discussed by Bong-won Kang (2005) in the context of Elman Service's (1975) evolutionary scheme of band, tribe, chiefdom, and state. Kang demonstrates that the states we call "kingdoms" are not fully states under the customary understanding of evolutionary stages, and yet kingdoms continue to be called states. Since kingdoms are more organized than chiefdoms but do not fit the definition of states, Kang proposes that kingdoms comprise an intermediary evolutionary stage between chiefdoms and states. While I am not a fan of evolutionary typology—and the pigeon-holing of archaeological polities that often follows—in early East Asian polities, the notion of kingdoms as neither chiefdoms nor states is helpful in thinking about leadership. This concept allows consideration of strong rulers whose claim to power depends on kinship, as well as possible access to the spirit world. In other words, it opens a space for East Asian polities that was previously unavailable.

An important characteristic that sets kingdoms apart from Service's category of states is that states have "a professional ruling class [which] was separated from the bonds of kinship relations" (Flannery 1972:403). Flannery, of course, meant a bureaucracy of workers who were the actual managers of the affairs of the state. However, when individuals in the bureaucracy are also members of the ruler's kin group, the situation differs. The shift away from kinship has not occurred, but the level of organization is distinctly greater than that of chiefdoms. For example, in the early Korean kingdom of Silla, as will be seen in chapter 7, the populace was divided into rigid endogamous classes, and only members of the highest group were allowed to hold government positions. Dynastic succession (not to mention the fact that the ruler's relatives were almost certain to be members of that bureaucracy) shows that kinship was a vital factor in such societies.

Kang (2005:23) suggests that "the establishment of hereditary royal succession has been a critical indicator of the emergence of a strong centralized government in many different areas." He emphasizes his point as follows: "the rule of hereditary succession for the political ruling class, and particularly for the kingship, was neither distinct nor separated from a lineal kinship relationship." Affinal relationships are also important, even in strongly patrilineal societies. The family members of the ruler's spouse (often, of course, related to the ruler by cousinship in any case) were almost always important players in the organization of kingdoms, going far beyond mere palace intrigues (Gailey 1987; Muller 1987). In the case of early Korean states, "power . . . was concentrated in . . . the aristocratic families, headed by the lineages of the kings *and queens* that dominated the rigid and hereditary social status systems and occupied a position of primacy in the political, economic, and cultural spheres" (Eckert et al. 1990:32 [emphasis added]).

Lewis (2000:25) describes a similar situation in the Shang period in ancient China. "The only significant nonkinspeople who were active in the Shang government were advisers and diviners, who came to the Shang capital from allied tribes. The point of bringing such people from other groups may have been twofold, to utilize their powers for Shang, and to deprive the groups from which they came of their powers." Chang (2005) and Tong (2002) suggest that in the process of state formation, shamanistic beliefs were co-opted into the service of particular kinship groups. The debate hinges on how shamanism is defined. Since more and earlier (mostly Neolithic) sites have been discovered and interpreted as evidence of shamanism, it will be useful to examine the evidence and ask whether, on the basis of East Asian archaeology (aided by texts), it is possible to infer that several early states in East Asia were grounded in shamanistic beliefs and practices in which the leaders were shamans.

Ideology

Ideology is an undertheorized path to power, but the role of ideology in legitimizing rulership is a vital one. Christopher Fung explains how shamanism in particular was important in creating legitimacy for the rulers of Shang China:

> The practice of shamanism underlies traditional Chinese notions of rulership. Shamanism is a form of religion based on the idea of a layered universe. Powerful beings (shamans) can travel from one place of the universe to another, aided by spirit doubles, animal helpers, or ecstatic trances brought on through meditation, asceticism, dance and

music, or hallucinogenic drugs and alcohol. The act of transport or transformation allows shamans to act as curers, spirit mediums, diviners, prophets, or magicians. (Fung 1994:55)

Thus if the populace perceived the ruler as a shaman, the power that accrued in a shamanic capacity legitimately could be applied in other ways. Perhaps the ruler did not need to express the idea that, for example, the need to sacrifice a particular number of pigs, oxen, and humans was an order from the spirits. If everyone accepted that spirits made requests that required sacrifices, obedience to the will of spirits would have been assumed. Fear of the spirits would have overridden any distaste for the sacrifice (or offering up one's own chattel) that might have been felt. The king himself was under the obligation to respond to the readings of the oracle bones regarding the desires of the spirits. It can be argued that in China the person of the king functioned as a central symbol, since the king was the person ultimately responsible for decisions about sacrifice and warfare, with the help of the spirits. The world of the Shang was a spirit-driven world, and the ruler was responsible for placating the spirits and the powers.

Charisma

Ching (1997:xii) suggests that the king performing as a shaman was legitimization in itself: "It is my thesis that the charisma associated with shamanic ecstasy created the aura for the office of kingship, giving it a sacred, even a priestly, character." She further asserts that "in the Chinese experience, shamanic figures, the original, spontaneous, and charismatic religious individuals, were often, though not always, also the political leaders or kings" (Ching 1997:xiii).

The charisma of a leader may be personal or may derive from high social status—or, of course, both. In East Asia, it seems that social standing was of primary importance. Even earlier than the Xia dynasty, a Yangshao cemetery in Qinghai shows that the "relationship between religious power and high social status is evident" (Liu 2004:158). Between the Dawenkou and Longshan periods a "marked change in ritual practice" occurs, but "by the Longshan period there was "a close association between highly ranked individuals, ancestral cults, status markers, and ritual paraphernalia"(Liu 2004:155).

Personal charisma may still have played a part in the choice of king (and queen) from among several eligible persons. The Shang records show that the king was always a male of the royal line, but not necessarily the first born, or even the son of the previous king. Similar rules are implied in the Korean kingdoms of Goguryeo and Silla (Grayson 1976). Sometimes, however, the female line is a direct one, suggesting that marrying the legitimate queen was the route to kingship (Gailey 1987; Muller 1987; Nelson 1991b).

Control of the Spirits and Powers

The fact that the shaman is able to respond to the spirits, not just contact them, is of vital importance to the respect and legitimacy that he or she commands. Much of the theater of séances is dedicated to demonstrating the control of spirits. In describing the performance of power, Kehoe (2002) calls ancient capitals "theaters of power," where the ruler enacts the power of the state. Temples and palaces provided the backdrop for such theater.

Shamans as leaders were not limited to states. "Burials associated with ritual paraphernalia . . . suggest that even in an egalitarian society some individuals with ritual power may have played special roles in the community" (Liu 2004:155). The fact that shamans could move between the world of humans and the world of the spirits without being harmed (whereas contact with spirits was dangerous to other people) was a basic reason to fear and respect them.

Divination

Evidence of divination appears early in East Asia. Several animal shoulder bones that had been pretreated by boring holes to enable the bones to crack in the fire were found as early as 4000 BCE in Inner Mongolia (Guo 1995a) and in several sites along the Yellow River (Liu 2004). Thus the use of scapulimancy was ancient long before the Shang period. It is interesting to wonder what future events were the subject of such divinations. Did the shaman ask whether an illness would be cured? How the weather would be for an impending ceremony? Whether neighboring groups were hostile or friendly? These seem trivial questions even in the context of a simple society, but they are not different in kind from queries in the Shang period. The subjects of divination as they are known from the Late Shang were practical rather than profound. It seems likely that this was the case from the beginning.

Divination was of supreme importance in the Shang. "Almost every aspect of royal activity was preceded by divination, accompanied by specific sacrifices, offered chiefly to the Shang royal ancestors. These were potent divinities in their own right and the sole intercessors with the high god Di, or Shang Di, a remote deity who lay beyond human offerings" (Lewis 2000:24). Sometimes the king himself divined, and sometimes others did. "The names of over 120 diviners who served the Shang kings have been discovered. By the end of the Shang dynasty, however, the king himself had become virtually the only diviner of record, suggesting that the last Shang kings, Di Yi and Di Xin, were now monopolizing an activity that under Wu Ding had been shared with large numbers of other notables" (Keightley 1994:73). Divination seems almost obsessive in Late Shang times, but this perception may be a result of the fact that earlier divinations have no inscriptions, and were not deliberately preserved.

The practice of divination with animal bones continued in East Asia into the Iron Age and beyond. Several scapulae with burned holes but without writing have been found in archaeological sites in both North and South Korea. Divining through scapulimancy continued in Japan through the Yayoi period and the Yamato kingdom. Even Genghis Khan read the future from bones (Humphrey 1994:203–4). The urge to know the future—and the presence of persons who can contact spirits to reveal the future—are a continuing theme in East Asia and Central Asia. Fortune tellers, who are widely consulted at present in Korea, use a variety of methods but are nevertheless still carrying on the ancient tradition of divination. Divination by computer is even available on the streets of Seoul during festivals.

Sacrifices

The scale of sacrifices in the Shang periods is impressive. Not only do the oracle bone inscriptions describe huge numbers of humans and animals to be slaughtered in a single sacrifice, but archaeology also confirms the scale of human sacrifices. Piles of skulls were thrown into ditches, humans were buried in the foundations of important buildings, and extra bodies are extravagantly included in noble tombs. Sacrifices were made to the sun, the cardinal directions, the wind, and ancestral spirits (Keightley 2000:4). A typical sacrifice might include a few sheep, dogs, or pigs. But human burials called for much larger sacrifices of human life. At the burial of Lady Hao, one of Wu Ding's major wives, fifteen humans and six dogs were sacrificed. Some of the bodies had been decapitated, and one was cut in half at the waist, which must have been an unpleasant way to begin the journey accompanying Fu Hao to the afterworld. Near the graves of the kings, rows of pits contained sacrificed victims, in groups of up to twenty-nine men (Thorp 2006). These large sacrifices hint at the way that wealth became part of the religious system in Shang, rather than the other way around. Both displaying and sacrificing wealth can be "dedicated to the gods, the dead, the ruler, and the elite" (Yoffee 2005:36). The number of bronze vessels placed in royal tombs is a cogent example. Lady Hao was laid to rest with 440 bronzes to contain food and wine to feast the ancestors (see Case Study D).

Warfare

Warfare loomed large in the origin of the state in East Asia. Chang (1983:69) notes that "ritual and war, as the twin instruments of political power, were the keys to the emergence of civilization in ancient China." Warfare of the Shang period seems to have been optional, as inquiries to the spirits concern whether or not to send armies to attack one or another enemy group. These were nontributary groups—thus outside the Shang state—but they were not necessarily threatening to initiate warfare with the Shang. Many enemies may have been far away territories that were not contiguous with Shang. Keightley (1983) suggests that the Shang state did not enclose a solid territory. Using a compelling metaphor, he compares Shang territory to Swiss cheese with holes rather than a solid chunk of tofu. This puts a different light on Shang warfare and suggests booty (including people and animals to sacrifice) as the motivation for warfare, rather than defense. Ching (1997:13) asserts that both sides used shamans in warfare, screaming into battle ahead of the troops to terrify the enemy. Much pageantry and showmanship also went into banners and decorated war chariots, pulled by horses whose trappings were made splendid with bronze and cowry shells.

Wealth could be acquired by raids on large towns, and vicious raids are evident in some Neolithic sites, where bodies were dumped helter-skelter into wells. It was originally thought the Shang city unearthed at Anyang had no walls, but recently city walls have been located. Although such city walls existed, with their chariots and horses the Shang city may have been considered too strong to attack for much of the period of their ascendancy.

Qualities of a Leader

Some discussions of leadership divide leaders into two types—managers and exploiters (see Shelach 1999:31–34 for a summary of these debates as they can be applied to China). Exploiters take more than they give, while managers are responsible for redistributing goods within the society. Shelach shows that this is not really a dichotomy—the same leaders both managed and exploited the populace. Leadership strategies analogously may be divided into corporate and network models (Blanton et al. 1996). Corporate strategies are oriented within the group, while network strategies concentrate on connections with other polities in long-distance trade or family alliances. These are useful categories, but both tend to omit the dimension of ideology. It does matter what people believe.

One important quality of leaders is access to esoteric knowledge. Leaders who were knowledgeable were also likely to be the inventors of knowledge, as well as keepers of knowledge passed down from their ancestors. Shamans needed to know many things—how to heal illness, how to bring rain, and in general how to make things right with the spirits, who were the cause of all troubles. It is likely that both writing and astronomy originated in East Asia in the service of divination—of finding out what would satisfy the spirits and what the future would bring. There is some suggestion that metallurgy—the miraculous transformation of ugly hard ore into shining liquid metal—was also associated with spirits (Eliade 1964).

Ideologies of Leadership

Four versions of the relationship of ideology to leadership in ancient China have been advanced by Shao, Tong, Chang, and Hsu. Each relates shamanism to kings, but makes different assumptions about how kings and shamans coincided.

Shao supposes that the king usurped the role of shamans. The king acquired the religious rights and duties that had previously been more accessible to ordinary people. "With the birth of civilization, religion became an attribute of kingship and another pillar of the emerging social order, but the circumstances varied from region to region. . . . Access to the spirits was now the sole right of the king and . . . served as an instrument of rule" (Shao 2005:121). In this scenario, secular leadership and religious responsibility became joined. Shao believes that "with the birth of civilization, religion became an attribute of kingship and another pillar of emerging social order. . . . Once the institution of kingship emerged, rulers radically reformed the primitive religious practices in which all members of a society were able to communicate directly with spirits and perform their own services. Access to the spirits was now the sole right of the king and, together with the secular system of rites, served as an instrument of rule" (Shao 2005:121).

Tong also sees the elite and shamans as separate entities to begin with. He suggests that at the time of the Longshan (or the legendary Five Emperors), the status of the *wu* changed: "As some elite members of the community came to function as *wu*, the elite and a small number of *wu* merged together" (Tong 2002:41). His argument is similar to that of Shao, but he believes the status of the *wu* improved as they became members of the elite. Tong cites a number of ethnographic accounts as well, ones in which the religious and secular leaders (male and female) were the same people or their close relatives. Tong notes that "Sometimes one can hardly distinguish early political leaders from religious leaders" (Tong 2002:54)— and that is the very point.

Chang advances the idea that the king was the chief shaman because he had access to heaven "where all the wisdom of human affairs lies" (Chang 1983:45). Thus esoteric knowledge allowed the king to be chief shaman—and allowed the chief shaman to be king. Chang asserts that "the most important instrument that was used to accomplish these undertakings was political power in the hands of the elite" (Chang 1994a:62). The emergence of civilizations in China was closely associated with the use by political leaders and shamans of various symbols, especially ritual symbols, of political power for the purpose of acquiring, retaining, and increasing such power.

Another possibility is described by Hsu (2005) who suggests that serving deities and serving the ancestors were "two different sets of faiths" (Hsu 2005:452). Eventually a "hybrid culture" developed, with aspects of both. This occurred around 2000 BCE, at the end of the Longshan period. The combination, in his view, led to the rise of civilization.

My version of the process of state formation is somewhat different from any of these, although it is likewise based in archaeological discoveries. The evidence suggests to me that the *wu*, having been leaders already, themselves became the elite. For example, both Chang (1980, 1983, 1986a, 1994a, 1994b, 2005) and Tong (2002) cite a number of texts about the legendary emperors that demonstrate their shamanistic power. These emperors were perceived as possessing supernatural traits and as being able to commune with the spirits. The Yellow Emperor (Huang Di) was said to know how to summon spirits. Di Ku created a calendar that coordinated the movements of the sun and the moon and was familiar with spirits (Tong 2002:41-42). Perhaps it is only a matter of emphasis, but it may be that the Yellow Emperor was a shaman first and subsequently a powerful leader who united several groups. Or perhaps he was simply a shaman leader who was euhemerized.

Women as Shamans and Leaders

The question of whether women could be shamans/rulers in state-level societies is a sticky one. The vehemence with which female shamans have been denied by some prominent scholars is quite surprising, especially given the abundant ethnographic evidence of women as shamans. Atkinson (1992:317) notes that "scholarly constructions of shamans reveal highly gendered assumptions." The data show that both men and women could be shamans in most East Asian cultures, but that the majority were women. Insisting on men as the only leaders and women as necessarily inferior is, I suggest, a means of following a Confucian "party line" (in which a woman should know her place vis-à-vis father, husband, and son). It is the result of reading the present into the past, and it fails to appreciate the fact that Chinese history texts have omitted almost anything that would show women as leaders or women as shamans. The gynophobia of Chinese historic texts may mask considerable power in the hands of women. A deity called the Queen Mother of the West, who was worshipped in Han times, could be a folk memory of ruling women.

Chinese history is deliberately biased against women (Chang 1986). Bronson (2000) notes that by the Han dynasty the intelligentsia are the arbiters of the ideology of rule. They followed a Confucian perspective with a gendered aspect, in which "virtuous women" are described and praised (O'Hara 1971). Presumably this was necessary because some elite women refused to conform to the Confucian requirements of women as always subservient to a male kinsman. Although little actual evidence of ruling women in China exists, recent scholarship has brought to light women of power in many societies where history has neglected them (Andaya 2000; Connelly 2007; Sered 1994; Teubal 1984). It is possible that historians deliberately distorted the past. Roger Ames (1983:1) has noted that "history, far from being an objective account of incontrovertible fact, is a highly interpretive undertaking." For example, there is a tradition of a woman tribal leader of Chu in ancient times—"a mysterious female Yi Yin who was an early tribal leader of Chu" (Cook and Blakeley 1999:3). Women warriors seem to be the stuff of legend, but such women warriors are known from burials in China. Even later than the Shang dynasty, when Lady Hao and Lady Jing were both buried with weapons and helmets (see Case Study D), the most elaborate tomb of the Baiyin site belonged to a woman with a helmet (So and Bunker 1995). These women warriors also may have been rulers.

To find the women requires reading between the lines, and using poetry and art as data, as pioneered by women historians (Hinsch 2004; Connelly

2007). Paper (1995) shows that women shamans had power in parts of ancient China, and Major (1999) emphasizes the fact that women shamans were active and influential in the state of Chu. In fact, a number of prominent male scholars, especially the Chinese scholar Chen Meng-jia (1936), have been able to see beyond the Confucian overlay (which finds women rulers out of place and therefore erases or condemns them) to the possibility of equality in gender relationships.

A concern with the gender of shamans seems to be ubiquitous in research on shamans in East Asia—whether they are current, in the historic past, or in the archaeological past. For example, Yang-chung Kim (1977:14) asserts that in the early Silla period in Korea, female shamans "had already outnumbered male shamans. Therefore a reference to shamans generally meant female shamans."

But in spite of the weight of evidence favoring women shamans (or perhaps because of it), contrary writings are worded strongly. Some, like Chang (2005) and Keightley (1999a), eagerly show that women were not equal to men in ancient China. For Chang this belief takes the form of going to unusual lengths to emphatically deny that women were shamans. For Keightley, the denial of power for women is more subtle and linked to "the status of women," which allows him to lump all women together as inferior to men. The few women of power he acknowledges, such as Lady Hao, are construed as exceptions, hence require no explanation.

The interpretations of gender by the two scholars are quite different. Chang wants to show that kings could be shamans and shamans could be kings. [Note: I believe these gender blunders are the result of cultural blinders, and in no way do I mean to be disrespectful of these scholars whose work I admire, and who were personally gracious to women scholars.] Perhaps, given the historical belief in the superiority of men in China, Chang felt it necessary to exclude women as shamans in order to protect his main concern about the identity of kingship and shamanism. He may have believed that raising the gender issue would cloud his argument about leadership. For whatever reason, Chang makes a specific point about the shamans being male. In a book published posthumously, Chang (2005b:129) insists that there were ring ornaments on the penis, which he appears to equate with shamanism. Perhaps he meant this comment to refer to the Maya of Mesoamerica, where bloodletting of the penis and tongue was a ritual event. I know of no penis rings found in archaeological settings in East Asia. Even if there were penis ornaments—and a chain of reasoning could link them to shamanism—it would not deny the possibility of female shamans. And yet Chang is insistent that shamans were men, even trying to explain away any suggestion of female shamans: "The extant evidence indicates that shamans were males, but sometimes they enacted both male and female roles" (Chang 2005:129).

In discussing the women of ancient China, Keightley relies on texts, although he is cognizant of archaeological discoveries and their various interpretations. In a lengthy paper for the inaugural issues of the journal *Nan Nu,* he addresses the gender issue in Neolithic archaeology and the Shang oracle bone inscriptions (Keightley 1999a). He takes a prefeminist approach to women by concentrating on the status distinctions between women as a group and men as a group. This tactic repeatedly has been shown to be inadequate as a way to study gender. Women were "Mates, Mothers, Mystics, Militarists, Maids, Manufacturers, Monarchs, Messengers, and Managers" in ancient Japan, to quote a recent title (Barnes 2007). Barnes drew these activities of women from the *Nihon Shoki,* which was written to legitimize and glorify the Yamato line of males. The multivalent activities and roles of women could not be omitted from the story because some women in early Japanese history had been both active and powerful, and they were well known in legends and stories.

Anne Pyburn (2004:1ff), Rosemary Joyce (2000:3ff), Jocelyn Linnekin (1990:3ff), and many others have shown that lumping women together into a single category results in an ahistorical approach to history, one that interprets women as unchangeable and without history. This tactic only works when readers are unaware of extensive feminist critiques of archaeological explanations (see Nelson 2004 for an extended discussion of those critiques). Women, like men, were (and are) differentiated by class, kinship relationships, age, occupations, and many other attributes. To begin with the assumption that the culture had such a category as "women," which overrode all other individual characteristics, not only biases the results but fails to create meaningful categories and therefore lacks meaningful data.

Keightley (1999c:1) is not entirely unaware of the feminist critique of historical scholarship. He recognizes that Chinese historical texts were compiled by men and potentially biased for that reason, but he takes male scholarship as an indication in itself of women's supposed lower status. It seems not to occur to him that this argument does not apply retroactively to preliterate eras. Most likely, male bias has omitted and trivialized much female history (Lerner 1986). The fact that *any* women shamans appear in Chinese texts suggests that they were too well known to deny—and perhaps powerful enough to make it dangerous for the author to omit them. As has already been shown, more than a sprinkling of women shamans appear in written Chinese history.

Keightley's perspective is similar to that of Levi-Strauss, who thought the village was empty and he had been left "alone" because all the men had rowed away in their canoes, leaving the women and children (cited by Wylie 1991:38). For an analogous example, Keightley (1999c:6) writes, "the way *they* treated women in death . . . may reveal much about the way *they* treated women . . . when alive." It is worth pondering who "they" might be—clearly not women, who were on the receiving end of the treatment. In the context it is clear that Keightley means men, who are the actors in his story. The culture—male—is the actor, which treats (all) women in particular ways.

Keightley does, however, concede that some women may have high status because women may be worshipped as ancestors. Discussing Neolithic burials, he (1999c:11) suggests, "that women, as well as men, received secondary burial is important evidence . . . that their memory was preserved and that some kind of cult involving ancestresses, not just ancestors, may already have been developing in the Chinese Neolithic." This is important evidence about the status of women—not of women in general but of some women, probably elite and powerful women, who may have drawn their power both from their lineage and from their perceived ability to convince others that they could command spirits.

Another way of devaluing women shamans is to assign low status to shamanism. In Korea, where women shamans are the norm in the present, shamanism is understood as degraded and devalued, unlike in the distant past when shamans were kings. As will be discussed in chapters 7 and 8, the shamanism of early rulers in Korea and Japan could not be denied because of the authority of ancient texts—and additional verification is found in archaeological sites. For example, in southern Korea the crowns of early rulers are acknowledged with pride to be covered with shamanic symbols, but the crowns are assumed, even against archaeological and textual evidence, to belong to kings.

In several papers, I have addressed the apparent anomaly of the largest and richest burial of Old Silla belonging to a queen, while her husband's burial is replete with weapons but no gold crown or belt. The first paper entered the feminist discussion about women and the origin of the state. The papers that had been published at that time used archaeological evidence to describe the lowering of women's status, mostly following Engels' notion that the advent of private property and the state caused that downfall (e.g., Rapp 1977; Rohrlich 1980). I gathered data supporting a contrary case, the only ruler's burial that could be sexed—a queen of Silla who was buried with the shamanic crown and belt of royalty (Nelson 1993b). My second paper speaks to the written evidence, addressed to a Korean audience familiar with the texts, and makes a case for matrilineal descent of queens, with kings becoming kings as a result of Holy Bone status and marriage to the legitimate queen (Nelson 1991b). In the third revisiting of the data, I analyzed the way that rulership was conceptualized in Silla. I concluded that the Silla queens were perceived to have preferential access to the spirits as the highest level of the elite (Holy Bone) and as descended from mountain goddesses, thus they were shamans with access to the spirits (Nelson 2002a). If status is to be measured, the costliness of burial goods and the symbolism of the shaman crown make it obvious that rulers were indeed shamans, and women were indeed rulers—perhaps even the most honored and powerful rulers.

Conclusion

Many paths to leadership are possible. In state-level societies, leaders are associated with power. In the case of shaman leaders, that power is connected directly with spirits. Thus shamanism can provide a path to power. Early scholarship concludes, with Wolfram Eberhard (1950), that shamans in ancient China could be female. In a study of Chinese religion, Paper (1995:217) points to the "fundamental misperception" in the sixteenth century by the Jesuit Matteo Ricci in understanding Chinese religions. He considers that "although China has a patriarchal social system, its religious system considers male and female spirits of equal importance and power." More recently, Lionel Jensen (1997) has made an even stronger critique of traditional Chinese history, showing that the Jesuits in sixteenth-century China misunderstood the differences between China and the West, and "manufactured" Confucianism. These two critiques together open a space for a different version of ancient China. Rather than perceiving women in China as subordinate, Paper points to the complementarity of genders. Mountain and water spirits are both female (Paper 1995:227), as indeed they are also in early Korea (Nelson 1991b). In China, the summit of Mount Tai, the most sacred mountain, a temple to the First Princess of Purple and Azure Clouds was erected (Paper 1995:228). Women were potent, Paper suggests, because of pregnancy and childbirth. In addition, women were at the forefront of several cultural transformations, as will be detailed in the following chapters.

ANYANG, CHINA, TOMB No. 5—LADY HAO

The first intact tomb to be excavated at Yinxu was the tomb of Lady Hao, one of Wu Ding's queens (Figure D.1). It is an interesting coincidence that the excavator was a woman, Zheng Zhen-xiang, who described to me with excitement still in her voice the sequence of the excavation. It was a difficult excavation, waterlogged in the bottom, but with everything in place.

Wu Ding is the Late Shang king who brought in oracle bones, with the new practice of writing the charges on the bones. Another innovation from his time was the horse-drawn chariot. It is possible that Lady Hao was a bride from the north, and that she and her kin were responsible for the introduction of the chariot and supplied the horses. Lady Hao is mentioned on oracle bones many times. From

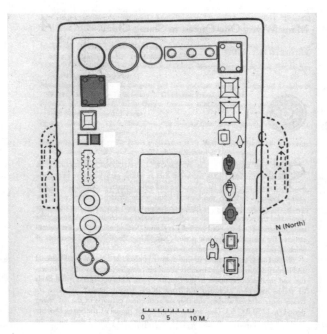

Figure D.1 Plan of Lady Hao's inner burial. After Wenwu Press 1994a

these texts it is known that she led large armies into battle, owned and managed estates, and helped prepare the oracle bones for use. She even may have been a diviner herself (Keightley 1999b).

Lady Hao's burial was extraordinary, overflowing with artifacts made of bronze, jades, and ivory (Qian Hao 1981; Zheng 1997). Some of the bronzes are inscribed with her living name, Fu Hao (Lady Hao), while others are marked with the name Mu Xin, which is presumed to be her temple name after death. Temple names were used to worship ancestor spirits, thus Lady Hao became Mu Xin in her ancestral temple. Several Northern Bronzes—in nomadic style, found mostly across Inner Mongolia and Manchuria (Guo 1995c)—were found in her tomb. These included mirrors with geometric designs and knives with animal heads and jingle bells for finials (Linduff 2002, 2003) (Figure D.2). Lady Hao may have come from this region (So and Bunker 1995).

Besides unusual bronzes, Lady Hao's 750 jades are of fine quality as well as large in number (Ma 1980). Many of these jades are small human and animal figures, carved in the round. One of them is a phoenix with a long tail and a crest, prefiguring the use of the phoenix as an emblem of an empress (Figure D.3). It has been speculated that

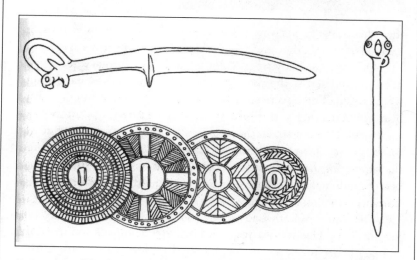

Figure D.2 Northern bronzes from the grave of Lady Hao. After Wenwu Press 1994a

Figure D.3 Jade phoenix. After Wenwu Press 1994a

Lady Hao may have used some of the small jades for divination purposes. One of the most graceful artifacts is a pair of ivory cups with designs inlaid with turquoise (Nelson 2002a) (Figure D.4).

A grave of a charioteer, likewise unlooted, contained the only other Northern Bronzes, which also seems to relate the horses and chariots to the north, rather than the northwest. Although the other grave goods were not as elaborate or numerous as those in Lady Hao's tomb, they are spectacular for a charioteer.

The tomb of Lady Jing (M260), Wu Ding's primary queen, has been located across the river in Xibeigang, where the Shang kings were buried. There were some artifacts remaining, although it had been robbed along with those of the kings. Lady Jing's tomb lacks ramps, which are characteristic of most of the king's graves, but the tomb is more elaborate than Lady Hao's. Lady Jing's tomb contained the largest *fangding*—square caldron raised on four legs—that has ever been found, including those in museums around the world that must have been robbed from kings' tombs.

The tombs of both Lady Jing and Lady Hao included sacrificial victims. Lady Hao was accompanied by sixteen humans and five dogs in her journey to the spirit world; Lady Jing was buried with thirty-eight sacrificial victims and thirty-three additional skulls. Lady Jing, however, was gifted with artifacts similar to those of Lady Hao. Each

Figure D.4 Drinking cup of ivory with inlaid turquoise. After
Wenwu Press 1994a

of the royal women's tombs contained weapons as well as gender sig-
nifiers—musical instruments, jade effigies of silk worms, and spindle
whorls (Linduff 2003). Each also had a bundle of hairpins with knobs
made of costly materials and created with elaborate workmanship.

Lady Hao appears often in the oracle bone inscriptions, indicating that King Wu Ding was particularly concerned about her welfare.
Should she be sent with troops against the Qiang? Would her deliveries be auspicious? (A lucky birth apparently was one that resulted in
a son [Keightley 1999a]). Lady Hao and other queens often prepared
the oracle bones for divination, but few were allowed to be diviners

themselves. Lady Hao, however, sometimes was the diviner. The oracle bones show that she owned property and led armies as a general. Her tomb contained weapons as well as objects often associated with women in China, implying that she might weave and embroider as well as prepare oracle bones and charge into battle in a chariot in front of the troops. She must have been an extraordinary person. One of the oracle bones tells of a dream that Wu Ding had about her after her death, which might have suggested that she was an angry spirit. But it was divined that her spirit was not causing trouble, perhaps to the relief of any of her relatives living in the Yin capital.

Interpretations of oracle bone inscriptions suggests that King Wu Ding may have married many wives, perhaps as many as sixty-four, but it is unlikely that they all received this kind of burial treatment. Only three of the women bore the title of Lady (Linduff 2002; Wang 2004) and were official queens. It is probable that each of the three queens was the mother of one of Wu Ding's three sons, who were designated as crown princes. Lady Hao's son apparently did not live to rule, but the other two inherited the nine *ding* and are listed as Shang kings.

FIVE

SHAMANS IN THE
EAST ASIAN NEOLITHIC

Twenty-four people of Bird Mountain Village stood in a semi-circle facing the sea, while Birdwing beat the ancient drum stretched with reindeer hide. They gathered in an open space made sacred by a tall pole topped by a wooden bird. . . . As the red sun began to reflect on the shining waves, the villagers shuffled their feet and murmured the daily incantation for safe passage through the day.

—*Spirit Bird Journey*, Nelson 1999:41

When the sun was at the top of the sky, Jade adorned herself with the treasures the spirits craved: yellow silk headband, shell bracelet, jade pig-dragon and jade earrings. She tied a yellow headband on Piggy, too, and a belt of shells around his waist. . . . When the flutists and drummers and stone ringers arrived at the top of the mountain, Jade clapped six times, poured out millet wine for the rain spirits, and distributed wine to the musicians . . . Jade took off her straw sandals and began to dance. She whirled clockwise around the ring of musicians, her shell belt rattling.

Jade Dragon, Nelson 2004:206–7.

THE QUOTES above are excerpted from novels, which represent my attempt to understand the people who left archaeological remains by writing stories about them. *Spirit Bird Journey* takes place in Neolithic Korea, while *Jade Dragon* is a reconstruction of the Hongshan culture of northeast China. Both novels are constructed from artifacts, features, and the landscape of sites that I know firsthand. This fiction is an attempt to understand how shamanism might work in small-scale and medium-scale societies. One problem I encountered in creating the stories is a dearth of perishables so that it was necessary to imagine clothing as well as daily and ritual activities based on a limited set of clues. Another, more basic problem was to intuit how shamans operated as leaders (Nelson 2003c).

In the opening four chapters, background was presented and theories were discussed. Now it is time to join data to theory. To what extent are the theories sustained by discoveries in East Asian archaeology? If shamanism provided leadership in the various regions of East Asia, was Siberian-type shamanism the model for it? Did other elements of ritual and belief, such as ancestor worship and animism, mix with shamanism to form something new? It is likely that the answers to these questions differ by times and regions, and that looking for the contours of an ancient pan-East Asian shamanism is chasing a situation that never existed. This is not surprising. Even Siberian shamanism as described by Russian and other observers differed according to local circumstances (Balzer 1990; Znamenski 2003). Turkic shamanism shows additional variations (Van Deusen 2004). There is no single pattern of shamanism today, even within, for example, the relatively small region of South Korea (Howard 1998a).

East Asia in Neolithic times was a cultural mosaic as well as an ideological mosaic. It is of course anachronistic to speak of China, Korea, and Japan as Neolithic entities, but because archaeologies are reported within national boundaries and according to national perceptions, they are often treated as national ancestry. This observation may seem obvious, but in practice when archaeology is summarized by current political boundaries, differences are often glossed over, rather than highlighted. Shelach (1999:47) notes the tendency to lump sites together in China: "Chinese and Western views are the same in that both see China as a homogenous cultural entity shaped by a unilinear sociopolitical process." As will be discussed in the chapter 9, many groups of people are known to have moved both within East Asia and into East Asia in prehistoric times. Therefore, even if a site seems to be clearly shamanistic, the presence of shamans cannot be generalized to its neighbors—and certainly not to all of East Asia.

A close look at shamanism shows a great deal of variability. Shamanism may not have been practiced everywhere, and where shamans did exist rituals differed. Regional differences are notable, although it is interesting that sites with possible shamans in China tend to cluster in the north and along the east coast of China (Figure 5.1).

One problem with the archaeology of shamanism, especially for China, is that while many kinds of artifacts and their contexts suggest the presence of shamanism, no two sites are alike. Of course archaeology often depends on chance discovery, and many sites remain uninvestigated, but rituals do not show the same characteristics at every site. In addition to this variability, the archaeological data are uneven in the ways they are reported, leading to problems in comparing the sites. A third variable is that attention to possible shamanism in the Neolithic by archaeologists is irregular. For example, the chapters on the Neolithic and Bronze Age in a recent book enthusiastically present the case for shamanism in China, lavishly adorned with

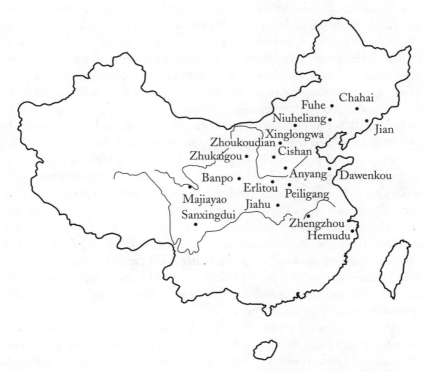

Figure 5.1 Map of Neolithic sites mentioned in the text. Map by Andrea Reider

crisp color photographs (Chang and Xu 2005). On the other hand, Under-hill (2002) spends less than a page on the topic of shamanism in the Shan-dong Neolithic, and that only in the context of fermented beverages. Liu's (2004) recent book, which covers the Yellow River region in the Neolithic, takes an intermediate view, noting figurines with Caucasian features and pointed hats as possible contact with peoples to the west, as well as sites that have been associated with shamanism, without placing any particular emphasis on these occurrences.

Postulating a "Jade Age" in China after the Stone Age and before the Bronze Age (Mou and Wu 1999; Teng 1997) is another view that tends to homogenize Late Neolithic in China. While many Neolithic regions do have spectacular jades, jade artifacts are not found throughout the Neolithic, and jade is used lavishly only in a few regions in China. Sites with exten-sive and elaborate jades are limited to the eastern part of China, especially the Hongshan, Longshan, and Liangzhu cultures. The eastern bias of jade usage appears not to be based on the prevalence of the raw material in the east, so jade usage must instead be cultural, either reflecting related peoples spreading down the coast, or stimulus diffusion through trade.

Even in the regions where jade is conspicuously used for ritual, styles of jade carving are markedly different in these regions and time periods. "Pig-dragons" and elaborate plaques with cut-out designs dominate the Hongshan assemblage. Almost all jades have been found in burial contexts adorning the deceased. Jade ornaments are prevalent in Longshan, mostly rather small but intricately carved with delicate inlays. Hairpins, which appear to have been worn exclusively by women, had skill and care lavished upon them, and presumably they marked the living elite as well as the deceased (Huang 1992). They were surely elite markers, but were not obvi-ously devoted to ritual. In the Liangzhu region, shapes with no obvious use, such as *cong* and *bi*, are conspicuous. Chang (1994b) believes that they are shamans' instruments. In addition to the fact that these three regions used jade in different ways, they are not contemporaneous. Hongshan is much earlier than Liangzhu and Longshan. What they have in common is the fact that jade appears to have been used exclusively by the elite. Working jade requires skill and training and was expensive in terms of labor, as well as the (probably) imported raw material.

While a standard joke in North American archaeology has been that an artifact otherwise unexplained must be a "ritual object," in China there is a different twist. Rituals and beliefs known from literate eras are read back into the prehistoric past to explain archaeological features and artifacts.

Although it is not unreasonable to suppose that many beliefs were ancient by the time they were recorded, archaeological verification requires multiple instances, and these are not always forthcoming. Furthermore, Chinese texts that refer to prehistoric and early historic times were almost lost in the third century BCE, when the infamous first emperor of China, Qin Shehuangdi, ordered all books in private hands to be burned. He was the victor who would have history written his way. Some palace records written on stone survived, and these were recopied and abridged in the succeeding Han dynasty by the Sima Qian, the Grand Historian of China. But much that was previously written must have been lost. Some older versions of ancient books miraculously have been preserved in a few tombs (the Bamboo Annals), and are carefully compared to later versions by scholars, but much is still missing. Nevertheless, skepticism is not always called for in assessing ancient records. Astronomical data, for example, suggest some truth in the ancient annals, whether they were passed along as oral history or some form of writing on perishable materials.

Neolithic sites and artifacts relevant to shamanism in Korea and Japan are fewer in the peninsula and islands than those in China, and less attention has been focused on evidence of shamanism. Perhaps simply it is taken for granted, since shamanism still exists. It is nevertheless interesting to compare the island and peninsular sites to those of China, especially in the retrospective light of later shamanism that still flourishes in Korea and Japan.

Neolithic Chronology

Possible ritual sites are distributed in many parts of China, and found as well in Korea, Japan, and the Russian Far East. A strict chronology of these sites is not possible, but since several millennia are involved, it is possible to divide sites into Early Neolithic, Middle Neolithic, and Late Neolithic.

Neolithic Origins

In East Asian archaeology the term Neolithic does not imply plant and animal domestication, but is used in the presence of pottery. Some recent discoveries show that the earliest pottery in East Asia is found in Japan at about 14,500 BCE (Ikawa-Smith 1999). This is a step back farther into the Late Pleistocene than the previous date for Incipient Jomon of 12,000 BCE. Although surprising, the dates are unassailable because the newest site was sealed under a well-dated layer of volcanic ash. But pottery-bearing sites elsewhere in East Asia are also being discovered in ever earlier contexts. By about 10,000 BCE, scattered sites from southern China to the Amur River in the Russian Far East include crude pottery in assemblages that are otherwise no different from those in purely Mesolithic sites. Little is known of the culture of these sites beyond the presence of pottery, although often the lithic technology includes sophisticated microliths and a variety of blade techniques (Pearson 2007; Underhill and Habu 2005). It is clear that even before the glacial melting and the significant rise in sea level in the Holocene, East Asians traveled long distances by boat and could have spread ceramic technology rapidly (Ikawa-Smith 1986).

Neolithic Japan is called Jomon, subdivided into Incipient, Initial, Earliest, Early, Middle, Late, and Final. Incipient includes the first pottery. By Earliest and Early Jomon, some groups lived by the coasts as shellfish collectors, and others hunted deer and boar in the mountains and collected nuts (Habu 2004). Some nonpottery sites in Korea up to about 6000 BCE likewise have few suggestions of plant or animal domestication, but indicate hunting and collecting. Rice grains dated to 14,000 BCE have been found in peaty soil in western Korea, but so far this discovery stands alone (Lee 1986). Some east coast sites appear to be largely dedicated to fishing sites. Boats must have been used because large fishhooks suggest deep sea fishing in the wide and deep sea between Korea and Japan (Nelson in press). Perhaps most surprising of all, in the Russian Far East a period of pottery use without domestication of plants also exists, but within this time range a maritime adaptation is evident along the coast (Vostretsov 2007; Zhushchikovskaya 2006).

Evidence of plant domestication occurs at least by 8000 BCE in both northern and southern China. Domesticated rice was found at Pengtoushan on the Chiangjiang River, and earlier evidence shows the harvesting of wild rice (MacNeish and Libby 1995; Yan 1992, 1999, 2005). By 6000 BCE at Hemudu rice is abundant in this waterlogged site (Chang 1986b). Because the unusual preservation of wood allows appreciation of carpentry skills in building houses of mortise and tenon structure, and intricate carvings on other objects made of wood, this site demonstrates the richness in variety and artistry of the Hemudu culture and shows how much of Neolithic life is missing when perishable materials are not preserved. The carvings of double-headed sunbirds (Figure 5.2), reminiscent of designs from the Northwest coast of North America, are delicate and evocative, and suggest myths and beliefs beyond mere decoration.

In northern China, abundant millet was found in the Peiligang/Cishan culture, including stalks and chaff. Much of it was found in storage pits,

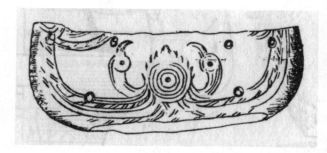

Figure 5.2 Carving of double-headed sunbird from Hemudu. After *Kaogu Xuebao* 1978/1

demonstrating a fully agricultural society. The amount of grain suggests that still earlier sites are yet to be found, especially if it is posited that millets were domesticated independently in North China. Pigs were domesticated, and many figurines of pigs were found in the sites (Chang 1986b).

Farther north, in Liaoning province and Inner Mongolia, another important region of early farming flourished. The northeastern region is often omitted in summaries of early agriculture in China, but it is crucial to understanding the early cultural mosaic of Neolithic China (Li 2003; Shelach 2000). Any discussion of the adoption of nonlocal plants and animals, and possible connections with Central Asia, must include this region. Domesticated pigs and millets are reasonably secure for the earliest sites such as Xinglongwa, Xinglonggou, and Chahai, suggesting possible connections with the more or less contemporaneous Peiligang culture. Xinglongwa is a particularly interesting site, because it appears to have been constructed all at once, with houses built neatly in rows with the whole village surrounded by a ditch, implying a population that moved together to find new land to farm, not a people just commencing on plant and animal domestication. Domesticated pigs were present in large numbers, including burials of whole pigs. Pig figurines may indicate a cult of pigs as occurred in the Hongshan period (Nelson 1995a, 1998). Sheep also appear, ecologically appropriate for the grasslands to the north and west. Indeed, sheep are more prevalent farther west and also become more important through time (Linduff 1995), although they are also notable in Peiligang, which strangely enough also had crocodiles.

Middle Neolithic

The Middle Neolithic of China brings increasing complexity in pottery types, houses, and village layouts. Many named cultures are lumped together under the general rubric of Yangshao, a term applied to sites with painted pottery along the Yellow River in north China. The habitation areas of Yangshao sites are often surrounded by a ditch, while pottery kilns are grouped together and separated from the dwellings. Cemeteries were placed outside the village. Silkworms were raised, and the presence of spindle whorls implies that other textiles in addition to silk provided clothing. Wool from sheep (or perhaps long-haired dogs) could have been spun. Hemp is implied by cord-marked pottery and was probably used for thread woven into cloth as well as cord (Ho 1975:81). Cattle were domesticated and may have been used to pull a wooden plow attached to the plowshares of stone that are found in many northern sites. The Middle Neolithic levels of Zhukaigou in the Ordos region have more sheep and oxen than pigs (Linduff 1995), which suggests increasing grasslands within the region as desiccation occurred (Wagner 1993). Domesticated sheep might indicate a connection with the Central Asian steppes, but the question of where and how domesticated sheep appeared in East Asia has not yet been studied.

The Middle Neolithic also contains small amounts of metal in the northeast and northwest. Both Qijia and Hongshan have hints of copper smelting as early as 3000 BCE (Linduff et al. 2000).

Late Neolithic

The Late Neolithic in China includes a number of complex features, with the result that some regions have been called incipient states (Su 1986, 1999). Walled towns became more common, notably in the Shandong region (Underhill 2002). Large ritual areas have been excavated in Hongshan (Sun and Guo 1986a), but no towns have been discovered. Burials with suggestions of elaborate rituals are found in the Liangzhu culture, the Shandong region, along the Yellow River basin and in Gansu province, suggesting increasing social differentiation. Warfare or raiding is implied by the discovery of bodies thrown helter-skelter into wells, suggesting the vulnerability of cities despite their walls. Marks on pottery suggesting proto-writing are another indication of increasing complexity (more on this topic below).

Possible Evidence of Neolithic Shamans

With this brief overview of the Neolithic in East Asia for context, archaeological evidence of possible shamanic activities is reviewed. Elements of material culture that could indicate shamanic activities include musical instruments and depictions of dancing, exotic clothing, paraphernalia of shamanic performances, unusual burials, depictions of humans and animals, ritual buildings, and containers for making, serving, and consuming intoxicants. Also relevant are symbols that have been used by shamans, materials that have been said to have spiritual qualities and relate to spirit worship, landscapes and ancient astronomy, and divination, including writing. After the broad picture of possible shamanistic manifestations has been examined, differences by regions and changes through time can be better appreciated. The next section considers material evidence wherever it appears. It needs to be kept in mind, however, that although some sites have obvious and sometimes spectacular rituals implied, they are rare and unusual sites.

Music and Dance

Energetic dancing is one of the hallmarks of shamanism, as a means through which shamans induce trance. Music and dancing are partners, as seen in the Chinese word *gewu*, combining song and dance into one concept. Kinetic movement of the dance and repetitive sounds of the drum or other percussion help the shaman to invoke spirits. It is likely that the first musical instruments were percussive and that they were parts of the human body—clapping hands and stamping feet—or extensions of them. Sound is a call for attention, and in many cultures the attention of spirits may be attracted with hand claps or simple percussion instruments such as wooden gong or even a pair of sticks. Jingles or clappers worn on arms or legs would have had the effect of accentuating bodily movements, but shamanism as it is known ethnographically in East Asia tends to jingling belts and dangles sewn onto clothing more than armlets and anklets, and Neolithic archaeology seems to reflect the same convention.

   Ching (1997:19) enumerates ritual dances as described in ancient texts. Each kind of dancing occurred in its proper ritual context. For example, "a military dance took place at sacrifices to mountains and rivers, while feather dances were performed at sacrifices to the spirits of the four directions." The rain deity was believed to have the form of a dragon, and dances to this spirit were mostly performed by women. These texts refer to historic times, but may also describe earlier forms of dance.

   Drums may be the original shaman's instrument, especially the handheld variety, because such drums were used throughout Central Asia and Siberia, as well as among the Inuit, for calling spirits. Such shaman drums are not identical, however. Many are played with a stick rather than the hand. Siberian drums are beaten on the top of the stretched hide, while Chukchi and some Inuit drums are played from underneath. Drums also differ in size, decoration, and other characteristics. It is the sound of drumming that is relevant to shamanism, not who plays the drum, how it is played, or physical characteristics of the drum. Small drums were probably the earliest in China, for several have been found in Chinese Neolithic sites. For example, in the Early Neolithic, probable drums were found at Hemudu, in the form of hollowed wooden objects. Late Neolithic drums were stretched with crocodile hides. Ceramic cylinders may have been drums, as well, stretched with hides on one or both ends.

In the Late Neolithic at the site of Taosi, in Shanxi province, definite wooden drums with crocodile skin tympani were excavated (Shao 2005:92). Since the Taosi site is about five hundred miles from the Shandong peninsula where crocodiles infested the rivers and swamps—and where such drums were placed in the graves of the elite—it raises questions of trade or migration. It has been suggested that women from Shandong married into Shanxi, bringing the drums with them. And, if women brought the drums and the drums imply shamans, were the women shamans? Besides the crocodile-skin drums, possible pottery drums and stone chimes were also found at Taosi. Played simultaneously, they would have produced sounds no spirit could resist.

Although Nuwa, the woman originator god, was said to be the creator of music, invention of musical instruments was also connected to Yao, one of the legendary Five Emperors, who possibly lived in the third millennium BCE (Wu 1982). Neolithic archaeology shows that musical instruments had been around for several thousand years by the time of Yao. Early instruments mentioned in texts include a drum made of a deer skin stretched over a pottery jar, musical stones, and a lute with five strings (Karlgren 1946:292). The musical stones were said to have power over animals: "When I knock on the musical stones, the hundred animals all dance" (Karlgren 1946:258).

The human voice was surely the first melodic instrument. But a more sophisticated (and perhaps more mysterious) method of extending the range of musical sound is found in Early Neolithic China by 5000 BCE with the discovery of bone flutes, which were well enough preserved to be played and their tonality studied (Zhang et al. 2004). For example, a seven-holed flute made of a bird leg bone was unearthed in the Peiligang culture at Jiahu, Wuyang, Henan (Yan 2005:34), along with several other flutes. In later times, flute music was considered to have magical properties. A legendary flautist, Xiao Shi, ascribed to the sixth century BCE, taught his wife to play the flute and both of them, floating as they merrily played, rose into the sky, immediately becoming spirits. Bone whistles were unearthed at Hemudu, near Shanghai, along with a pottery *xun*, an irregularly-shaped object with holes like an ocarina (Paper 1995:96). Music was obviously available for shamanistic séances, other rituals, or simply entertainment.

By the Late Neolithic, musical instruments had become more sophisticated. By their placement in burials these instruments can be assumed to have been valuable as well as sacred. In a rich burial at Taosi, spaces between the inner and outer coffins were filled with musical instruments on one side and finely made colored ceramic artifacts on the other. This distribution of burial goods suggests that the tomb inhabitant was not only a member of the elite, but also a ritual leader who provided music, food, and drink for rituals. Personal leadership and communal ceremonies seem to be emphasized together.

A few copper bells from Neolithic times have been unearthed. A single copper bell was placed at the waist of a burial, also from Taosi, but in a middle-level grave, in terms of both size and grave goods (Shao 2005:91). The small clappered bell is called *ling*. It is quite different from those that occur in graduated sets—like the chimes and bells placed in noble burials from the Eastern Zhou—which suggests a different origin. Sets of metal bells were not provided with clappers but were struck from the outside. If the Taosi bell was attached to a shaman's costume, it would have rung with a loud clamor as the shaman danced. Falkenhausen (1993:134) remarks that such a bell would "produce noise rather than music." He further notes that later uses for clapper bells included horse and chariot trappings, dog collars, and wind chimes—all functioning to attract attention. Therefore it seems likely that this *ling* was attached to a shaman's coat. It would have had an appropriate effect for a shamanic séance. But it is interesting that, although some very rich burials were unearthed at Taosi, none of them contained any copper artifacts, and the burial with the copper bell was only a medium-sized grave. This suggests that copper was not at that time considered a high-status object, and/or that shamans were not among the wealthiest individuals. Or the bell might have belonged to a person connected to sites in the western part of China, where copper objects were beginning to be produced and were used more widely (Fitzgerald-Huber 1995).

While musical and rhythmic instruments obviously do not imply shamanism necessarily, some kind of sound was required for a shamanistic séance. Similarly, dance is another aspect of shamanism, and dances depicted in various kinds of art, including painted scenes on Early Neolithic bowls, have been used to suggest shamanism in the Chinese Neolithic (e.g., Chang 2005; Shao 2005). The problem with interpreting these painted bowls as evidence of shamanism, however, is that the dances painted on Early Neolithic pottery in China do not show individual dancers flinging themselves about. Instead orderly lines or circles of dancers dressed in identical costumes hold hands. Painted pottery bowls from the Majiayao culture around 3000 BCE are the most frequently used to illustrate this style of dancing. One basin from Shangsunjaizhai in Qinghai depicts three groups of five dancers on the inside of a large shallow bowl (*pan*). A similar bowl found at Zongri, Qinghai, shows two groups of eleven and thirteen dancers. Two other bowls each depict a line of five dancers, which are interpreted as a group of woman on one bowl and a group of men on another. The "women" have round lower bodies or wear skirts (Figure 5.3). The people in the line of dancers that are alleged to be males are painted with objects that point down and slightly to the left near the top of their legs. These figures are described as "ithyphallic males" (Shao 2005), but the designation is open to question. The "ithy" part of the word implies erect, but the painted stripes hang down at about 6:35 o'clock. They look like feathers or ribbons, with slightly uneven ends (Figure 5.4). These painted marks are more likely to represent part of a costume,

Figure 5.3 Painted Neolithic bowls depicting "female" dancers. From brochure, Yangshao Culture

Figure 5.4   Painted Neolithic bowl depicting "male" dancers. From brochure, Yang-shao Culture

perhaps the feathered tail of a bird that is imitated in this particular dance. A similar object falls from the head, likewise pointing down and to the left. The most likely interpretation of both objects is that they indicate feathers or ribbons, rather than either tails or phalli. A shell pendant from Zhoubao-gou in the northeast shows a possible shaman in costume, with a belt that seems to end in feathers, similarly trending off to the left, although in this case it is unambiguously part of the belt (Figure 5.5). Devlet (2001) asserts that feathers and fringes on shamans' costumes are references to the flight of birds. Because of their orderly positions, however, the dancers depicted on these bowls are likely to be performing a community ritual rather than participating in a shamanistic performance. That it was a ritual of some importance can be reasonably inferred, but any connection with shamanism is a long, uncomfortable stretch.

Shamans' Clothing

Shamans do not dance and perform rituals in ordinary clothing unless, like some impoverished tribes of Siberia, they have little access to colorful clothing or embellishments. The séance is a theatrical performance, for which special clothing is worn, used only for this purpose. The shaman's costume is intended to honor the spirits and to allow the shaman to reach them, while it also sets the scene for the audience. The shaman's coat was often covered with colorful paintings, mirrors or other flashy devices, or objects that rattle. Robes or coats shown in ethnographic photographs do not conform to a single pattern. What was appropriate probably depended on local custom and available materials, as well as the idiosyncratic ideas of a particular shaman. In any case, clothing is too perishable to be found in most archaeological contexts.

Shamans' headgear tends to be constructed of shapes that distinguish the event from daily wear. Headgear worn by recent or current shamans includes pointed hats, circlets with uprights, and strings of beads dangling over the face. Some hats are depicted in bronzes from Siberia, including bands with antlers, trees, or birds springing upward from them (Federova 2001:59). A Mongolian hat from Xiongnu times features a golden bird (Kessler 1994). Devlet (2001:50–52) illustrates rock art with upright "rays" on hats. She explains, "In the Altai, shamans who wore bands decorated with feathers and shells were called 'birds.'" DeWoskin (1983:16) also notes bird or feather headdresses for shamans. The Yellow Emperor is often depicted wearing a flat hat with bead curtains dangling from the front and back, perhaps intended to indicate his ability to communicate with spirits.

Headdresses are not well represented in the Neolithic, except in Northeast China and along the Yellow River (Liu 2004). In a burial at Zhaobaogou, a small shell humanoid figurine suggests an otherworldly creature from outer space, with a pointed hat or a peaked head (see Figure 5.5). Many burials of the Hongshan period contained a

Figure 5.5 Shell figure from Zhoubaogou with a belt. After *Hongshan Jade*, Liaoning Province, no author listed, 2004

hoof-shaped jade ornament that was usually under the skull. It has been suggested that the function of this artifact was to hold long hair, perhaps fastened with a knot at the end. Drawing long hair through this tube would have created a "ponytail" bobbing rhythmically in a shaman's dance.

A raptor bird carved from jade was found under the head of a Hong-shan burial, but it has no device for attachment to the head, so it must have functioned as a pillow rather than a headdress. Some figurines from the Yellow River region wear pillow-shaped hats, while others have pointed hats. Liu (2004:91) implies that they indicate contact with Central Asia, because the faces have big noses and round eyes.

Belts may also feature prominently in the shaman's costume. Often belts include streamers that whirl outward during a dance. When made of metal or shell, they also clack and clank against each other. In the Northern Zone of China during the Bronze Age, bronze plaques with dangling objects were joined together to make belts. Similar belts made of gold are found in royal burials of Silla in fourth- and fifth-century Korea, and also occur somewhat earlier in northeastern China (Nelson 2008). A rope belt is depicted on a fragment of a clay statue from Dongshanzui, Jianping, Liaoning (Figure 5.6). A double strand of thick rope with a distinctive knot of Z-shape is depicted. A photograph of a similar rope from a site in North Korea suggests that this knot is symbolic, perhaps designating the person wearing it as a spirit medium.

The séance is a performance for which elaborate costume is compulsory; unfortunately, clothing is among the most perishable of human-made

Figure 5.6 Rope belt, part of broken female figurine from Dongshanzui. After Sun and Guo 1986b

objects. While attachments made of less perishable materials—such as shell, bone, stone, and occasionally metal—may be present in burials, distributed in a way to suggest attachment to clothing, they are often ambiguous without the robes or coats to which they were attached. Painted or embroidered designs would have vanished entirely. Furthermore, it is difficult to distinguish mere ornament from objects meant to rattle, jingle, and sway with the dance. Tinkling and glittery objects can be a part of elite clothing as well as shamans' outfits, likewise intended to attract attention to an august personage. Figurines sometimes indicate ornaments, especially round earrings, but other ornaments, if depicted at all, are often sketchily shown.

Human Figures and Masks

Sculptures meant to represent human beings are relatively rare in Neolithic China (Yang 1988). Most of those that do occur are found in the northeast in what is now Liaoning province and Inner Mongolia, and along the Wei River, a western tributary of the Yellow River. These two regions are possible southern and northern corridors of contact between the heartland of central China and Central Asia, where human representations occur earlier. The earliest figures known so far within any part of the present borders of China are from Xinglongwa in Inner Mongolia (Hinsch 2004; Li 2003). The Xinglongwa period in Inner Mongolia features lumpy and crude stone figures, which appear to represent women because breasts are sculpted (Figure 5.7). These figures were found in household contexts, therefore are thought to be representations of a hearth goddess. Several of these figures— kneeling, sitting, or squatting—have been found at the site of Houtaizi on the northern side of the Yan Mountains. Liu (2004:91) suggests that they were made by individuals for special occasions, although Hinsch (2004) and Li (2003) accept them as household deities, perhaps personifications of spirits. A small female figurine from Sinamni was found in southeastern Korea (Choe 1989), and a similar figure was found in Japan (Kidder 1966).

Human representations in the Early Neolithic have been described as "fertility figures" (Childs-Johnson 1991:88) or "goddesses" (Hinsch 2004) because they are possibly or definitely female. "Fertility" is one of those catchwords that often is used as if it were self-explanatory. It is assumed that primitive people would have desired more children. This is a dubious proposition, as Kelley Hays-Gilpin (2004:50) points out: "Research on historic hunter-gatherers suggests that they typically avoid having large families." If fertility means the ability to become pregnant, that might have been less of

Figure 5.7 Liangzhu jade figure with mask headdress. After *Kaogu Xuebao* 1984/2

a problem for Neolithic people than the safety of births and mortality of mothers and infants. Burial data in Neolithic China suggest that maternal and child mortality figures were high (Keightley 1999c:7). The skewed sex ratios found in some Neolithic cemeteries (Gao and Lee 1993) could indicate high maternal mortality, which required disposal of the bodies in some other place rather than the village cemeteries. Therefore it seems that rather than wishing for "fertility," the figurines could represent requests to the powers for safe deliveries and healthy mothers and babies.

Some faces made of shell and clay have been found at Baiyin in Inner Mongolia. This is a large complex site north of the Xilamulun River, with two walled settlements and three cemeteries. It is divided into five phases. The faces are from Phase II B, contemporaneous with the Xinglongwa culture (Wagner 2006:26–35). In the same phase, the site also had one of the Xinglongwa-type lumpy female figures placed near the hearth. The site of Nasitai contains humanoid figures as well—one kneeling, with a tall hat or turban, the other sitting, with horned protrusions on its head. Typical Hong-shan jades are also found at this site.

By the Middle Neolithic, small heads from the Houwa site, near Dandong on the Liaodong peninsula, represent grotesque humans and animals. They occur in both levels of the site, but steatite heads (sometimes with torsos suggested) are more common in the earlier level. Headgear on a few heads is interpreted as turbans (Xu 1995). A realistic face said to be female because of its delicate features was found in the upper level (Yang 1988). A figurine was found in the Xinkailiu culture, on Lake Khanka, near the Russian Far East. Faces or masks were also found in the Zhoubaugou culture. They are realistic, not otherworldly or grotesque. Liu (2004:91) notes that small human figures in the Yellow River region probably depict ritual practitioners. Some of their clothing includes tall headdresses. The features of these figures are Caucusoid, which leads to speculation about shamans or magicians arriving from the west during the Middle and Late Neolithic.

The life-sized statues from the Hongshan culture are realistic, well-executed, and absolutely unique in China. They are some of the earliest life-sized human figures in the world. Similar statues are not known to occur elsewhere in Asia. Childs-Johnson (1991:84) suggests that Hou Tu (Sovereign Mother Earth) is represented at the site of Dongshanzui and asserts that the "sacrificial altars were used in worshipping an earth mother who was treated as a fertility goddess," but my studies of Hongshan suggest that this is not a likely scenario. The "goddess" face at Niuheliang is part of a life-sized statue found within an unusual building (see Case Study A) that has been assumed to have a ritual use. A groove for a band or circlet above the forehead must have contained something made of cloth or other perishable material. The intention could have been to represent a goddess, but the specificity of the face suggests a real person, who might have been a seer or shaman, or possibly a founding female ancestor. Jade plaques with similar headbands and upturned shoulder-length hair have been noted in museum collections (So 1993). The female figure is accompanied by fragments of life-sized statues of a pig and a bird. The animals could be present as spiritual assistants to a shaman. Pigs and birds were important in local mythology, a topic which will be discussed later.

There is nothing about the altars that would imply sacrifices. Earlier, Sun and Guo (1986a) suggested that the life-sized face with inlaid jade eyes at the "Goddess Temple represents a fertility goddess who is also a mythified ancestress." The pregnant and possibly nursing figures at Dongshanzui send a different message about birth and growth. I have suggested that Dongshanzui represents the celebration of life, and Niuheliang the celebration of spirit ancestors (Nelson 1991a). The two ceremonial centers thus comprise ritual venues for the beginnings and endings of human life.

In some séances, shamans wear masks. For example, copper masks were worn by Tungus shamans (Paper 1995:69). However, masks may be worn in other kinds of rituals and even entertainments, so masks are not necessarily indications of shamanism. Chang (1983:84) notes that sites with masks are found in the Yangshao, Dawenkou, and Longshan cultures, especially near the southeast coast. Some masks with perforations in the ears for tying the mask over the face have been found in both China and Japan. Masks were probably more commonly made of wood, gourd, or lighter materials, such as those used in Korean masked dances. Human faces on jars in Yangshao are said to imply the mask of a *wu* or *xi* (Yang 2000:52).

Perhaps most convincing as specifically depicting humans wearing masks are the Liangzhu jades from the Early Neolithic. These show a face topped by a hat or crown that is also a face. Although both faces are humanoid, with large round eyes, neither represents a naturalistic human face. Some art historians have suggested that the Liangzhu figures are the origin of the *taotie,* the monster mask on Shang bronzes (Allan 1993).

Masks are not common in the Korean Neolithic, but they do appear along the east coast. A shell from Tongsamdong, near Pusan, has been made into a simple mask, with holes for eyes and a round, open mouth. A mask-like object of pinched clay was found at Osanni, in the middle of the Korean east coast (Im and Kwon 1984). A smaller face made of clay and surrounded by coils of clay that may represent hair was found in a coastal site of the Russian Far East (Zhushchikovskaya 2006:5) (Figure 5.8). In the Late Jomon of Japan there are definite masks made of clay and some human faces that are mask-like (Kidder 1965).

Figure 5.8 Faces from Korea and the Russian Far East. Above, photo by Im Hyo-jai; below, after Zhuschchikovskaya 2006

Burials

Some unusual burials in the Early Neolithic of China have been offered as indicating shamans. They are each distinct, which suggests cultural differences, rather than a single type of widespread ritual. A unique configuration of burials is found in the Yangshao period at Yuanjunmiao, where an adult cemetery contained only a few children (Zhang 1985). These juvenile burials included long hairpins on top of the head and were sexed as female. They were lavishly buried compared to others in the cemetery, especially having many ceramics and beads. Tomb M429 was the joint grave of two (probable) girls, one of whom was richly adorned with 785 bone beads. A girl buried in M405 was supplied with a bone hairpin and a shell knife in addition to bone beads, which are shown around her head in the drawing of the burial, as if they had been attached to a headdress. A woman and girl buried together in M420 were provided with an unusual number of pottery vessels, in addition to bone beads, bone hairpins, and a pierced shell ornament (Figure 5.9). The girl in this burial wore a necklace made of 1,147 bone beads. While the sex of these juveniles has been questioned on the ground that subadults are difficult to sex (Lee and Zhu 2002), the artifacts, especially the hairpins, do suggest females, especially since one such child burial is accompanied by a woman with an identical hairpin placed in the same way (Zhang 2005). A great deal of labor went into the necklaces, but whether the special treatment indicates that these women and girls possessed the power to call down the spirits is not possible to know. In regard to a different burial site, Zhang (2005:73–74) speculates that "craftsmen, skilled hunters, successful warriors, and sha-

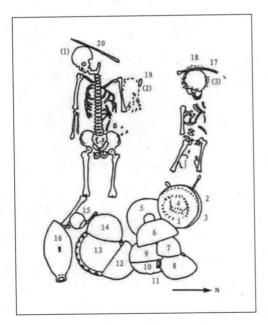

Figure 5.9 Burial of woman and girl from Yuanjunmiao. After Wenwu Press 1983

mans (*wu*) possessed more wealth than ordinary members in the lineage." These girls were unlikely to belong to any of his categories except that of shaman, but the wealth of their burials could well suggest special relationships to the spirits.

Another unusual burial from the Early Neolithic Xinglongwa culture consisted of an adult male buried within a house with two whole, articulated adult pigs beside him. One of the pigs was male, the other female. These full-grown pigs together were nearly as long as the person they accompanied in death. It is possible that the buried person was a shaman accompanied by pigs representing spirit familiars. The pigs were unlikely to have been food for the afterlife in this context. Although they could have been buried as pets, this also seems an unlikely explanation for such a unique burial. The man was buried with 715 other grave offerings made of jade, bone, ceramic, and shell.

The Hongshan culture, which succeeded Xinglongwa in the Late Neolithic, also was notable for pig ceremonialism (Nelson 1995a, 1998), which took several forms. The main burial at the site of Niuheliang, in Locality 2, M1, had been plundered in antiquity, but it still contained pig and cattle bones. Pigs were sacrificed in Manchu rituals and are still important in Korean shamanism. A pig head or whole pig is often part of the rite. Animal bones were unusual as grave offerings in Hongshan sites. In fact, this is the only burial at Niuheliang from which animal bones are recorded. Sheep bones were found in a pit near the Goddess Temple, along with broken pots, suggesting a sheep feast dedicated to the spirits, making it necessary to dispose of the pots and bones in special pits.

Hongshan jades are the earliest figured jades in China, although jade earrings were found in the preceding Xinglongwa culture (Liu 2003). They include many *zhulong*, or pig-dragons, which feature a pig's head attached to a curved body. The body is plain but the head has sculpted ears, large round eyes, and tusks indicated by incising. These objects were perforated for suspension from a cord and were often found on the chest of the deceased. Another form also called *zhulong* (in my opinion inappropriately) is larger than the typical one, has a thinner "body" and ends in the head of a horse with almond eyes and a long, flowing mane. I have argued that these creatures represented horse-dragons, not pig dragons, and should be called *malong* (Nelson 2008). It is possible that both pigs and horses were spirit animals, or animal assistants to shamans. However, *zhulong* seem to be more generic than personal, since so many have been found. Each shaman has his or her own particular animal helper, while these "dragons" are made to a pattern

that must have had a specific meaning. More likely they signaled rank, occupation, or other status—perhaps even different clans of Wu.

The jaw and trotters of a pig from the Goddess Temple at Niuheliang
have already been mentioned. Pigs clearly figured in many rituals. Another
possible indication of pig symbolism is a mountain visible from the Goddess Temple that has the outline of a pig head with upright pointed ears and
a snout and is known locally as Zhushan—Pig Mountain. It seems likely
that this was a sacred mountain, since it is also visible from most of the burial areas. The idea that it might be seen as a bear has been floated (Barnes
and Guo 1996), that is unlikely because the shape of the ears is porcine
rather than ursine, and there is no other indication of bears in the Hongshan iconography (although a small bear head and partial torso was found
at Nasitai). Thus pigs seem to be important in the whole society, not just as
a shaman's familiar.

Zhang (2005:83) suggests that the temple at Niuheliang was for the use
of the dead, not the living: "Erecting a temple within a mortuary complex
shows that the dead, although in a different world, were supposed to still
worship the deities, as they had in life, and to seek these deities' protection."
However, the long narrow building seems to resemble a shrine more than a
temple, and, if the beliefs were animistic, "deities" is probably too specific a
word for the statues placed inside. A shrine honoring a former shaman or
priestess seems to be a more likely explanation

Possibly relevant to interpreting the burial is the fact that the Puyang
site is near the Dragon Temple of Leize on the north bank of the Yellow
River. This region was a marshland in ancient times and might actually have
sheltered crocodiles. It is said that the culture hero Fuxi was conceived when
a young woman stepped in the footprint of the God of Thunder. Thunder is
associated with rain and dragons (Da 1988).

Dragons and Other Animals

The question arises about what dragons represented for Neolithic peoples.
Yang (2000) notes the common use of lizards (he calls them "gekkos") in
the art of Neolithic China. However, it is possible to speculate that they
might represent crocodiles rather than small lizards, because of the relationship of Chinese dragons with rivers (Schafer 1973). Perhaps the presence
of crocodiles in rivers and marshes led to the idea of the dragon in China
as a folk memory after crocodiles had become extinct in central China. It is
known that actual crocodiles occurred in the Shandong region, since croco-

dile skin was used for drumheads and crocodile bones were found in the Longshan period as well (Underhill 2002). Perhaps the most dangerous animals for human populations were the crocodile and the tiger—the only carnivorous ones large enough to attack and consume humans. Jean James (1993) suggests that the Puyang burial actually is an alligator.

In addition to the large dragons and other animals already mentioned from the Puyang burial, two similar dragons (or crocodiles) were made of stone or clay instead of shell. An enormous dragon, 19.7 meters long, was found in Liaoning province at Chahai, near Fuxin. It is from the early Neolithic level, belonging to the Xinglongwa period around 6000 BCE. Smaller clay dragons (each about a meter long) of the Xinglongwa culture have been found at Yangjiawa in Liaoning province (Yang 2000).

A smaller stone dragon mosaic belongs to the Daxi culture of the Late Neolithic, about 4000 BC. It is in Jiaodun, Huangmei, Hubei, and is of considerable size at 4.46 meters long. Such mosaics have been described in the literature as representing totemic animals, although they are unlikely to be totems in the classic sense of animals from which the group is believed to be descended (Schafer 1973:143). It is said that earthen images of dragons were constructed to pray for rain in times of drought (Ching 1997)

While Hongshan jades depicts recognizable birds, turtles, and insects, composite figures of animals with human heads are found elsewhere in the Early Neolithic. The earliest composite figures known include a lizard with a human head molded on a pottery jar in Qianmao, Shaanxi. These composite images are said to suggest transformations from human to animal, as might occur in a shaman's séance (Yang 2000:53). In the Yangshao culture, many fish are depicted on bowls, and some of them seem to have human rather than fish faces. Yang (2000:51) suggests that, "the human face pattern was an anthropomorphic fish spirit that can be also be found in personified animals in the Liangzhu and Majiayao cultures."

Symbols

Many kinds of symbols suggest shamanism in East Asia including suns, birds, and turtles. Chang (1994b:62) emphasizes the importance of the visibility of symbols. "Symbols adorn ritual garments and paraphernalia to imbue them with power, and by their presence provide the only clues to the workings of the rituals in political or any other terms."

In later East Asian cultures, birds were perceived as message carriers from the world of spirits to the world of humans. Therefore it is not surprising that birds play a prominent part in the ritual symbolism of Early Neolithic cultures, especially those along the eastern side of China. In the Middle Neolithic Xinle site in Liaoning, an elaborate wooden baton was carved with the figure of a bird. The artifact was interpreted as a symbol of leadership. In the Late Neolithic Hongshan period many of the birds represented are owls and raptors, which are depicted realistically. Other birds are more obviously symbolic. Images of a long-tailed bird, perhaps a forerunner of the mythical phoenix, were carved into bone daggers.

Birds sometimes symbolize shamanic flight, representing the souls of shamans seeking the spirits. DeWoskin (1983:16) emphasizes that feathered headdresses and costumes are common among shamans. Birds may also represent the sun, as in the ancient myth of the ten suns, in which Archer Yi had to shoot down nine of them (Allan 1991). In the Hemudu culture (4900–3900 BCE) a carved pig included the design of a bird on its flank, and double-headed birds with solar symbol in the middle were carved on wooden artifacts (Yan 2005:39). Birds are also prominent in depictions of deities of skies and directions in the ancient shamanistic book, *Shanhaijing* (So 1999).

Pigs, as already noted, are frequently depicted in the Neolithic. At the Peiligang site, small realistic figures of pigs are common, and similar clay figures are found as far north as Heilongjiang province. Pigs represented wealth in later China and may have acquired that symbolic meaning quite early because they are an excellent source of food, reproduce prolifically, and are able to digest plant parts and waste that humans cannot, and therefore they do not compete with humans for food. Painted jars from Zhaobaogou, Nantaidi, and Shaoshan depict "spirit" deer, pigs, and dragons (Guo 1995a).

Turtles also had special meaning in ancient China. Allan (1991) shows that the *ya* shape that represents the earth is also the shape of a turtle shell. The Jiahu site of the Peiligang/Cishan culture, one of the earliest sites with extensive millet agriculture, contains turtle plastrons in burials. Realistic jade turtles of different types were grasped in the hands of a burial at Niuheliang in the Hongshan period. Turtle plastrons were used to make inquiries of the spirits in the Late Shang period. A jade turtle with an inscribed plaque placed inside it was part of the rich burial goods (M4) at Lingjiatan in Hunan (Figure 5.10). The eight-pointed star drawn on the plaque is said to be a sun symbol and has also been connected with archaeoastronomy because the Shang were known to emphasize the cardinal directions, even as powers (Keightley 2000). This same pattern is found on sites in Central Asia and is found on an early mirror of the Qijia culture. Major (1984) links this pattern with cosmology.

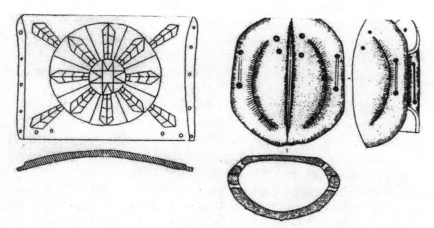

Figure 5.10 Plaque from Lingjiatun, Hunan, engraved with eight-pointed star found inside a turtle box. After Chang and Xu 2005

Real turtle shells were found in the Dadianzi cemetery, but they were relatively rare, occurring in only eight (out of 186) tombs. One turtle shell contained bone needles, another was the repository for six bone awls. Both needles and awls suggest "women's work" of sewing and basketry. However, only one of the wealthy burials is recorded as a woman.

Dragons, as we have seen, are associated with water in East Asia, including bodies of water and rain, symbolized by clouds. The symbolism of yin and yang makes water female. Although this association is said to come later, women shamans were specifically called upon to dance for rain (Ching 1997). It is possible and even likely that dragons were associated with women in the Neolithic (Nelson 1991a; Schafer 1973).

Sun symbolism appears in various patterns. Circular patterns were painted on pottery of the late phase of the Yangshao culture at Dahecun near Zhengzhou, Henan. The circles represent the sun and were related to solar worship (Yang 2000:54). A Han dynasty document records that the Goguryeo people of Korea and Manchuria worshipped the sun, and the mythical founder of Japan is Amaterasu, the Sun Goddess, who is linked with shamanism. Birds are shown with suns in several regions, notably at the Middle Neolithic Hemudu site and the Late Neolithic Liangzhu culture, both near Shanghai. The myth of Archer Yi shooting down nine of the ten suns likewise suggests solar worship (Allan 1991). At least for some groups, the sun was a central power.

Artifacts including Hongshan bracelets and joined rings, which are round on the inside and squarish on the outside, may be related to the round-heaven/square-earth concept and are invoked as shamanistic as well. "Altars" in the Hongshan culture are either square or round and are said to represent earth and heaven. The Puyang burial, described above, has a rounded side and a squared side, and it has been similarly interpreted as representing heaven and earth. The Liangzhu culture produced tubes called *cong* in Chinese, which likewise are seen as related to this belief. It has been speculated that these objects were used by shamans to sight specific stars, or to "communicate between heaven and earth" (Chang 2005:133).

"X-ray" figures are common in the rock art of the Amur River (Okladnikov 1981). Such figures are sometimes seen on shamans' robes in Siberia and Central Asia. They are not common in East Asia, although a skeleton was painted on bowl of Yangshao culture. Rock art at Ulchu in southeastern Korea also includes some petroglyphs of animals showing ribs inside, as well (Kim 1986).

Triangles and short lines are used as decorative motifs from Central Asia to Japan, possibly with symbolic meaning. They first appear on Neolithic pottery, especially in Korea and the Russian Far East, but also in northern China and Japan (Nelson 1991b). Triangles also appear on Yangshao pottery in connection with horned figures (Paper 1995:64). A stove recovered from the Fu Hao burial of Shang China is decorated with large triangles, a similar decorative motif is used on Northern Bronzes such as knives and mirrors, and a shrine depicted in Eastern Zhou shows the same set of triangles along the hill under the shrine (Chang 1994b).

The eight-pointed star appears to have had a special meaning. It was carved on a turtle shell at Jiahu, and painted on various Neolithic jars. For example, the motif is found at Nantaidi in the Zhaobaogou period. It is also found in sites in Gansu, and even as far west as the Namazga culture (Kohl 1981).

Proto-writing

Because the earliest identifiable writing in sentences in East Asia is an early form of Chinese engraved on the oracle bones of the Late Shang dynasty, nearly everything that is known about that time period from contemporary written materials is connected with divination. The writing found on Shang oracle bones is a well-developed script, and clearly must have had a long period of development (Boltz 1986, 1999). It is therefore not surprising that many Neolithic objects have been found to have marks on them from which writing could have developed. One pottery bowl has a series of marks that can only be explained as writing, although it cannot be read. The search for the Neolithic origins of writing has led to much closer scrutiny of pottery and bones, confirming that the origins of writing go well back into Neolithic times in China.

Evidence for the beginnings of writing in the Neolithic of China, even the Early Neolithic, is extensive already and is expanding as archaeologists scrutinize Neolithic potsherds more carefully (Li et al. 2003). The number of sites with signs that have been suggested as proto-writing have increased exponentially as excavators examine their artifacts more closely.

Few of the marks that may be proto-writing have much in common with the oracle bone script. The differences may reflect different writing systems and even different languages, which would be consistent with the cultural mosaic that was China at the time. Chang (2005:6) suggests that "it is possible that different regions began to create their own writing systems during the Longshan period." I would go further, for it seems that different scripts were likely, as different dialects and even languages were probably spoken in the variety of Neolithic cultures in China.

Probably the most convincing marks suggested as proto-writing are the complex marks at the site of Jiahu in Henan province. Although only three marks are present, two of them resemble characters found on oracle bones, so they have received considerable attention. More extraordinary, and underlining the possible oracle bone connection, is the fact that the marks are carved on a turtle plastron. They will be discussed more below under the heading of Divination, but the connection between writing and knowing the future is an important one for the discussion of shamanism in ancient East Asia. The Jiahu site begins in the Early Neolithic, which would suggest a long gestation period for the development of writing—something to be expected. Wu (1982:31) supposes an accretion of written characters of only 10 percent per century. At that rate the three thousand characters written on oracle bones in the Shang period would have begun with just a few characters as early as 6000 BCE. Wu computes that in the twenty-seventh century BCE, the time of the Yellow Emperor, there should have been 766 written characters. Certainly astronomical and calendrical records appear to have been kept at that time.

The Yangshao culture of the Early Neolithic includes several sites with patterned marks on pottery that are assumed to be meaningful. Banpo is one of the earliest of such sites, where 113 potsherds and two intact bowls had "incised marks of simple strokes in regular compositions" (Yang 2000:48) (Figure 5.11). In examining the marks further, the excavators identified thirty-four types of marks. These were described as potters' marks, or possibly designations of owners because similar marks were commonly unearthed together in one storage pit or nearby (Yang 2000:49). Thus, early marks were used in a consistent way, although they cannot yet be considered as a script.

Figure 5.11 Marks on pottery from Banpo. From Yeh 1973

Another Early Neolithic Yangshao site with interesting marks is Beishouling, Baoji, Shaanxi, which had four complicated marks painted on a jar with a pointed-bottom. One pattern drawn on a jar from Dazhu village of the Dawenkou culture (Shao 2005) looks remarkably like a shamanic emblem on the back of a drawing of a Mongolian wind horse. This is described as a "*syombo*, consisting of a crescent moon with its horns pointing upward and holding a sun disk, topped by the three flames of time: part present and future. Chingis Khan's battle standard, and nearly every Mongolian flag afterward, included these important shamanic icons" (Tedlock 2005:97) (Figure 5.12).

The early phase of Jiangzhai, in Lintong county, Shaanxi province, is dated between 4800 and 3600 BCE. Unbroken deep bowls (*bo*) and large shallow bowls (*pan*) were found with twenty "notations." Eighty-two more marks were discovered on potsherds. These go beyond the simple one or two-stroke marks that comprise most of the Banpo incisings. Several marks have more than ten strokes, and a few resemble oracle bone graphs (Yang 2000:49). Bowls usually were marked with only a single graph rather than a sequence that might be interpreted as a sentence. Most were carved on the unfired clay, which would suggest marks identifying potters, although a few were scratched on after firing, more likely to designate owners.

Painted marks occur on Laoguotai pottery, likewise applied after firing. The vessels have wide red bands around the lip and small tripod legs; both are traits that could imply use in a ritual context (Yan 2005: 33). Although tripods were often used for cooking in early China, the idea that being raised on three legs or a pedestal stand might have been respectful to the gods or spirits has been proposed (Keightley 1986). Thus red-banded pottery may have had a ceremonial function in the Zhaobaogou period.

Figure 5.12 Mongolian symbol compared to a symbol on a Longshan jar. After Tedlock 2005; Jar symbol redrawn from Chang 1986b

By the Late Neolithic, especially in the Longshan culture, evidence of proto-writing expands noticeably (Shao 2005:105). One of the most promising as an example of real writing is a sherd engraved with eleven characters, which was found at Dinggong village in Zouping county, Shandong. The Liangzhu culture is also alleged to have had primitive writing (Shao 2005:115). Writing itself may have been seen as a kind of magic for communication between the gods and ancestral spirits (Ching 1997:136; Paper 1995:4), before it was used widely among humans.

Divination

Animal scapulae (shoulder blades) and turtle plastrons (the turtle undershells) are the major materials used for divination in the Shang period, as noted above. Both of these are foreshadowed in the Chinese Neolithic. The earliest animal scapula that has been treated with holes and burning in the manner of later oracle bones is from the Fuhegoumen site in Inner Mongolia, about 4000 BCE (Guo 1995a; IMT 1964). Other sites in the north and west also have treated bones without writing (Debaine-Francfort 1995; Wagner 2006). Similar bones with prepared holes for cracking are found in the Hwangniangniangtai and Xindian sites in the western part of China. Later they turn up in larger numbers in the Longshan culture (Shao 2005:97), and as late as Iron Age sites in the Korean peninsula and Kyushu, Japan (Seyock 2004). But only the Shang scapulae are inscribed, recording the question for the spirits and sometimes the answer (Keightley 1978).

One of the most intriguing artifacts from Neolithic China is a turtle plastron with an engraved sign, which was found at Jiahu, in the Peiligang culture, dating between 6000 and 5000 BCE. Since turtle plastrons were used for divination in Late Shang, there is every reason to believe that this is an example of divination (Zhang 2005:74). Yang (2000:48) describes the marks on turtle shells at Jiahu as resembling known oracle bone graphs. He notes that one resembles the graph meaning "eye" and another is identical to that for "sun." The third is "difficult to describe," suggesting that although it is a complex graph it does not have a clear analogue in the Shang script. Yang concludes that these marks are similar to the Shang bone inscriptions in four ways: both were made on turtle shells; both employed an engraving method with very fine linear carving; both possess stylized, nonnaturalistic, and almost identical "graphs"; and both could have served some magic or divinatory function. It seems reasonable to conclude that this is a glimpse of pre-Shang divinatory practice.

The Jiahu discovery is not alone in having possibly divinatory turtle shells. The Xiyin site at Liulin contained turtle shells in several graves. In one case, two shells were tied together, with six small pebbles inside. Again, it is reasonable to conclude that the pebbles in the turtle box were thrown or otherwise used to divine the future. Large carved stone turtles were used in later East Asia as bases for commemorative stone tablets, showing that turtles continued to play a part in the belief system. The burial (M4) in which the jade turtle box was found contained an unusually rich artifactual assemblage, including ninety-six jades, twenty-seven stone artifacts, and four ceramic vessels. Nonfunctional axes—symbols of royal authority later in the Shang dynasty—are also present. The combination of elite burials with the means of divination suggests that leaders were in touch with spirits.

Late texts relate that divination by throwing milfoil stalks was another early practice (Zhang and Liu 1981–1982). Its discovery is attributed to the culture hero Fuxi. According to Paper (1995:4) the clothing and activities of the milfoil diviner were prescribed. He or she had to face east wearing white silk underwear and a white deerskin cap. Later divining with milfoil stalks was codified into specified meanings, as recorded in the *I Ching*.

Temples and Shrines

The earliest rituals connected with buildings occur in the Early Neolithic. For example, in the Banpo site human skulls were placed under the walls of a large house (F1) that is thought to have been a communal structure (Zhang 2005). The skulls could represent a ritual of human sacrifice that occurred when the structure was built. Such skulls, and even entire skeletons, continue to appear in burial foundations into the Late Shang (Li 1977).

Several ceremonial buildings are found in the Late Neolithic. At the site of Niuheliang, Liaoning, the structure that was dubbed the Goddess Temple was surrounded by high-status graves on nearby hills (see Case Study A). House F411 at Dadiwan in the Late Neolithic is believed to have been a religious construction because of its strange floor paintings. It is hard to discern what the human-like figures on the floor are meant to represent, but it is said that it "allows us to see a fragment of a shamanistic scene." The figures seem to be very limp and suggest death, but they may be meant to represent dancing.

Medicines, Alcohol, Narcotics, and Stimulants

Materials that could have been used to aid shamans to achieve a state of trance are many, but none of them are exclusively associated with shamanism. Chang (1983:48) asserts that the *wu* originated medicine, which would reflect Balzer's assertion that shamans were primarily healers, but the connection is tenuous. Texts attribute the discovery of medicines to the Yellow Emperor, who is sometimes also described as a shaman.

There is no question that wine is implied as an element in ancestor worship in ancient China. Fermented beverages were almost certainly used in funeral context. A drink called *chang* was made from broomcorn millet while *li* was made from rice or foxtail millet (Underhill 2002:82–83). In the Neolithic, there are signs of possible feasting and wine at burials (Fung 2000; Liu 2000; Nelson 2003a; Underhill 2000). Traces of probable wine have been found in a Neolithic pot at a site in Shandong province (Bowers et al. 2006) and another at Jiahu about 7000–6600 BCE (Henry 2005). Chemical analysis suggests that some of the ingredients are honey and hawthorn fruit. It is only a guess that the wine was made from grain such as millet or rice, but grains seems a more likely ingredient than grapes, given the fact that even at present wine in China, Korea, and Japan is made mainly from grains. Grape wine is a recent import. Furthermore, rice wine has continued to function in ceremonies in East Asia, including *mudang* rituals in Korea. The wine appears to have been warmed in small tripod vessels with pouring spouts. Warm rice wine is still consumed in East Asia. Paper (1995:32) suggests that the wine was heated for the ancestors so they could smell the vapors. Ching (1997:24) notes that Confucius in the *Analects* describes the great summer sacrifice in which wine was poured to cause the deity to descend. Clearly the powers were attracted to alcohol and appreciated it.

Bronze wine vessels are prolific in Shang burials, but the variety of shapes of the ceramic vessels that preceded bronze is also impressive. Several different shapes of wine vessels were used for storing, heating and serving wine. At the site of Dadianzi, tall cups for drinking wine lay on their sides in side niches above the burial, as if they had been drained of wine in the burial ritual. Other multicolored vessels stood upright, presumably containing wine not consumed at the burial but left for the deceased person (IACASS 1996; Nelson 2003a) (Figure 5.13).

Cannabis is a plant that was available to the Neolithic inhabitants. Hemp likely was grown in the East Asian Early Neolithic, as people made cordage (impressed into many potsherds) for nets, fish lines, traps, and so forth (Crawford 1992:27; Ho 1975:81). However, there is no evidence that hemp plants were used as a stimulant or narcotic in East Asia, as paraphernalia for

Figure 5.13 Painted *li* tripod from Dadianzi. After IACASS 1996

burning, needed to release the active ingredient, is unknown. Hemp seeds were burned in ceremonial censers in Central Asian burial, where they had clearly formed part of the interment ritual (Gryaznov 1969), but such evidence is absent in East Asia before the mountain-shaped censers of the Chu.

Spiritual Materials

Shiny materials with a soft glow that seems to emanate from within had spiritual value in ancient East Asia. These materials included jade and silk in the Early Neolithic, while copper and bronze were added in the Late Neolithic. Cowrie shells, used as money at least by the Shang, might have fallen into the same category, since they, too, have a pearly glow.

The earliest jade was made into slit circular earrings in the Xinglongwa culture of Inner Mongolia. Other sites in the Liaodong peninsula, in western Liaoning, and in Inner Mongolia continued to carve jade earrings. Hong-

shan jades from the same region have already been described. They are the earliest emblematic jades in East Asia. Later, and farther south, Liangzhu jades, especially shapes called *bi* and *cong*, were used for ritual (Figure 5.14). The *cong* is a tube that is round on the inside and square on the outside, often decorated on the corners with the double face and headdress. The *cong* is said to be a shaman's tool that "encapsulates the principal elements of the shamanistic cosmology"

Figure 5.14 *Bi* and *cong* from Liangzhu. After Chang 1986b

138 Shamanism and the Origin of States

(Chang 1994a:66). A great many *cong* are found at the Sidun site in a burial of a young male, where a complicated ceremony involving burning had occurred (Huang 1992). The Liangchingjen site in Jihao on the coast of Shandong also has many finely made jade objects (Chang 1986:31b).

The making of silk thread by unrolling the cocoons of silkworms was known as early as the Yangshao period (Ho 1975). Silk shares with jade a lustrous quality, which made it sacred to the spirits, as well as appropriate for emblems of the elite. Ritual bronzes of the Shang period often retain silk impressions, suggesting that they were wrapped in silk. Silk and jade were both "essential ritual objects" (Shao 2005:114–15).

Metals are likewise shiny, although they were not as highly treasured in ancient China as jade and silk. Nevertheless the Three Dynasties beginning with the Xia made vessels of bronze for worshipping spirits. The nine *ding* were such important symbols of kingship that the Shang took them from the Xia, and the Zhou appropriated them upon conquest of the Shang. Eliade (1964:470ff) points out the relationship between smiths and shamans. Bronze must have seemed magical because of its transformation from an ugly metal into the shiny appearance of the finished product.

Copper appears in the Late Neolithic in many parts of north China, including the northwest, northeast, and even Shandong. The earliest may be the Jiangzhai site of the Banpo culture in north central China (Zhang 2005:66). This was a scrap of copper piece and a tubular brass artifact that was alloyed with zinc (Fitzgerald-Huber 1995; Bunker 1997). Copper smelting remains and copper artifacts were found in the Hongshan period at Niuheliang, and copper slag was found at the Yuanwozhen site. Evidence of local copper production increases in the west. The Majiayao site in the northwest produced a bronze knife and copper slag. Metal contained copper and iron and was cast in a double mold. A copper-smelting crucible was found in ash pits at Meishan, Henan, and a bronze awl at Zhukaigou, Ejin horo banner, Inner Mongolia. Qijia in the northwest included the most copper, including bronze knives and mirrors related to Central Asia. These were small artifacts that could be cast in simple molds; nevertheless, some metallurgy was carried out at all these sites.

Conclusion

In the Early Neolithic, household rituals are said to be the norm (Liu 2004:71; Lee and Zhu 2002; Li 2003), while Late Neolithic evidence of ceremonialism (and possible shamanism) is attributed to elites, often related to feasting at graveside (Underhill 2000). This suggests that a set of beliefs and rituals had developed within common areas. The Hongshan culture focused on rituals and birth and death. In Longshan and the Yellow River region, graveside feasting seems to have become important. Ceremonies including ritual burning of jade occurred in Liangzhu.

Many aspects of shamanism are found in several parts of East Asia, beginning in the Early Neolithic. The rituals imply animism and ancestor worship, and symbolism focuses on suns, birds, turtles. The spirits, especially ancestor spirits, appreciate intoxicants, which could imply feasting. Music and dance are evident, but this association with shamanism is unclear. The most puzzling aspect of the archaeological evidence is that there is no pattern. No two sites seem to reflect the same ritual activities, the same set of symbols, or the same beliefs.

CASE STUDY E

KAMEGOAKA, JAPAN

Female figurines in prehistoric Japan are found from Early Jomon to Late Jomon, in many parts of the Japanese islands, especially Honshu. These figurines are not distributed evenly in either time or space, but the styles can be differentiated according to both time and location. The Early Jomon versions are not impressive—they are flat pebbles with scratched lines that seem to represent a string skirt below female breasts. The female figurines of Middle and Late Jomon are in the round. Their overall shape is definitely human, but their faces and limbs are so strange that they must have been representations of spirits (Figure E.1).

Kamegoaka, in the northern part of Honshu, is an important center of the production and use of figurines and other ritual objects. There are some seventeen hundred related sites in northern Honshu and southern Hokkaido. Kamegoaka flourished in the Final Jomon period, about 1000 to 100 BCE. Evidence of influences from Kamegoaka is spread from the Nara basin in southwestern Honshu to central Hokkaido. The "Kamegoaka phenomenon," to use Ikawa-Smith's (1992) phrase, was contemporaneous with the first evidence of Yayoi rice farmers. Ikawa-Smith believes that the people from Kamaegoaka were actively resisting the rice farming culture. Although

Figure E.1 Figurine from Kamegoaka. After Kidder 1965

the Kamegoaka groups cultivated buckwheat, they were still predominantly a gathering and hunting culture.

The Kamegoaka culture can be visualized as the center of a social network that extends from the Nara basin in Honshu to the middle of Hokkaido (Ikawa-Smith 1988), because the finely made ceramic wares were traded over this distance. Some of the vessels are ornate and were made in a variety of shapes that imply ceremonialism—spouted jars, bottles, dishes on pedestals, and objects with loopy handles that are sometimes called incense burners. Some are painted red and polished, like those of Mumun in Korea, but others are more varied—black or red-on-black or even unpainted.

Kamegoaka figurines are usually found with beads, stone cylinders, and complete pots, "all of which suggest magico-religious significance" (Ikawa-Smith 1988).

The figurines are quite stylized and look otherworldly, although they are mostly female and humanoid. Sometimes large numbers of them are found together. Often they are broken, but at times they were deliberately buried in a pit or surrounded by a stone circle.

Kamegoaka ceramics are found in impressive numbers far from Kamegoaka itself. Most of the shapes suggest storing and serving of liquids. Ikawa-Smith (1988) suggests that the liquid could be fish oil, but other possibilities are fermented beverages, or a substance either medicinal or poisonous. Lamps and spouted jars diminish near the end of the Kamegoaka phenomenon, while pedestal vessels increase. Ikawa-Smith suggests that the ceremonialism that was based on some sort of liquid was replaced by something more like Yayoi rituals.

Richard Pearson examines the elaborate ceramics, lacquer, and grave goods to explore Jomon social complexity. Contrary to some earlier understandings of Jomon, recent research shows that some cultivation of plants occurred as early as Initial Jomon (Pearson 2007:363). At the site of Sannai Maruyama, a Middle Jomon site, large two-story buildings were erected within a complex settlement (Habu 2004). One six-post structure is said to be sited for the purpose of rectifying the calendar (Pearson 2007:363).

In the Initial Jomon a burial was found at the Kakinoshima B site in Hokkaido, with lacquer beads and other ornaments, some of which appear to have been attached to a twined textile. Some twelve thousand small lumps of red ocher were also found among the houses at the site.

Late Jomon burials of (possible) females in Hokkaido are particularly rich, with lacquered combs, ornaments on the head, ears, neck, fingers, waist, and arms. Because red ocher is scattered on the bottom of the graves, it is suggested that they are "shamanesses" (Pearson 2007:368).

SIX

SHAMANISM IN
EARLY CHINESE STATES

Under the Xia dynasty [the wu] served the spirits of the departed and respected the Spirits, keeping them at a distance. Under the Yin [Shang] dynasty they honored Spirits and led the people to serve them, and spirits were more important than ceremony. In the Zhou they honored the cer-emonies, and kept the spirits at a distance.

—Paraphrased from Chang 1994b:15, citing *Biaoji of Liji*

It was the king who made fruitful harvest and victories possible by the sacrifices he offered, the rituals he performed, and the divinations he made. If, as seems likely, the divinations involved some degree of magic making, of spell casting, the king's ability to actually create a good har-vest or a victory by divining about it rendered him still more potent politically.

—Keightley 1978:213

THE EARLIEST states in Chinese history are referred to as the Sandai, the Three Dynasties of Xia, Shang, and Zhou (Chou). Much of the current knowledge about the first two states comes from archaeological excavations, and archaeology has added detail in understanding Zhou texts and inscriptions (Falkenhausen 2006; Li 2006). Although the exact center of each of the Three Dynasties differed, and the capitals of each moved several times (Price 1995), they were all generally in the Chungyuan—the central plain of the Yellow River valley (Figure 6.1).

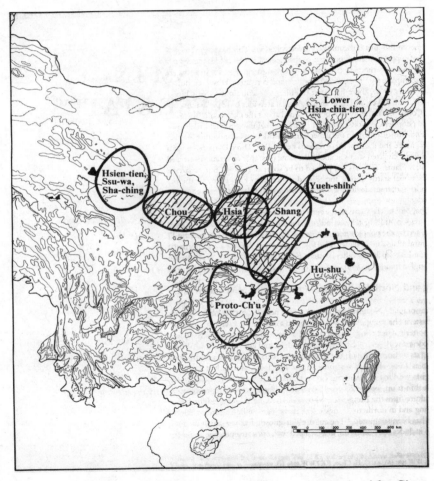

Figure 6.1 Map of locations of Sandai and contemporaneous peoples. After Chang 1986b

Texts that claim to have been written in the first years of the Zhou dynasty refer to both Xia and Shang. Although the historicity of the Xia has been questioned, there are reasons, outlined in chapter 4, to suppose that some form of Xia historical narrative was available from at the beginning of the Zhou if not the beginning of Shang. But while Chinese historical writing is centered on the Yellow River plain where the Three Dynasties developed, archaeology demonstrates that the context of the development of civilization in China includes a wider territory than is included in the histories. The archaeological "outliers" are in all parts of present-day China. They are described later in this chapter.

The most reliable data about the Xia is archaeological. Archaeological sites that many archaeologists believe are remains of the Xia are located in Zhengzhou, especially the Erlitou site on the Yiluo River, a tributary to the Yellow River. According to the Bamboo Annals, the Xia dynasty was founded by Yu the Great, but his feats are larger than life and unreliable for reconstructing a history of the Xia. Yu is known for controlling the floods of China's east-flowing rivers. At the time of Yu, about 2200 BCE, sea level was rising in the Gulf of Bohai, so perhaps some historical memory lingers in the legend of overpowering floods. The Yellow River has overflowed its banks so dramatically that it carved new channels multiple times (Huang 1984). Several old channels, which flow both to the north and south of the Shandong peninsula, can still be seen.

The Shang dynasty was similarly thought to be legendary until in 1899, when almost five hundred inscribed animal shoulder bones and turtle shells became available to scholars (Li 1977:4). Systematic excavations at the site of Anyang, begun in 1928, have greatly expanded the number of oracle bone fragments, which were deliberately broken and buried together in pits. The writing on these fragments is an early form of Chinese characters, which can be read by specialists in the ancient Chinese. These artifacts are called *jiagu*—meaning simply shells and bones in Chinese—but they are known in English as "oracle bones" because the inscriptions show that they were used for divining the future. The translations of these divinations into modern Chinese provide a valuable window into Shang beliefs, rituals—and to some extent their daily lives (Keightley 2000). The diviners were kings and persons closely connected to kings. The purpose of writing on the bones was to contact the powers and spirits to learn about the future and to discover what sacrifices would make the powers and spirits favorable to the Shang fortunes. Thus the Shang is considered a truly historical period because it has these contemporaneous texts—indeed, unlike texts from the Zhou period, they are writing that no one had an opportunity to change. Recopying texts introduced errors, and others may have been deliberate distortions.

Nevertheless, Zhou has fairly reliable histories, as well as informative inscriptions on excavated bronzes, rather than simply naming the owner as is largely the case for Shang bronzes (Li 2006). People who could reach spirits and powers are called *wu* in Zhou histories, and the word also occurs in Shang oracle bones. In the Zhou dynasty there was an attempt to turn *wu* into bureaucrats by giving them specific duties. To some extent this plan succeeded, putting *wu* "on the payroll of the Ministry of Rites" (Falkenhausen 1995:282). Both female and male *wu* officiated in rituals, and some officials were designated as managers of the *wu*. Thus the *wu* from the Zhou period do not seem to be individuals who reached the spirits through trance and dance but followers of controlled ritual steps that began to be canonized.

In spite of the control extended over *wu* by standardizing their rituals and placing a manager above them, shamanism continued to flourish in some states, most notably Chu, into the Warring States period. Some sculptures and paintings from excavated Chu tombs show apparent shamans, some of them wildly dancing (Rawson 1980). Tombs excavated in a number of places, but particularly at Mawangdui near Changsha, attest to beliefs in spirits and the continuation or revival of beliefs in unearthly powers, especially Nuwa and Fuxi, whose lower bodies are depicted as snakes with intertwined tails.

Evidence of Xia

Scholars agree that religion was an important building block in the creation of the Shang state. Lu and Yan (2005:140) infer from oracle bone inscriptions that in Shang society, kingship and divine power were intertwined, and "religious power was the central pillar of political authority." "Successive generations of Shang kings monopolized the power of sacrifice to heaven through the status accorded to the worship of their own ancestors" (Lu and Yan 2005:142). Archaeology indicates considerable continuity from Xia to Shang, thus the centrality of Shang religion was presumably derived from the preceding Xia dynasty, which shows evidence of ritual events and ancestor worship—even including oracle bones, although they were uninscribed. The beginning of writing goes back to the Neolithic, so there could well have been Xia records of various kinds.

The Discovery of Xia Sites

When the first site was found in the right time period (third millennium BCE) and at the right location (in the Chungyuan) to attribute it to the Xia dynasty, there were enthusiastic predictions that more evidence of the Xia state would be forthcoming. While at first many archaeologists remained skeptical, as excavations have continued, most scholars have come to agree that the discoveries at Erlitou do indeed represent the elusive Xia dynasty (e.g., Liu and Chen 2003:26ff). The discoveries are important for understanding state formation in early China, as well as continuities (and discontinuities) in culture from Xia to Shang. Although few artifacts from either the major site of Erlitou or similar contemporaneous sites throw light on activities of the *wu*, a great deal has been learned about the Xia, especially the Xia elite.

The earliest known bronze vessels are from Erlitou. They were almost certainly used in ancestor worshipping rituals, likely to have been intertwined with shamanic beliefs and practices (Figure 6.2). Some jades that could have

Figure 6.2 Bronze *jia* from Erlitou. After Wen 1980

been used in rituals were deposited in burials. Buildings identified as temples were presumably the site of ritual performances. Inferences from Shang practices are made about what kind of events took place in the buildings, because so far the archaeology at Erlitou and contemporaneous sites imparts little new knowledge about shamans or the organization of the Xia state.

In spite of the thinness of the evidence, it is important to include Xia in the search for shamans as early leaders in Chinese states for three reasons. First, histories written in later times include Xia in a succession of competing states, which were at least partly contemporaneous (Chang 1983). Xia was preceded by complex Neolithic cultures with indications of shamanism, and followed by Shang, where evidence of reliance on spirits is strong. Second, the continuity of bronze ritual vessels from Xia to Shang suggests that the containers were used in the same way in Xia and Shang. Not only were such vessels made specifically for rituals in the Shang period, but the Xia also were famous in later history for having created nine ritual bronze tripods. Third, a Zhou text (quoted at the beginning of this chapter) relates the differences among the *wu* and their practices in Xia, Shang, and Zhou. Even if this was folklore written at a later date, it suggests a memory of different ritual practices in the past.

Discoveries at Erlitou in Zhengzhou are divided into four phases from about 1900 to 1500 BCE (Liu and Chen 2003). A stamped earth platform roughly 100 meters on each side raised up foundations of large buildings that have been reasonably described as palaces. They have rectangular floor plans with impressions of large wooden pillars placed at regular intervals along the periphery of the building. The diameter of the pillars suggests lofty roofs. The palace area expanded through time (Bagley 1980). By Phase III, an area of 7.5 hectares was devoted to large buildings probably for the exclusive use of the elite. Temples were surrounded by areas in which as many as two thousand people could congregate to watch and participate in ceremonies (Bagley 1999).

In addition to buildings, elite burials have been excavated. These tombs contain rich funerary offerings, including jade ritual objects. White pottery vessels made from kaolin (the material from which porcelain is made) are found exclusively in rich graves and were finely crafted. Two types of small tripods were made for heating alcoholic beverages, and a third shape served as a drinking goblet. This suggests continuity with Neolithic graveside ceremonies, such as have been considered in the previous chapter. The same shapes later were used for the first bronze ritual vessels, which represent the very beginning of the construction of bronze containers (although not the first use of bronze in China). The tripods are unadorned at Erlitou, compared to the elaborate decoration that was to follow. Although the vessels are plain and awkward in shape, the complexity of the shapes bespeaks a well-developed bronze industry (Bagley 1980). The bronzes at Anyang and other Shang sites were made in elaborate piece molds in which the decorative elements were carved intaglio into the molds. Although a huge gap in elegance exists between the first Erlitou bronzes and those of Late Shang, their function likely is to have been the same.

As noted in chapter 5, small metal objects were found in Late Neolithic sites in the outlying regions of China, especially the west and north, during the Late Neolithic. But of these, only a few mirrors from the Qijia culture (Debaine-Francfort 1995; Fitzgerald-Huber 1995) suggest possible ritual—and mirrors imply ritual of a very different sort. The bronze vessels at Erlitou were placed only in the most elaborate burials, suggesting that the high elite were managers of rituals. Although it was a technological breakthrough to create wine-pouring vessels in bronze, the shapes have earlier analogs elsewhere—in far away Inner Mongolia, in the culture known as Lower Xiajiadian.

Lower Xiajiadian

One of the reasons that Lower Xiajiadian is seen as a possible precursor of Shang is that containers in similar shapes—but made of pottery instead of bronze—were found in Lower Xiajiadian sites (Fitzgeral-Huber 1999; Guo 1995b). The burial ground at Dadianzi, which was entirely excavated (IACASS 1996), is particularly interesting. Its graves, numbering nearly a thousand, were divided into several grades. Like later Shang burials, the depth of the grave was correlated with the richness of the grave goods. Not only were more numerous and elaborate grave goods in the deeper graves, but the deeper graves were more elaborate, with wooden coffins and side niches.

Burials with the highest status showed evidence of graveside rituals, which included drinking from tall goblets with trumpet-shaped mouths and painted containers that were left with the dead, presumably filled with food and drink for his or her spirit journey in the afterlife. The tripod vessels with pouring spouts also stood in the burial niches, while the goblets were on their sides, as if they had been used to drink a final tribute to the deceased (Nelson 2003a). Wu (2004) argues that artifacts placed in the niches reflect social status, while objects in the coffin reflecting personal identity presumably were on the body at burial. Rowan Flad (2002) suggests that the markers of social status suggest a variety of kinds of status by examining the different groups of grave goods within a single grave.

Mayke Wagner (2006) uses histograms to show that both sex and age affect the graves and their contents, but again, in different ways. For example, the number of graves with side niches increases with the age of the deceased, but the niches are approximately equal by sex. The same is true of grave depth. This is also an attribute of Shang graves, except that queen's graves were never as deep as those of the kings. The painted ceramic vessels of Lower Xiajiadian are very similar to Shang bronzes in both shape and design—and since they are earlier, it is a reasonable inference that they influenced Shang bronzes. Exactly how and where the Lower Xiajiadian people interacted with those of Xia and Shang is unknown, but the existence of a relationship is clear. While distance between the two regions is great, as we have seen, people covered long distances on foot, even before horses were available, for the purposes of trade, warfare, and perhaps marriage. In the case of Lower Xiajiadian, horses were raised and presumably ridden, so that long distances could be covered more easily. The Northern Zone even has a few bone artifacts that could have been cheek pieces for riding horses. At Danangou there are six pairs of these objects, while at Zhizhushan spoon-shaped objects (Wagner 2006) are similar to artifacts demonstrated to be cheek pieces in the Northern Zone, in Eurasia, and along the Yellow River during the Shang period (Yang 2007).

Yueshi

The Yueshi culture of Shandong province is an archaeologically defined culture that is contemporaneous with parts of Erlitou and Erligang, about 1800 to 1450 BCE (Cohen 2001). Yueshi includes large walled cities, bronze production, a ritual system, and a writing system. Other characteristics include many indications of ritual, such as turtle shells for divination, human sacrifices in graves, jade *cong*, and cattle sacrifice. The elite are marked by wooden burial chambers with second level ledges and rich grave furnishings including white kaolin pottery, carved bone spatulas, turquoise inlay, and animal designs. These are all precedents for the Shang at Anyang.

The Yueshi culture is found throughout Shandong province, as well as in eastern Henan, northern Jiangsu, and Anhui provinces. Yueshi seems to begin during the Longshan (Late Neolithic). It is perceived by some scholars as the direct predecessor of Shang, who presumably moved their capital from Shandong to the central Yellow River plain. Various early Chinese geographic writings describe a group of "barbarians" called the Dongyi, the eastern barbarians, who are associated with Shandong and Manchuria. The archaeologically recognized Yueshi may be a branch of those Dongyi people, and the Shang themselves were descended from the Eastern Barbarians. It is possible that the Shang cult center, known as Da Yi Shang (Great City Shang) was in the east (Cohen 2001), although no site has been specifically identified as such.

One of the legendary Sage Kings was Tuan Xu, who was linked to the east coast. It is possible that Yueshi is the archeological manifestation of this legend. Tuan Xu may have taken control of shamanism for his own ends. It is said that he "depended upon ghosts and deities to institute the rules, clearly indicating that he was the Great Shaman or Religious Leader" (Chang 1994b:18). So far, the mystique of the Yueshi is not completely unraveled, but it seems to have had a role in the development of the early state in China.

Evidence of Shang

The Shang dynasty follows the Xia in time. Shang not only conquered Xia with military might, but claimed to have appropriated as evidence of their right to rule the (no longer extant) nine bronze tripods representing the nine districts of China. Although there is no trace of them now, it seems reasonable to suppose that the vessels really existed, because they were clearly important in ancient China. A Zhou document boasts that the bronze vessels were taken from the Shang as a sign of the Zhou conquest and a change of dynasty. The conquest of Shang by Zhou occurred at the time of a conjunction of the five visible planets, which was used as further evidence of validation for the Zhou conquest of Shang. As has been explained in chapter 4, it was important for the spirits to demonstrate that the Mandate of Heaven had passed to Zhou (Pankenier 1995).

The case for shamanism in Shang rests on several types of evidence. These include later written material, the testimony of the oracle bones that are contemporaneous with Late Shang, and artifacts including the bronzes and their iconography. Chang (1983, 1994b, 2005) argued forcefully for Shang shamanism in several articles and books, and brings to bear these several lines of evidence.

Chang's most thorough and systematic statement of his research on *wu* in the Shang royal court considers the word itself, the social status of *wu*, the activities of *wu*, and "instruments and means" to accomplish these tasks (Chang 1994b). *Wu* is of course a Chinese word, but Chang is completely satisfied with translating *wu* as "shaman." He explains that "using the word shaman to translate *wu* is common sinological practice and does not imply a prior definition" (1994b:10, fn1). He supposes that the content of shamanism is common knowledge, and a shaman is the same thing as a *wu*. Chang uses "textual records and archaeological remains of ritual paraphernalia" to elucidate his case.

The basis of shamanism, according to Chang, is the concept of a contract between people and spirits in ancient China. The spirits were believed to be just as "real" as humans, but only some special people could communicate with them. The specialists ("descendants of ancient sages and famous clans") were called *wu* and *xi*. Spirits descended into them at rituals where sacrifices were offered to the spirits. In later times, two kinds of shamans are described: *chu* shamans who were in charge of the forms of ritual, and *cong* shamans who were in charge of the behaviors of rituals. Only *wu* are mentioned in the oracle bone divinations, however.

Chang (1994b) enumerated some characteristics of Shang shamanism as follows:

1. A belief that the cosmos is divided into upper and lower levels. The upper is the sky, or heaven, where spirits dwell. The lower is the land of the living. The two worlds can be "interpenetrated."
2. Deities and spirits knew the future, and it was possible for humans to discover what the spirits knew about the future. Chang explains that "the logical next step would be that those who were in possession of such knowledge were possessors of political power. Accordingly, during the Shang period shamanism and political power were closely linked."
3. Shamans contacts with the spirits were "the result of shamanistic action, requiring certain techniques and paraphernalia."
4. The interrelationship of humans and animals was important. Animals could help shamans reach the spirits. Animals could be transformed into something else (human or spirit) or they could be spirit helpers.

Chang is not alone in describing kings in the Shang dynasty as shamans. Elizabeth Childs-Johnson (1989, 1995, 1998) in several art-historical papers supports the view that shamans were important in Shang. Shang bronzes, produced for use in elite rituals, were created individually. Each was poured in a mold that had to be broken to remove the vessel, thus each vessel is unique. It is reasonable to suppose that the iconography of the bronzes can be said to reflect an ideology of the elite, but even that perspective has spawned a variety of interpretations. Childs-Johnson explains Shang bronzes as depicting shaman's masks, transformations of various kinds, and animal intermediaries between shamans and spirits. She notes that the kings were diviners, and ordered sacrifices on behalf of ancestral spirits and powers. Still, the question of whether kings conducted séances is unclear. Chang interprets some bronzes as relating to the shamans trance, such as the juxtaposition of a person and a tiger, a motif that appears on axes as well as bronze containers, although written evidence of ecstatic trance is lacking.

Falkenhausen, discussing the *wu* in the Zhou period, translates *wu* as "spirit medium" rather than shaman, implying that the spirit connection was reached in ways other than soul flight. It seems likely that the Zhou dynasty bureaucratized the *wu*, perhaps removing whatever direct access to trance and ecstasy they may have previously possessed. According to the *Zhou Li*, Rites of Zhou, the *wu* dance the rain-making ritual, cause the spirits to descend at funerary services, and, most enigmatically, the directors of *wu* led them "in enacting the long-standing practices of the *wu*, which must have been so well known it was unnecessary to specify what they were" (Falkenhausen 1995:294).

Shang Archaeology

The last capital of the Shang dynasty was at the present city of Anyang. It was long known that large and elaborately decorated bronze vessels were looted from this vicinity, but the exact location of the graves that were being destroyed was not immediately discovered. However, archaeology began in earnest when caches of oracle bones were found at the site of Yinxu, in Anyang. The archaeology there has proven to be very rich, and surprising discoveries continue to be made, over a span of almost eighty years (Li 1977).

The last Shang capital is divided into several areas with different functions, demonstrating the complexity of the city. Bronze foundries, pottery kilns, and bone workshops were arrayed around the city. Palaces larger than those at Erlitou were grouped together into an elite compound. It was thought until recently that the Late Shang city at Anyang (which was anciently called Yin) had no wall, but an extensive wall has been located. The cult center was at Xiaotun. The burial ground of kings was to the north across the river, in an area called Xibeigang. Although the tomb robbers had left few artifacts—and they were of little value—the shape and size of the tombs themselves were of great interest, as well as the human and animal sacrifices that accompanied them (which had been of no interest to the looters).

The kings' tombs were clustered in two groups (Chang 1980). Twelve kings ruled at Anyang, and it is thought that each king who ruled in the city was represented in one of the large and impressive cruciform burials. Near one group of four kings' tombs were hundreds of pits holding sacrificed humans and animals. The kings' tombs at Xibeigang were mostly cross-shaped, with ramps on four sides. The south ramp continued all the way to the bottom where the coffin was placed, while the other ramps reached only to the level of the grave goods. One of the ramps was 60 meters long, a statistic that gives a sense of the monumentality of these constructions. The main burial chamber was constructed of wood, with room inside for a coffin and many grave goods. The floor of the chamber was stained heavily with cinnabar, a red coloring matter that may have been used as paint on the coffins, or simply sprinkled on the floor surface. Sets of ritual vessels were placed in the central chamber, presumably along with other rich grave goods. Lines of sacrificed humans protected the king, lying head to toe along the ramps up to the surface. The king was protected from spirits below by a small pit under the coffin, which contained a dog or even a human guardian. Tomb 1001 from the Late Shang period, about 1250 BCE, is one of the largest. It is thought to be the tomb of King Wu Ding (Bagley 1999), the husband of Lady Jing and Lady Hao and the diviner on many of the oracle bones. Inscribed oracle bones earlier than King Wu Ding have not been found.

Oracle Bone Inscriptions

Each oracle bone contains a record of which spirit or power was addressed, the question being asked, and sometimes the answer (Figure 6.3). In spite of the simplicity and formulaic nature of the writing, the sheer number of oracle bones reveals much about Shang rituals and beliefs (Keightley 1978, 1983, 1999c, 2000). The questions asked regard such diverse concerns as weather, illness, warfare, and sacrifices.

Most of the oracle bones concern topics such as weather (the wind was a particularly troublesome power), battles to be fought, illness and its causes, whether the harvest would be bountiful, and success in the royal hunt. Using this wealth of material, Keightley (1999c, 2000) has shown that much can be learned about the Shang. For example, each day was named, and from

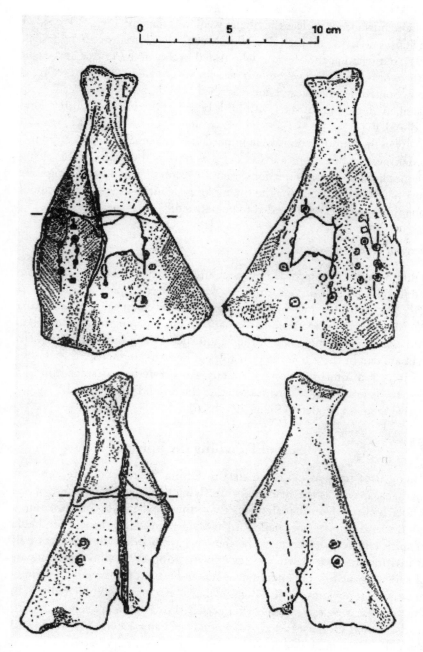

Figure 6.3 Oracle bone from Shang. After Wen 1980

that circumstance it is clear the Shang week was ten days long. A legend of ten suns, one rising on each day of the week, was current in Shang (Allan 1991), but whether the ten suns who rested in the mulberry tree at the end of the world when they were not in the sky was treated as story or reality is moot. Sometimes the ten suns are described as birds, but, as has already been described, depictions of suns with birds began in the Early Neolithic, long before Shang.

Even the four directions were important in the oracle bone inscriptions. Sometimes the directions are addressed as powers themselves. The Shang enemies lived in all four directions from the "center," which was Shang. Life must have been anxious for the Shang kings, continually worrying about non-Shang peoples who needed to be pacified.

Textual References to Wu

A number of *wu* are recorded by name in the oracle bones, some of whom had the family name of Wu. Other *wu* were relatives of the Shang king. The *Shu Qing* records that in the second year after the conquest of Shang, King Wu (not the character meaning shaman, but one meaning martial) of Zhou paid a visit to Jizi the uncle of the vanquished Shang kin. Jizi, who was a shaman, taught the Zhou the principles of heaven's methods—that is, divinations and interpretations of omens. An oracle bone names him as a diviner: "Jizi of Yi (n) . . . divines whether the South Palace official Yi ought to give them a banquet" (Chang 1994b:16).

Means of Reaching the Spirits

Chang uses texts as evidence that in China spirits could descend on shamans, as well as the shamans' souls flying to the spirits. In spite of the scholarly distinction that shamans fly to the spirits while spirit mediums call the spirits down (see chapter 3), in Shang and in later times both kinds of spirit contact could occur. The shamans ascended to the spirits as well as inviting the gods down. One example is King Wen, who "yoked a pair of jade dragons to a phoenix figured car, and waited for the wind to come, to soar upon my journey" (Chang 1994b:21). An inscription on a *xing* bell, the same type we have seen earlier attached to a shaman's coat in burial, reads, "Great God ascended, descended" (Chang 1994b:22). Gods and shamans with equal ease could transgress the boundary between heaven and earth.

Mountains

Mountains were the dwelling places of spirits and deities. The mists that rise from many Chinese mountains must have contributed to their otherworldliness. For example, the Queen Mother of the West (a concept that first appears in texts in the Han dynasty, perhaps with earlier roots) resided at Jade Mountain. Jade itself, as we have seen, was sacred to the spirits. Mountains were also used as ladders to reach heaven. Some Daoist sages attained immortality by flying to the sky from the top of a mountain. Chang considers it relevant that the characters for both ascend and descend have the mountain radical.

Not every mountain was sacred to the gods and spirits, but the mountains where shamans ascended and descended were named. One of them was even called Mount Wu. Some scholars maintain that *Shanhaijing* [*Classic of Mountains and Seas*] represents the shamanistic culture of the state of Chu. The word *shan* (mountain) occurs frequently in oracle bones (Chang 1994b:23). Sometimes sacrifices and other rituals took place on mountains.

Trees

The *Huainanzi* notes that spirits ascend and descend by means of trees. The mulberry tree (where silk worms feed) is called the *fusang* tree. The mulberry tree often appears in myths at the beginning and end of the world, where huge birds perch (Allan 1991). Perhaps this myth is reflected in artifacts. Large metal trees with jade ornaments were found in many elite Warring States burials. Large bronze trees also appear in Sanxingdui, in the far west of China at the same time as the Shang. Small mountain-shaped censers are found in Chu and Han sites, often covered with trees and birds.

Birds

We have already seen that birds were important in Neolithic myth and symbolism. In later writings, legends relating birds to spirits and suns are numerous, especially in eastern coastal areas, generally the same regions where Neolithic bird figures were common. In later writing, not any bird would do. It was the phoenix—an imaginary magical bird—that was the messenger between the shaman and the spirits. A jade bird in the grave of Lady Hao of the Shang dynasty may already represent the phoenix (see Case Study D). Carved from yellow jade, the bird has a splendid presence, with a crest and a long tail. Other birds, owls for example, are depicted in Shang as well, in bronze or jade. Lady Hao is unique for a woman in having owls (and tigers) depicted in her tomb. Perhaps owls represented wisdom in China, as they did in the Greek world.

Animals

Domesticated animals were targeted as sacrificial victims in large numbers. They clearly belonged to the spirits, but it is not clear whether the sacrificed animals come from royal herds or were requisitioned from other elites. Horses were given special burial when sacrificed, often including a chariot and even the charioteer. A young elephant was even found in a sacrificial burial.

While domesticated animals were offered to the spirits, animal images on artifacts, especially bronzes, included few domesticated animals. Horned animals, such as rams and water buffalo, were the major exception. For the most part, wild or composite animals were depicted. Some bronze motifs suggest human-animal transformations to Chang. However, few legends are related to such transformations. One ancient legend pertains to a king of Xia transformed into bear (Wu 1982), and a Korean legend involved a female bear to human transformation, but these stories are not reflected in the bronzes, where bears are absent. In any case, composite figures that are part human and part animal are present in the Neolithic Yangshao period, but are rare in Shang art forms. Shang instead depicts mythical animals with parts of different animals joined into a single image.

Rituals

Five important rituals were named in the oracle bones. *Jung* involves drum music, *xi* involves the feather dance, *chi* uses meat, millet was used for *chai*, and *xie* was comprehensive (Ching 1997). Wine was conspicuously used at all these rituals. The spirits were thirsty, or as Paper (1995) has it, the spirits were drunk. Shang rituals required food preparations as well as drink, including vessels for warming wine and cooking and serving millet and meat. These elements of rituals can be verified with archaeological data. Not only are bronze vessels for wine and food plentiful, but Lady Hao uniquely had a bronze cooking stove accompanying her in death. She was clearly equipped to prepare feasts for other spirits in the world of the ancestors.

Alcoholic Beverages and Drugs

Oracle bone inscriptions contain many references to wine. The number and quantity of bronze wine vessels is astonishing. Several different shapes were used for serving as well as mixing and storing wine. Perhaps there were several kinds of wine, fermented from different grains and/or flavored with honey or fruits. Ma (1980) illustrates nine different shapes of bronze containers that were used for ritual wine. They are often found in matching sets. The wine offered to the ancestors was probably heated in the tripod bronze vessels called *jia*. The essence of the wine may have been enough for the ancestors, wafting up to them by the warmth of the fire. Then it may have been "used by the shamans to help elevate their own mental state to facilitate their communication with the ancestors." Chang (2005:33) makes this speculation on the basis of a line in the Shu Qing, which says that wine "should be drunk only on occasion of sacrifices." By the end of the Shang dynasty, however, the kings were indulging in wine for pleasure. The records of the Zhou dynasty declare that the overthrown final Shang king was a drunkard and a womanizer.

Chang suggests that hemp was used to "communicate with the spirits and to lighten his body," but there is no archaeological evidence of burning aromatic materials before the Chu, when censers in the shape of mountains became fashionable. Chu and Han censers were miniature mountains, with trees, buildings, and people sculpted on the side of the mountain-shaped object. Smoke rose through holes in the top, imitating the mist of mountains. Some were made of pottery, but many were metal. A famous example was found in the Korean state of Baekje. It is not known what substance was burned, but hemp seeds are a likely possibility.

Music and Dance

The best-known shamanistic dance in ancient China was *jiu tai*, which was danced by King Chi of Xia (Ching 1997). Another famous dance was called the Dance of Yu, the founder of the Xia dynasty. A dance named *li* was performed to bring rain. Inscriptions describe the Shang king dancing for rain. Arthur Waley (1955) translated *The Nine Songs*—shamans' songs from the state of Chu. He explains, "In ancient China intermediaries used in the cult of Spirits were called *wu*. They figure in old texts as experts in exorcism, prophecy, fortune-telling, rain-making, and interpretation of dreams. Some *wu* danced, and they are sometimes defined as people who danced in order to bring down Spirits. . . . They were also magic healers and in later times at any rate one of their methods of doctoring was to go, as Siberian shamans do, to the underworld and find out how the Power of Death can be propitiated. Indeed the functions of Chinese *wu* were so like those of Siberian and Tungus shamans that it is convenient . . . to use shaman as a translation of *wu*" (Waley 1955:9). The Chu songs are in the words of male and female shamans who dress in their finest clothes and sing and dance to music in order to bring the spirits down from the sky. Sexual attraction is implied as a way to induce the spirits to descend.

It is only much later, with the appearance of tomb murals, that a full picture of dancing costumes emerges. Dancers depicted in Han and Chu painting and sculpture flap long sleeves that extend well beyond the hands (Wu 1999; So 1999; Rawson 1980). This type of dancing is still performed in Korea as court dancing. A Goguryea (Kaoguli in Chinese) tomb outside of Jian is known as the Tomb of the Dancers. A mural shows several dancers performing in a line, perhaps as a ritual, as entertainment, or both. Their spotted (fur?) robes cover their hands. Robes differ in length between the men and women, but otherwise are similar. Both women and men appear to be wearing boots. Thus, while dance is depicted in the mural it does not have the individual characteristics of shamanic dances. It apparently differs from the dancers depicted on Yangshao bowls in representing men and women dancing in the same line.

Ritual Materials

Burials of royalty and nobles who were to be treated as ancestors contained enormous numbers of objects. According to Chang (1983:134), in both Shang and Zhou the principal sacrificial objects were ritual bronzes, musical instruments, and weapons. However, the tomb of Lady Hao suggests that jades were also extremely important. Lade Hao had ritual functions herself—she was able to divine with the oracle bones. The small jade pieces, of which there were several representing animals and humans, may have been part of her ritual paraphernalia, not merely decorative pieces. The same could be true of the small bronze mirrors and knives that were found in her grave (but not elsewhere in Anyang). They may be both souvenirs of her homeland (Linduff 1996), part of a northern ritual that she brought to her marriage to Wu Ding (Wang 2004) (see Case Study D).

The bronze industry in Shang was almost entirely devoted to ritual vessels made of copper and tin, although traces of additional metals are found when the alloys are tested. The apparatus of the Shang state was involved in the process of making bronze from start to finish. The sources of copper and tin had to be discovered and obtained through mining. Then the ore was smelted and refined, and finally workshops with highly skilled craftsmen designed the vessels, carved them in wax, made casts of clay, and poured the molten alloy into the molds. The technique of bronze-making was very precise, and the quality of design has never been equaled (Wen 1980).

The vessels were designed in sets dedicated to ritual, and are found in sets in tombs (Rawson 1996). Some bronze vessels were square or round food containers (*ding*), most of them elevated on legs, perhaps to be warmed on a fire beneath. Other shapes were related to the storage, presentation, and consumption of wine. Some of the vessels were in the shape of animals— owls, tigers, and elephants, for example. Most of the designs included animals or parts of animals rearranged into *taotie* (monster masks), or composite animals with horns, legs, tails, and so forth from different animals. These were all crafted for the purpose of entertaining the ancestors, so that the favors of the ancestors could be enjoyed by the living elite. Bronze axes, on the other hand, look like they were intended to decapitate—possibly humans as well as animal sacrifices (Figure 6.4).

As noted at the beginning of this chapter, in the Three Dynasties, there was a tradition of the nine *ding*, or ritual vessels, which represented the center and the eight other directions. In the beginning these were created and owned by the Xia dynasty. Archaeology has confirmed that bronze

Figure 6.4 Shang ritual axe. After Wen 1980

vessels were made in Erlitou, a site that is thought to reflect the beginnings of the Xia dynasty. However, these first vessels are not *ding*, but wine pouring vessels shaped like *jia*. Thus the original nine bronze vessels may have been for pouring wine. According to tradition, the Shang took the vessels from Xia as a sign of their exclusive right to contact the spirits, and Zhou appropriated the vessels upon their conquest of the Shang. The spirits may have had to be drunk before they would be helpful.

Bronze was important for a number of reasons, not the least of which was for making weapons that were more effective than those made of stone or bone. Success in warfare, however, may have depended on horses and chariots as much as on bronze weapons. Chang (1994b) emphasizes that connection with the ancestors was also power, which was partly attained through bronze production.

Keightley (2000:101) suggests, "The great wealth of ritual bronzes buried with dead elites was presumably provided so that the recently dead could continue their sacrifices to the more senior ancestors." Presumably the living needed bronzes to worship their ancestors, too. Kija is said to have been allowed to take the ancestral Shang bronzes with him, along with a retinue of five thousand people (perhaps the royalty and nobility of the Yin city at Anyang, along with their servants) to the northeast. If such bronzes were discovered, it would solve the question of the location of Kija's state, but they have not been found.

Critiquing the Shaman Hypothesis

Sarah Allan (1999:71) is skeptical about the kings of Shang performing as shamans for several reasons. She finds no evidence for shamanism in Shang religion as known from the oracle bone inscriptions. In her opinion, ancestor worship, in which the dead continued to exist and to need food provided by the living, was at the heart of Shang beliefs. The cult of sacrifice is seen by Allan as the focus of Shang religion, with ritual sacrifices and food offerings to the spirits as the avenue to contact spirits. She suggests that the cracks in the bones obviated the need for a shaman's flight. The spirits were believed to descend to make the cracks—there was no place for the ecstatic experience.

Furthermore, the tigers—said to be the shaman's spirit helper by Chang—that seem to be devouring humans are discounted by Allan because "bronzes with tiger motif are primarily southern" and not representative of the Shang (Allan 1999:73). This argument is less compelling. Tigers were found in the north as well; in fact, they still roam the north. Allan (1991:86) suggests that "*wu* were originally specialized priests who could call souls and whose spirits could travel to those four uninhabitable lands" far in the four directions, which sounds rather like shamans after all.

Warring States

Proponents of shamanism in the Sandai often use the archaeology and writings from the later part of the Zhou dynasty to show that shamanism continued to flourish even after the Shang. Where excavations have been carried out, texts written on bamboo slips appear in tombs, some of which suggest shamanic beliefs and practices. The most extensive information comes from the state of Chu, but Song also was said to be related to Shang and to feature dragons, while excavations in the Zhongshan kingdom indicate the use of oversized weapons as symbols of the power of the state. The cult of the Queen Mother of the West may date from this period, although this deity became particularly important in the Han dynasty.

Chu

Archaeology of the Chu capital city of Jinan has revealed a city of 16 square kilometers enclosed by an earthen wall at least seven meters high, pierced by seven gates (Höllman 1986). Texts record that Jinan existed from 689 to 278 BCE, when it was destroyed by the conquering army of Qin. More than eighty-four house floors were unearthed, as well as three hundred wells. The city is surrounded by about eight hundred graves. Elite graves contain objects that could be related to shamanism. For example, large drums were mounted on elaborate stands. The stands were often in the shape of a pair of long-legged birds standing on tigers. Another wooden bird has antlers instead of wings. Other carvings are of double-headed monsters with antlers and long, protruding tongues (Figure 6.5). Sets of bells and horse trappings were also included among the grave goods.

Three graves excavated at Mawangdui were remarkable, but the grave of the Lady of Dai was particularly valuable because it was completely waterlogged, which preserved entirely the organic contents—even Lady Dai's body and her final meal. In terms of shamanism, a painted textile was of great importance. It shows Lady Dai being interrogated by the spirits. Nuwa and Fuxi are represented with human heads and entwined snake tails. The moon has a rabbit and the sun a three-legged crow.

The state of Chu was considered to be shamanistic by its contemporaries (Major 1978), and it is the state with the most archaeological evidence of shamanism. Literary evidence includes some shamans' songs that have been preserved, describing how the shaman lures the spirits (Waley 1955).

> The Spirit in great majesty came down;
> Now he soars up swiftly among the clouds.
> He looks down on the province of Chi and far beyond;
> He traverses to the Four Seas, endless his flight.

Thus multiple lines of evidence show that Chu had a lively shamanistic culture.

Some scholars see Chu as a remnant of Shang—or somehow a continuation of Shang religious practices and beliefs (Major 1978:228). A shaman of Chu is said to have served King Wen of Zhou in the Late Shang period as a ritualist (Blakeley 1999:10). Chu religious practices preserved some aspects from Shang, including iconography of snakes, dragons, predatory birds, and tigers. Some motifs are quite different from Shang, however, including protruding tongues, bulging eyes, and antlers (So 1999).

Major (1999:121–23) shows that the state of Chu allows a glimpse into the operation of shamanism in a state-level society. He suggests that it is possible that the shamanism of the state of Chu was linked to that of northeast Asia and Siberia. Lacquer was traded as far north as the Lake Baikal region, and it also appears in the northern Korean peninsula. An embroidered silk textile like that of Mawangdui was found in the Pazyryk burial in southern Siberia contemporaneous with Chu (Major 1999:137). Chu definitely had cultural links with the north via

Figure 6.5 Monster from Chu with antlers and hanging tongue. After Wenwu Press 1959

Shandong and Liaodong (the states of Qi and Yan). Shandong did a lively maritime trade. As is shown by the archaeology, Yan was a state with mixed Chinese and non-Chinese population (Sun 2006). Chu had previously held lands farther north, but was awarded lands in the south in the early Zhou dynasty (Cook and Blakeley 1999:1–5).

Ban Gu, the author of *Han Shu*, defined shamans as people who worshipped ghosts and spirits. Their activities involved dancing, singing, and animal sacrifices. As Major (1999) notes, this is part of folk religion even at present. But as closely as shamanism was associated with Chu, Daoism also flourished there (Major 1999:143). Many gods were also worshipped and appear in the iconography of various kinds of material culture. These include not only Xiwangmu, the Queen Mother of the West—who also appears in Han iconography and apparently had a strong hold in popular religion—but also Dongwangmu, the Queen Mother of the East. The two queen mothers were described as founding deities of Chu, Fuxi, and Nuwa, portrayed on the famous Mawangdui painted textile as intertwined serpents with human heads. The myth of Archer Yi is also portrayed on decorated chests. There are deities for each of the twelve months, some of which are portrayed with antlers. Tomb guardian also sprout antlers, and their large tongues protrude (So 1999).

Astronomy was connected to religion, and recently uncovered evidence from Chu confirms its importance. Astronomical entities that we have seen to be important earlier were those that include the Big Dipper, the Dragon of the East, and the Tiger of the West. These are all portrayed on a chest from the tomb of Prince Zeng at Sunxian, as well as the lunar lodges. Names have been added, so it is clear what was intended (So 1999). A game or divining board shows evidence of cosmological beliefs as well. The image of the Big Dipper is used as a pointer, perhaps spinning around to tell fortunes.

Zhongshan

The Zhongshan culture was a small state among the Warring States, but it stands out from its archaeology as a likely shamanistic state. It was said to have been founded in the sixth century BCE by a barbarian group called Baidi, or White Di, from the Ordos region. The capital city of Zhongshan included a large palace, and elaborate royal graves were excavated near Shijiazhuang, south of Beijing. The artifacts in the grave of King Cuo show that the state had adopted many Zhou practices and the accompanying artifacts. However, many motifs are reminiscent of Northern and Central Asia

(Figure 6.6). Heads of birds of prey are particularly common, appearing on combs, architectural elements. Tigers (or some other feline) with wings are another frequent motif. These motifs are related to the Central Asian Steppes. Another similar motif is that of a tiger eating a deer. Xiaolong Wu (2004) has suggested that these artifacts are related to exchange along the Silk Road, and he shows that an important branch of that trade route went through Zhongshan. The inhabitants would have known the routes through the Taihang Mountains because they presumably used that access to the region they settled from the Ordos.

Conclusion

It is difficult enough to sort out the multiple ethnicities of ancient China without complicating the question by asking which styles and artifacts represent shamanism and which may simply reflect the fashions of the day—or fascination with exotic artifacts brought from distant places. Given Chang's criteria for shamanism, cited at the beginning of this chapter, can we recognize shamanism anywhere in China in the Sandai period? The cultures of the eastern side of China offer more evidence of shamanism than those in the central plain. New elements introduced into Late Shang—at the time of King Wu Ding—are those that Chang finds compelling for his argument that the Shang king was a shaman. These innovations include chariots and horses, writing on oracle bones, and new bronze styles. The bronze

Figure 6.6 Zhongshan bronze trident. After Wen 1980

decorations have some similarities with the paintings on Lower Xiajiadian pottery. It is possible that all these innovations during Wu Ding's reign were brought by one of his wives. All of the new elements definitely or possibly come from the northeast. Lady Hao's burial contained Northern Bronzes including mirrors and small jade figures that could have been used for divining. We know that Lady Hao prepared oracle bones and led armies (presumably driving a chariot). While no evidence points to Wu Ding performing ecstatic rituals, perhaps Lady Hao was the shaman. It is a possibility to ponder, especially considering it makes sense of all known discoveries.

SANXINGDUI, CHINA

A surprising discovery contemporaneous with Shang occurred in the far west of China, in the Szechuan Basin, at the site of Sanxingdui near Chengde (Bagley 2001; Chen 1999; Ge and Linduff 1990; Shen 2002; Xu 2001b; Zhao 1996). Two pits contained hitherto unknown artifacts made of bronze, jade, ivory, and pottery, which had been layered in an orderly manner. Animal bones and shells were also in the pits (Shen 2002; Ge and Linduff 1990). The bronzes were in a unique style, but bronze vessels in Shang style were among the items in the pits.

While these pits are contemporaneous with the Shang dynasty, civilization did not spring up in this location without antecedents. Some sites in the vicinity of Sanxingdui are dated as early as the Middle Neolithic, around 2700 BCE (Xu 2001a).

In the Sanxingdui pits, the large and small figures of humans and humanoid forms are impressive, unlike anything found in Shang territory. The figures found here must have been related to both their beliefs and their rituals, as they include humans and supernaturals. The statues were created with "great technical skill" (Rawson 1996:60). The largest figure weighs more than 180 kilograms. Life-sized statues that appear to be male held something in their oversized hands that is now missing (Figure F.1). To fit through the round openings, the objects would have had to be curved as well as large. Elephant tusks, which were found in profusion in a layer in one of the pits, are a likely candidate. The tusks could

Figure F.1 Bronze figure with large hands. After Wenwu Press 1994b have been symbols of authority—or might have had a more mystical function.

The humans depicted have sharp features (Figure F.2), and are sometimes ornamented with gold leaf. Other statues have cylindrical protruding eyes, and perhaps represent an all-seeing spirit or power, not an actual human (Figure F.3). Birds are also prominent in the iconography (Figure F.4).

There is some evidence for burning in the pits. It is speculated that the remains may represent the "burning ritual" recorded in Shang oracle bones. Although the bronze statues are strange and unrelated to anything known in the Shang, the Shang bronzes found in the pit col-

Figure F.2 Bronze human head. After Wenwu Press 1994b

Figure F.3 Bronze head with protruding eyes. After Wenwu Press 1994b

Figure F.4 Bronze bird. After Wenwu Press 1994b

lection suggest trade within the Shang sphere (Xu 2001b). The sacrificial pits contain almost all that is known of the people who cast these strange statues in bronze. City walls from the Shang period are known, but little else.

SEVEN

SHAMANISM
IN KOREA

Garbed in red robes of an antique general or wielding the Spirit War-
rior's halberd as she drives malevolent forces from her path, [the
shaman] claims an imposing presence. . . . By virtue of the powerful
gods who possess her, she can summon up divination visions and probe
the source of a client's misfortune, exorcise the sick and chronically
unlucky, remove ill humors from those who have difficulty finding mates,
and coax a reluctant birth spirit into an infertile womb.

—Laurel Kendall 1985:6

CURRENT SHAMANISM has been described in many parts of
South Korea and earlier was studied in the north. But when did
shamanism come to the Korean peninsula? With the first inhabitants? In the Neolithic? Later? The evidence is thin for the earliest times,
but by the proto-historic period both texts and archaeological discoveries
are clear about the presence of shamanism and its importance in the developing societies.

171

Paleolithic and Neolithic

Evidence of human presence in the Korean peninsula is well established in the Paleolithic period, but little has remained that could throw light on religious beliefs and activities. The site of Seokchongri, on the Gum River in central western Korea, contained some large flat stones with scratched lines that the excavator described as art (Sohn 1978), but these were not connected to any belief system. Other Paleolithic sites contain carved antler pieces that were possibly used as pendants and a deer antler placed atop an articulated bear skeleton (Lee 1986). This is not much to spin a tale from, although perhaps a story about bear spirits and the importance of antlers could be attempted. A few deliberate burials suggest a belief in an afterlife (Sohn 1974). Perhaps ancestral spirits were involved, but it is not until the Neolithic period that some artifacts begin to suggest ritual patterns, and the case for shamanism becomes likely.

The Korean Neolithic is marked by decorated pottery, stone and bone tools, and semisubterranean houses in small villages dispersed along coasts and rivers. Early Neolithic has mixed subsistence, including fishing and shellfish collecting, some hunting of deer, and possible pig and dog domestication. Animal domestication has been claimed for sites in North Korea (Kim Shin-kyu 1966), but in the south the only bones come from shell mounds, and they are few and have not been sufficiently studied. It is reasonable to suppose that people who knew the properties of local herbs served as healers. But if the healers held séances, nothing is known of their beliefs, their music, or their costumes. Shell bracelets from southeastern shellmound sites and a few perforated shells are the only definite adornments.

In Neolithic Korea archaeological discoveries are fewer and smaller than sites in China (Figure 7.1). The relative paucity of artifacts is due to the fact that Neolithic cemeteries are rare because of poor bone preservation in Korean soil. The huge Neolithic cemeteries of China, with many grave goods that can be used to examine questions of rank and gender as well as shamanism, have no counterparts in Korea. Obviously, comparisons regarding age, sex, and social rank can be attempted only rarely with Korean data.

Artifacts that might be related to religious beliefs and activities are mostly found in shell midden sites. They include crude masks, such as simple shell faces from Tongsamdong and a pinched clay face from Osanni. A similar face was found at the Kievka site in the Zaisanovka period of the Russian Far East (Zhushchikovskaya 2006). Burial evidence from the Russ-

Figure 7.1 Map of Korean sites. Map by Andrea Reider

ian Far East includes a small burial ground at the Boisman 2 site, with a central burial of an old woman encircled by all the others burials. She probably was a leader of a family group—and possibly a shaman. But burials from the Pacific coast of Russia are too rare to know whether such a cemetery represented a recurring pattern.

Human representations are likewise rare in the Korean Neolithic. Some bone figures from northeastern sites in the Korean peninsula, such as Sopohang (Mikami 1961), may be fetishes or could represent gods or spirits, like the shaved sticks (*inau*) of the Ainu, which indicated sacred space. A small female torso was found at Shinamni near the southeastern edge of the Korean peninsula (Chung 1989). It could be related to shamanism, possibly as an object from a shaman's altar, but the context gives no clue. Objects representing gods were kept in shrines among the Daur, a Tungusic people of far northern Manchuria (Humphrey and Onon 1996). Where bone is preserved, such as at Tongsamdong (Sample 1974) or Sopohang (Sohn 1978), some apparently nonfunctional artifacts with markings on them could be hypothesized to belong to a shaman's tool kit. However, these objects could as well be parts of games, tallies, or have other unimagined uses.

Pottery designs in Early and Middle Neolithic are usually made of short, straight lines arranged in rows or triangles. Blacker (1975:105) has noted triangles as decorative motifs on *haniwa* that represent female shamans in Kofun, Japan. The triangle was used by shamans in later Korea, and triangular patterns with hatching are found on the earliest mirrors in Late Neolithic China. Shamans' robes in Korea today sometimes have tiny triangles in different colors embroidered around the neck. It is hard to build a case for (or against) shamanism from these few artifacts. And yet they do show that the Neolithic inhabitants of the peninsula maintained beliefs and rituals of some sort. While this evidence is too sparse to provide access to ritual behavior, it antedates obvious shamanic artifacts in the Bronze Age and may indicate an ancient stratum of shamanism in Korea.

Bronze Age

Around 2000 BCE archaeological evidence suggests new influences in the Korean peninsula. These include several new types of undecorated pottery collectively called Mumun, along with the establishment of rice agriculture and megalithic structures (Nelson 1999b). By about 1000 BCE a few bits of bronze began to appear in the northwestern part of the peninsula in the form of bronze knives and buttons (Kim 1978). Bronze mirrors and daggers were cast on the peninsula by 700 BCE. These early bronze objects were the same types as those of the Northern Bronzes in eastern Liaoning province, China.

Dolmens are megalithic constructions that were erected by Neolithic people. They dominate the landscape in many parts of the Korean peninsula, as well as Liaodong, China (Figure 7.2). A few dolmens are even found in Shandong (Mikami 1961). In the northern part of Korea, as far south as Seoul, the dolmens are called northern dolmens, or sometimes table dolmens, because they are raised on two to four tall stone slabs, with a large capstone extending far beyond in all directions. The uprights are about two meters high, assembled in an upright square like the sides of a box. One capstone in Hwanghaedo has been reported to weigh 40 tons. The question of how a stone of many tons was maneuvered to lie atop the supporting stones has not been solved. In any case, the weight of the stones implies a labor force of strong persons who could be deployed for this purpose.

Northern dolmens were often erected on hill tops, usually singly but sometimes in groups (Kim Byong-mo 1981). They are presumed to have been burials, but if so most were robbed in antiquity. Sherds of red pottery jars and fragments of stone tools are often the only remnants of the grave goods (Kim Won-yong 1986). The typical dolmen burial—if such can be guessed at—

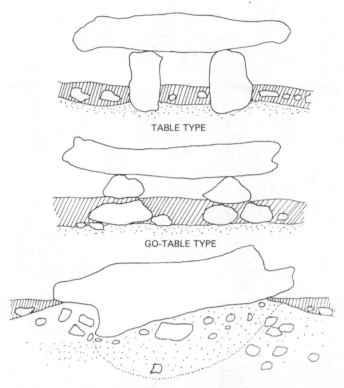

TABLE TYPE

GO-TABLE TYPE

UNSUPPORTED CAP STONE TYPE

Figure 7.2 Types of dolmens in Korea. After Nelson 1993a

seems to have been a single person of importance, buried with a necklace of tubular beads, often blue or green, with a curved jewel at the front. He or she (no bones have been preserved, probably from a combination of looting followed by dissolution) was buried with a fragile polished limestone dagger, which must have been purely ceremonial, and a pair of small red bowls (Figure 7.3). It is tempting to posit that a fermented beverage had been in those cups, perhaps as a final salute to the departed, but the possibility has not been tested. Some red cups are also found in houses, which could either argue for household rituals or that the red cups not only ceremonial.

Southern dolmens have a capstone that lies flat on the ground, sometimes above a pebble layer that covers an underground stone slab burial. These dolmens are not easy to rob and are less obvious than the northern type, accounting for the fact that more have been found with an undisturbed burial beneath the capstone when excavated. They are usually single burials, with small red jars, stone daggers, and necklaces with *gokok* (curved jewel). Liaoning style bronze daggers are sometimes found in these graves in place of the ceremonial limestone daggers. Dolmens continued to be erected into the Iron Age in the southern part of the Korean peninsula, sometimes as the markers for adult burials in huge jars, other times for cov-

Figure 7.3 Polished red cups. After Nelson 1993a

ering earthen pit graves without stone slabs. The dolmens have been interpreted as burial markers for chiefs and/or as delimiting a tribal territory.

Standing stones, called *menhirs*, have also been located, often in pairs.
Similar standing stones are also found in Japan along the inland sea, where
they are known as "husband and wife" stones (Gorman 1999:39). In Korea
the *menhirs* are interpreted as the forerunners of *jangseung*, the village
guardian figures carved from wood or stone, which persisted past the middle of the twentieth century.

Some groups of seven stones are arranged in the shape of the Big Dipper, indicating an astronomical connection for the stones (Holt 1948). Many
Korean shamans today cherish the seven stars of the Big Dipper as part of
their pantheon of spirits, and the seven stars were part of a divining board
from China, found in the Korean Nangnang region.

Rock art sites in the southeastern part of the Korean peninsula include
whales, tigers, fish, deer, and people paddling a boat. No C14 dates have
been possible to obtain, but the rock drawings are usually ascribed to the
Bronze Age, although Sohn (1974) suggests that some of the animals are
Late Pleistocene creatures. Some drawings depict bones inside the bodies
of animals, a trait said to reflect a shamanic belief—found also in rock art
as far north as the Amur River in the Russian Far East (Okladnikov 1981).

The megalithic stones may be unrelated to shamanism, although at least
one archaeologist has suggested a connection. Oval indentations were carved
into the tops of some dolmens. These are called "cup-marks," after similar
indentations on dolmens in Denmark, and are said to indicate eggs, which
Hwang relates to the myths of Korea in which culture heroes are born from
bird eggs (Hwang 1974). Data that would corroborate the relationship have
not been forthcoming.

Later in the Bronze Age, unusual forms cast in bronze have been said
to be shamanistic (Kim Won-yong 1986:167–68). Often they include jingle
bells cast into the artifacts. Similar bronze rattles are used by shamans today.
Kim suggests that one odd-shaped bronze piece is intended to be the figure
of a shaman holding a bell in each hand (Figures 7.4 and 7.5). "It must be
the representation of either a shaman performing a ceremonial dance or of a
shamanistic deity. It is probably the symbol of a ruler who, at the same time,
was the head shaman" (Kim Won-yong 1986:169). I have no alternative suggestion, but I do not find Kim's description convincing. However, the
"Korean-style" bronze mirrors and smaller bells are likely candidates for
shamanistic functions (Figure 7.6). The designs on bronze daggers and mirrors included the same triangles and short slanting lines that are found on

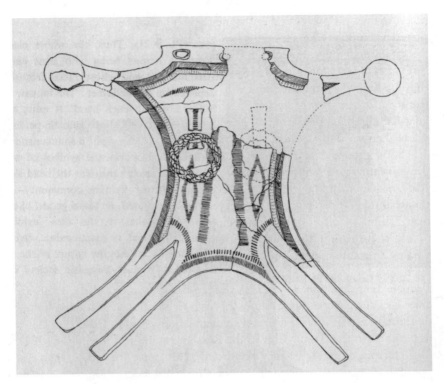

Figure 7.4 Bronze "shaman figure." After Nelson 1993a

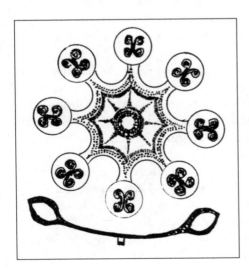

Figure 7.5 Bronze rattle. After Nelson 1993a

Figure 7.6 Korean bronze mirrors. After Nelson 1993a

Neolithic pottery. Mirrors are first found in East Asia in the Qijia culture in Late Neolithic China. The small bronze mirrors and knives that were placed in the tomb of Lady Hao of Shang China follow in the same tradition, as do slightly later mirrors from Liaoning Province in northeastern China. Korean mirrors have the same geometric patterns. The earlier mirrors have wide and irregular lines, but later ones are decorated with fine lines. Because partial molds for this type of mirror have been found in Korea, it is clear that they were not imported but manufactured in the Korean peninsula.

Furthermore, the *gogok*—the curved jewel that is better known in English language publications by its Japanese name, *magatama*—is present as early as the Bronze Age. *Gogok* are found on later gold crowns of shamanistic form in Three Kingdoms Korea and were one of the symbols of sovereignty in early Yamato, Japan. Early examples are often found in burials under dolmens, usually as the central bead in a necklace strung with tubular green beads. This necklace could designate a shaman leader, since they are found on *haniwa* (tomb figures from later Japan) that portray shamans. Such burials may also contain stone daggers (or rarely bronze daggers), which were clearly ceremonial, as they would have snapped when pressure was applied.

The Han Commanderies

When the Korean peninsula came into the view of literate China, texts describe the activities and belief systems of the inhabitants of the Korean peninsula. With the usual caveats, they can be used as an aid to construct an understanding of their religious beliefs. What we read is entirely consistent with shamanism, apparently the opinion of the authors, who sometimes use the word *wu* to describe persons in Korea.

The Han dynasty of China established commandaries in the northern part of the peninsula beginning in 108 BCE, bringing many Chinese artifacts and burial customs into the commandery known as Lelang (NMK 2001; Pai 2000). Resplendent tombs excavated in the vicinity of Pyongyang demonstrate that long distance trade was thriving. Shallow lacquer wine cups with ears in the style of the state of Chu were found in burials (Umehara 1926), as well as elaborately fashioned objects from Central Asia. A gold buckle with turquoise inlay resembles two others that have been found in southern China and far western China (NMK 2001; Pirazzoli 1982). Chariot parts were also found in burials, and occasionally bits of silk were preserved (NMK 2001). The upper-class Chinese who were sent to this distant outpost may have felt far from home, but they lived a luxurious life.

The documents that pertain to the southern part of the Korean peninsula contemporaneous with the Nangnang commandery are contradictory about the names and locations of the local polities. The *Houhanshu* describes a state called Chinguk comprising all of the southern part of the peninsula, but the *Weizhi* names three separate confederations of city-states—Chinhan in the east, Pyonhan in the middle, and Mahan (the Horse Han) in the east (not the same Han as the Han dynasty), and enumerates the "states" in each polity. The Han polities are located in the regions where the states of Silla and Baekje arose later, with the unaffiliated Kaya cities between them. Mahan was said to be the largest and strongest, comprised of more than fifty such towns (Seyock 2004:71).

The *guo* are interpreted as walled towns. Barnes (2007) states that archaeology does not confirm the presence of such walled towns, but names tell another story. Many towns in Korea are named Tosongni, meaning earth fort village. According to the account of Han in chapter 30 of the Chinese history *Sanguoji*, the people of Mahan believed in ghosts and spirits (Parker 1890). Chinese texts relate small bits of information about shamanism in the southern part of the Korean peninsula, especially in Mahan territory. The *Weizhi* describes sacred groves called *sodo*, marked by a tall pole, a drum, and a bell. One person called a "Heaven prince" was designated from each town to carry out the ritual sacrifices (Parker 1890:208). The same document describes an ordeal undergone by young men that might be related to shamanism, and is vaguely reminiscent of the Native American Sundance.

A piece of rope was inserted under the skin of their back, and they dragged a large log to show their strength and courage. The *Houhanshu* says that the people of Mahan "drew no distinction of age or sex" and worshipped the spirits twice a year—after planting and after harvest. The worship consisted of "a drinking bout night and day, assembling in groups to dance and sing." Hard work was rewarded by the spirits! Of the people of Chinhan who lived in walled towns, each town had its chief. They traded in iron. "When a son was born they liked to flatten his head by pressing it with stones." This practice has been verified in a Neolithic burial ground at Yeanni on the southern coast of Korea, in which some skeletons had artificially deformed heads (Kim Jong-Hak 1977).

On the east coast of the Korean peninsula, the *Houhanshu* records that the people venerated mountains and streams. Furthermore, "they knew how to observe the stars, and could prophesy the abundance or scarcity of the year" (Parker 1890:205). They sacrificed to heaven at an annual festival with singing, dancing, and drinking rice wine, and also sacrificed to the tiger. Siberian tigers still existed in this region into the twentieth century, so it is not surprising that tiger spirits were feared and respected, as among the Amur River peoples. Folk paintings of tigers are still popular. Spotted leopards, which appear along with tigers in Korean folk paintings, were said to be plentiful, along with ponies (Zaichikov 1952).

The Korean Three Kingdoms

The Three Kingdoms of Ko-Silla (traditional dates 57 BCE–668 CE), Goguryeo (traditional dates 37 BCE–668 CE), and Baekje (traditional dates 18 BCE–668 CE) are described in two Korean histories, written much later than the events they describe, but based on contemporary documents no longer extant.

Goguryeo

Although Korean histories give Silla priority as the earliest of the Three Kingdoms, Goguryeo (Koguryeo) is the first to be noticed in the Chinese records, and it probably became a state as early as the second century BCE (Rhee 1992). Neolithic discoveries in the region north of the Yalu River, from Jian to Huanren, show that the region where Goguryeo arose was already populated with agriculturalists in small but fertile valleys along north-flowing tributaries (Rhee 1992). The pottery from these sites is unlike the tall flower-pot shape with zigzag incising that characterizes much of the rest of Manchuria in the Early and Middle Neolithic. A new suite of pottery styles suggests the appearance of an unrelated group of people who made undecorated pottery around 2000 BCE. Plain pottery also appears in Manchuria about this time (Nelson 1990). Some dolmens are found around the Yalu River, suggesting some level of inequality. By the third or fourth century BCE, small piled stone tombs are found in large numbers. More than half the almost five thousand such tombs in the Huanren-Jian region were the earliest type, some having coins from the Warring States period to help date them. Obviously this region was within the trading network of the Chinese states. Iron implements found in the burials show technological sophistication or extensive trade. A city with an earthen wall was located beneath the present stone wall of Jian. Contemporary with the earthen walled city is a large square stone tomb that belonged to a strong leader. The region developed rapidly in response to trade with some of the Warring States.

Goguryeo emerged as a state sometime after the conquest by Han China of part of northern Korean peninsula in 108 BCE. By 75 BCE, Goguryeo had driven out the closest commandery of Hyondo and within a generation had brought large areas in northeastern Korea under its control. To be closer to the center of the newly conquered territories, the capital was moved to Jian in 3 CE. In the next century not only did Goguryeo challenge Han China militarily, it also imitated it, adding murals on the stone walls of tombs in the Han style. By the fourth century some of the population was literate. Both educational institutions and Buddhism had been established. A stele with a long inscription in Chinese characters, which was erected in 404 CE, boasts of the conquests of King Gwanggaeto, who is thought to have been buried in the most impressive stone tomb in Jian. The tomb is in the form of a stone-stepped pyramid and is partly constructed of gigantic monoliths. The place for the coffin is (uniquely) near the top of the pyramid.

Sites attributed to Goguryeo are found near Dandong and Luxun in Liaoning province (Hamada 1928), as well as Dongguo and many other sites in Jilin province (Rhee 1992). Some sites are Neolithic, but others belong to the Goguryeo state, with tombs covered with stone cobbles, or later stone-walled tombs with painted murals. The large ancient town of Jian was built on the north side of the Yalu (Amnok) River, surrounded by a rectangular city wall in the style of a Chinese city. An earlier mountain fortress nearby followed the Korean pattern of irregular walls enclosing a hill top. The fortress enclosed a lake large enough to contain fish and to be a useful water supply in case of siege. Many elite tombs were found in the vicinity. Later ones had slab stone walls, which were painted with scenes both of and for the deceased. Few Goguryeo artifacts have been collected because these tombs were looted long ago, but the tomb murals are full of lively scenes that reveal a great deal about the lives of the nobility who are buried in the tombs, as well as their clothing, architecture, and artifacts.

One Goguryeo tomb mural almost surely depicts a shaman (Figure 7.7). She wears a general's hat, which shamans today wear when they are calling the Spirit of the General. The famous Tomb of the Dancers depicts men and women in similar costumes, dancing in a line. They all wear boots and dotted gowns. Their robes cover their hands, as in later court dances (Figure 7.8). This is not an individual shamanic dance to contact the spirits, although it seems likely to depict a ritual rather than mere entertainment for the man and woman buried there. Laurel Kendall (personal communication) suggests that it might be entertainment for the gods, like Japanese shrine dances—or for the man and woman in their afterlife so that as powerful ancestors they would be well disposed toward their descendents.

A Chinese text that describes early Goguryeo festivals also suggests shamanism. The occasions sound rather raucous (no doubt shocking to the proper, ceremonial-minded Chinese scribes). These events were staged in a large cave and included singing and dancing, drinking alcoholic beverages, and worshipping the sun. "Of an evening and at night, the men and women assembled in dancing and singing groups. They were fond of sacrificing to the spiritual powers, the gods of the land, and to the stars. They worshiped

Heaven in the tenth moon, at a great assembly" (Parker 1890:186). The text further observes, "Koguryo believes in Buddhism, and worships the spiritual powers . . . there are many unorthodox shrines and there are two special divinities:

Figure 7.7 Painting of shaman in Goguryeo tomb. After Kim Wong-yong 1976

Figure 7.8 Dancers painted on the wall of a Goguryeo tomb. After Nelson 1993a

one is called Puyo divinity, a woman carved out of wood, who was the daughter of the god of the sea and the other is . . . the son of the Puyo divinity."

A tale in the *Samguk Yusa* involves women shamans being called upon by the Goguryeo king to dance for the spirits to help in a troubled time. The shamans danced to the spirits on behalf of the nation. Thus it is clear that shamans were respected and state-sponsored in Goguryeo, although the shamans were not rulers. It is also notable that the sex of the shamans is specified as female.

As can be expected, there are also Buddhist and Daoist references in the tomb paintings. Guardians of the four directions are found in the entry-ways of some tombs, and others are painted with the animals of the four directions on the four walls of the inner chambers. Shamanism was only one of many ways to reach the spirits. Goguryeo thus reflects its mixed place within East Asia.

Silla

The state of Silla grew out of a polity founded by six tribes in the valley around an ancient city that is now called Gyeongju (Kim Won-yong 1976).

The polity, first called Saro, was centered on a walled palace known as Banweolseong, Half Moon Fortress, on a hill in the bend of the south river. Later the town expanded as far as rivers on three sides, and was called Geumseong, Gold Fortress. Saro came to be called Silla probably as a result of the Chinese characters used to write the name. The *Houhanshu* recounts a tale implying that the elite had come from the northeast of China (Nelson 2008; Parker 1890). The location of the villages of Saro may have been chosen for the gold sand and gold nuggets found in the rivers. The newcomers brought traditions of mound burial, horses to ride and perhaps pull vehicles, and the lavish use of gold. The *Samguk Sagi* describes Silla's extensive conquests. In the first few centuries CE, Silla began absorbing or conquering nearby small polities, and by the sixth century it had absorbed all of Kaya, as well as other nearby unaffiliated towns.

Kim Won-yong (1986:240) concludes that "the indigenous faith of the Silla people was shamanism." He posits a connection with Siberia in the antler and tree shapes on Korean crowns. Six tall, sheet-gold crowns have been excavated, as well as many shorter gilt-bronze crowns (Kim Byongmo 1997). While no two of the tall crowns are identical, they are all pure gold crowns with uprights in the shape of antlers and trees, which lie near the head of the buried person. The crowns are covered with *gogok* and leaf-like spangles. Additional crowns are often found in the same tomb, in side chests containing additional jewelry, including necklaces, earrings, and bracelets. Precious items traded from afar, such as glass vessels and silver bowls, were also placed in the chests.

Similar but earlier crowns have been excavated near Chaoyang in Liaoning Province, China, an interesting fact in view of the statement in the *Weizhi* that "the old men of Chinhan used to say that they were Qin refugees who had come to the Han [Korean] states in order to escape the misery of forced labor, and that Mahan cut off the eastern portion of their state for them" (Parker 1890:209).

The crowns have been interpreted as shaman's crowns. The uprights are in two shapes (see Case Study G). One shape clearly represents antlers, and the other is more stylized—said to represent trees. Spangles cover the crown, attached to it with twisted gold wire. They are gold in the shape of birch leaves or curved jewels of glass, as well as jade and other stones.

Birchbark is another material found in these fourth and fifth century tombs, which further suggests connections to the forests of Manchuria. The broad-leafed evergreen environment of the southern part of the Korean peninsula does not include northern trees like birch. Some meaningful objects were made of birchbark, which must have been an imported commodity and quite precious. The material was probably favored for its white color, as well as possible connections with distant relatives. At least two such artifacts are painted with galloping white horses, and another has a red bird, possibly representing a phoenix (Nelson 2008).

Although histories of the Three Kingdoms were written in their present form more than five hundred years after Silla unified the Korean peninsula, the histories were at least partly based on ancient Silla records. Although the Confucian and Buddhist proclivities of the authors of these two histories would have precluded an interest in shamanism, there are still a few hints of it in the form of myths and stories. Some relate miraculous births of early kings, or the ancestors of queens who were mountain goddesses. Other stories feature swift white horses, such as were sacrificed by Mongols in shamanistic rites. One of the titles listed for early kings is said to mean "shaman" in the old Silla language.

Long-distance trade is evident in the elite graves from this period. One necklace features a face bead having a Europoid face. Face beads were a complicated form of glass beads made in the Mediterranean and India. Horses were also important—one burial consisted of nothing but a horse surrounded by a circle of stones and under a mound (Kim and Lee 1975), possibly a horse sacrifice.

While the written histories describe the activities of early kings and queens who built reservoirs for rice cultivation, for example, and held silk weaving contests between the women of different villages, archaeology shows that by the fourth and fifth centuries, the leaders of Silla had become powerful kings and queens who were buried with lavish gold jewelry in enormous tombs.

One of the first to connect the Silla crowns with shamanism was Karl Henze (1962), but Kim Byung-mo (1997) has elaborated this theme. He interprets the antler-shaped uprights as trees, arguing that the dangling ornaments represent "leaves and fruits." He believes that birds and trees were particularly important in Silla ritual. Kim notes that the mother of King Chijung was named Lady Chosang, meaning born of a bird, and notes that the inner gold caps that were found with some of the crowns resemble shamanistic caps, especially those of the Buryat region in Siberia. The gold cap from the Tomb of the Phoenix is decorated with three birds on the top, and birds are found on a small crown from the Kaya region. As we have already seen, birds had spiritual meanings for the peoples of eastern China in the Neolithic and later. These were the people known to central China as Dongyi, Eastern Barbarians. Some Korean historians make a connection between the Dongyi and the peoples of Korea.

Kim connects the love of gold with the Altai region. The name itself means gold in Altaic languages. Other characteristics that Kim uses to connect the gold crowns of Silla with the Altai are worshipping birds, respecting the horse, and constructing mounds for royalty. Kim also connects the occasional appearance of horn-shaped drinking cups to Central Asia. Two of the rhytons, which were apparently used in rituals, found in Silla burials have horse heads. This would connect them with the Turkic Sakha (Yakut), not the reindeer-herding Tungus and their presumed relatives in the Dongbei region. It is possible that they are trade items, or that people and influences from several regions joined together to form Silla.

Lee (2004:50) is one of many scholars who emphasizes that the main religion of Silla was shamanism, which formed the ideology of state rule. He asserts further that "shamanism came to constitute the mainstream of popular belief throughout Korea's long history." Referring to the fact that the title recorded for the second king of Silla means shaman, Lee emphasizes that shaman was a royal title and extends that fact to say, "from this one may surmise that the leaders of early Silla functioned as shamans." It is reasonable to propose that the early leaders of Silla were shamans, but the evidence suggests that the queens might have been the major shamans in Silla, rather than kings (Nelson 1991a, 1993b, 2002b).

The soil of Korea does not preserve bones well, and as a result there are no bodies of royalty to sex. The only tomb where the genders are clear is Hwangnam Daechong, the largest tomb in Silla (Kim and Pearson 1977). It is a double tomb, in which the male was buried in the earlier south tomb and the queen in the later north one. The male rated a rather unimpressive silver crown along with an enormous cache of weapons (Figure 7.9). However, the queen wore the gold crown and gold belt of royalty (Kim Wonyong 1983; Nelson 1991b, 1993b, 2002b).

Silla was divided into endogamous bone ranks, bone being an Asian metaphor for kinship and descent. The highest group was the Holy Bone, those eligible to rule, from whom the kings and queen were selected (Chong-Sun Kim 1977). Although by the sixth century, the Kim family had claimed the right to kingship and passed the throne patrilineally to sons, it seems earlier to have been a matrilineal succession, with queens' daughters becoming the next queen (Nelson 1991b). Both father and mother were required to be Holy Bone for the child to merit the rank of Holy Bone (Grayson 1976). The ancestors of royalty were those with mythical beginnings—they were brought by white horses, found in a golden box, or were daughters of local mountain goddesses. Nobles of the second rank were called True Bone. Sumptuary rules kept everyone in their place. They have the additional value for scholars of describing the richness of the clothing, horses, saddles, and houses of the elite (Chong-Sun Kim 1977; Nelson 2008).

Lee describes the shamans of early Silla: "In the early records of the Silla annals, shamans frequently appear as old women or mothers, sorceresses who possessed the ability to see the future, foretelling both fortune and misfortune." The king told the future by looking at the wind and clouds, and it was said that he knew in advance if there would be calamity from flood and fire and if the harvest would be bountiful or poor. But queens were also recorded as prognosticators. Queen Sondok was famous for being able to read portents. It is said that a shrine for the first king was erected in the seventh century where sacrifices were conducted for the four seasons. "The king's sister Aro was appointed to officiate at these ceremonies; one may generally recognize the spiritual predominance of females in Silla society" (Lee 2004:52). This same relationship of brother and sister as co-officiants or co-rulers is seen in Okinawa in the present, and in ancient Japan, as will be detailed in chapter 8.

Silla is known for an association called Hwarang. In later times its member were sons of the nobility who were taught to sing and dance for the spirits, and who traveled to mountains and rivers where spirits dwelled. Although these activities were considered training for warriors, it had previously been a girls' society called *wonhua*, in which elite girls learned to dance and appreciate nature. The switch from training girls to training boys perhaps suggests a shift from gender equality to patriarchy because of the need to train warriors, but the shamanism of the training is clear.

Kaya

A group of six city-states share the name of Kaya, but they were never united under one ruler. The Kaya states occupied a region along the south coast of the Korean peninsula, and up the Nakdong River, in a rough triangular shape. The archaeology of these polities is quite extensive. Almost all excavations are of graves, large and small. Iron weapons, iron ingots, and iron armor are prominent in these burials. Knife money from the Warring States period in China has been found in a Kaya grave in Yonyeongdong, as well as pedestaled lacquerware that contained peaches for the journey to the other world. Writing brushes were found at Dahori under a split-log coffin. Many bronze weapons also have been found. Early Kaya burials have black burnished pottery, small bronze mirrors, and small bronze bells (NMK 1998). Clearly the Kaya people were in touch with the trade networks in the East Asian world.

It is widely thought that shamanism was practiced in the Kaya kingdoms. A diorama from a special exhibit on state formation in Korea from the National Museum of Korea shows a scene in which a female shaman officiates at a burial like one that is on display. Buckles in the shapes of horses and tigers may have indicated high military rank.

Baekje

The Baekje kingdom began in the Seoul area (see Best 2006 for an overview of Baekje). In several regions of western Seoul, stepped pyramids in Goguryeo style have been excavated, giving some credence to the texts that describe the foundation of Baekje by two younger sons of a Goguryeo king. The fortress town of Pungnamni, along the Han River, has a rectangular wall and shows a number of other influences from China, including the layout of the town itself.

Goguryeo defeated Baekje and pushed them farther south, to two subsequent capitals called Puyo and Gongju. Baekje remains consist of tombs of the rulers, the ground plan of a large palace and an even-larger Buddhist temple. Some pagodas and *miruks*—standing Buddha statues—have also been preserved. A couple of sheep-shaped Chinese celadon pots have come to light in Mahan/Baekje territory, which are probably tradewares from southern China. Although Baekje artifacts are few, an important discovery is an incense burner shaped like a mountain, with small figures of birds, trees, and people modeled on it. This object is related to similar censers from the Chu and Han in China, but it was probably locally made in Baekje. The high artistic tradition of Baekje is particularly known from early Buddhist objects that have been preserved in Japan, including a standing wooden carving of Kwanyin, the Goddess of Mercy. Baekje was more closely related to southern Chinese polities than those of the north, as seen from the Buddhist art that was transmitted from Baekje to the Japanese islands, especially the Yamato state.

The discovery of an intact king's tomb—that of King Munyong and his wife—produced an intriguing mix of continental and peninsular artifacts (Kim Won-yong 1983). The gold head-dresses belonged to the same tradition as those of Kaya and Silla, although they were not crowns but more like the floral halos found on Buddhist statues. Gold burial shoes were also in the local tradition. However, the tomb was made of bricks decorated with lotus designs. The whole tomb was an arched vault, with flame-shaped niches that contained small lamps. An inscription in Chinese characters was placed within the tomb. Thus, the direct influence from China was clear, and evidence of shamanism is less striking.

Current Shamanism in Korea

If it is defined by dancing for the spirits, Korean shamanism is probably more closely related to the Tungus shamanism of Manchuria/Siberia than that of Late Neolithic China or that of the Chu state of the Warring States period in China. It is the same tradition as Siberian shamanism. The name for Korean shaman ceremonies, *kut*, is the same as that used among Mongols and other Inner Asian groups.

Shamanistic traditions in Korea, however, are also related to ancestor worship, like those of China At shamanistic rites called *kut*, ancestors are propitiated along with an assortment of local and household deities. The *kut* is an event that is part theater and part entertainment, as well as a serious interaction with spirits. "*Kut* are dramatic and entertaining: shamans take turns beating drums and gongs, singing mythical narratives, performing comic skits, and impersonating supernatural beings" (Janelli and Janelli 1982:148).

Some of the participants play musical instruments and dance at the end of the *kut*. Everybody, including the ancestors, has a good time. Some informants say that when *kut* is performed for ancestors, "they all come" (Janelli and Janelli 1982:149). The *kut*, however, is only partly about ancestor spirits. Other spirits are important, too, and are more powerful, although ancestor spirits and those considered gods may overlap. Powerful ancestors may assume the status of gods. Thus, the relationship between ancestors and gods is complicated. However, both ancestors and gods need to be fed, as they are fed from the objects on the shamans' altar—often including a cooked pig's head, dried fish, rice, *makkoli* [rice wine], fruits, and cakes. "Shamanism attempts to ward off or alleviate suffering by placating a broader range of supernaturals; participants at *kut* also want to have a good time" (Janelli and Janelli 1982:165).

Korean shamanism also includes particular clothing the *mudang* (female shamans) wear to entertain and impersonate each spirit. The color of the robe as well as the headgear and paraphernalia alert the audience to which spirit is being invoked. Each Korean shaman also has a spirit shrine, with artifacts which signal that it is the home of the shaman's special spirits. Unlike most Siberian shamanistic rituals, the *kut* has three distinct parts: calling down the spirits, entertaining them, and sending them away. Although several hundred spirits can be called upon, only ten to twenty may be called down in any particular *kut*. Both nature spirits and ancestors are called upon in this manner. The list of nature spirits is long, including "heavenly spirits, sun spirits, star spirits, mountain spirits, earth spirits, dragon spirits, water spirits, fire spirits, and animal spirits" (Kim Taegon 1998:22).

Conclusion

Some characteristics of peninsular (Korean) and island (Japanese) shamanism seem to be more closely related to North and Central Asian shamanism than are the *wu* of China. Aspects of wuism, however, also influence Korean shamanism. Even ancient Chinese wuism, about which there is written material, did not remain exactly the same through time and space. While similarities can be pointed out, the direction of influence and its timing are still unknown.

HWANGNAM DAECHONG, KOREA— BURIAL OF A RULING QUEEN?

The first of the elaborate tombs of Silla to be excavated was discovered by accident when a railroad was being laid through Gyeongju during the Japanese occupation. The richness of the tomb startled everyone, especially the tall crown covered with curved jades and gold dangles (Figure G.1), and the belt with many pendants (Figure G.2). Both of these artifacts were beautifully crafted and made of pure gold. Subsequently, nine other Silla tombs with gold crowns have been excavated. Smaller crowns have also been found—some of them made of silver, bronze, or gilded bronze—but the tall gold crowns and belts are believed to represent the actual rulers of Silla.

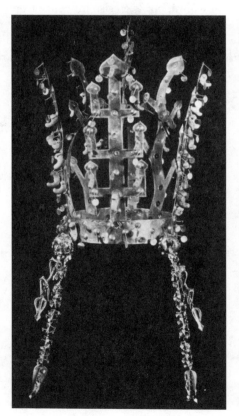

According to the traditional dates, the Old Silla kingdom of southern Korea lasted from 57 BCE to 668 CE. While the other two of the Three Kingdoms were in the north and west of the peninsula, Silla occupied part of the southeast. Silla was farther from China and was not influenced as early by Buddhism, the

Figure G.1 Gold crown from Tomb 98. After Nelson 1993a

Figure G.2   Gold belt from Tomb 98. After Nelson 1993a

Chinese language, or Chinese governmental forms. Thus, while Baekje and Goguryeo adopted Chinese burial styles that included tombs with a corridor intended for reentry, Silla used mounded tombs without a corridor (Figure G.3). This crucial difference meant that Silla tombs could not be easily robbed, and the remarkable inclusion of gold, beads, bronze, glass, and other valuables is thanks to the way Silla tombs were constructed.

The third to fifth centuries were the time of the flowering of Old Silla, when enormous tombs were erected. The tomb of interest here is Tomb 98, also called Hwangnam Taechong, the big tomb in the suburb of Hwangnam. It is a double mound, the largest of all the Silla tombs, both in length and height. Double tombs are always those of a husband and wife, and there are several in the vicinity of Gyeongju. The tombs are in the middle of the city, and houses were built upon them. When a park was made to surround the largest of the tombs (Figure G.4), the houses and trees were removed, and two remarkable tombs were excavated. One is Tomb 98, the other is called Chonma-chong, the Tomb of the Heavenly Horse (Figure G.5).

The soil of Korea does not preserve bones well, and as a result there are no bodies of royalty to sex. The only tomb where the genders are clear

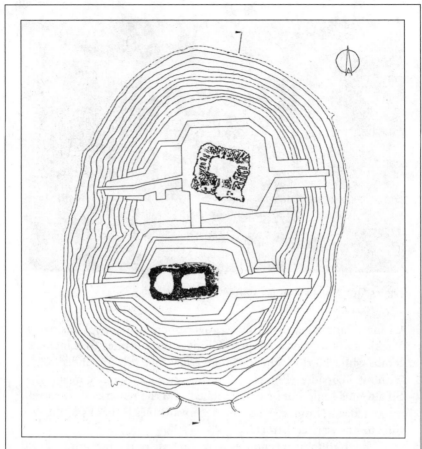

Figure G.3 Plan of Tomb 98. After Nelson 1993b

is Hwangnam Daechong, the largest tomb in Silla (Kim and Pearson 1977). The clarity comes from two circumstances: The male tomb is full of weapons and armor, and the female tomb has a rare inscription on the belt, "belt for milady." Thus there is no doubt which is the husband and which the wife. The male rated a rather unimpressive silver crown along with his enormous cache of weapons and a number of imports from the Mediterranean world. He was buried in the earlier south tomb and the queen in the later north one. Styles of artifacts in the queen's tomb suggest that she was buried many years after her husband. However, the queen wore the gold crown and gold belt of royalty (Nelson 1991b,

Figure G.4   Gyeongju tomb park. After Nelson 1993a

Figure G.5 The Heavenly Horse painted on birchbark, from the Jeonma Jeon. After Nelson 1993a

1993b, 2003b). It seems likely that she actually ruled for many years after the death of her husband. A computer study of the artifacts in the tomb found a cluster that implied greater status for women (Pearson et al. 1986), but the authors merely presented the data and did not arrive at the conclusion that queens were particularly important.

Although the archaeology is unequivocal in presenting us with a ruling queen, there is no such queen listed in either of the two histories of Korea—both written more than five hundred years after this queen died. Why is she omitted from the king list? I suggest it is because the authors of both books, *Samguk Sagi* and *Samguk Yusa,* were copying Chinese attitudes toward women and suppressed any queens they could under the name of their spouse. There were three ruling queens of Silla who are recorded in the texts, but they either had no husband, or a husband ineligible to rule, so they could not be suppressed in the narratives, as the earlier queens were.

Queens' names are included in the documents, as well as, often, the names of the queens' mothers and fathers. For this reason it is possible to construct a kinship chart of royalty. The first chart (Figure G.6)

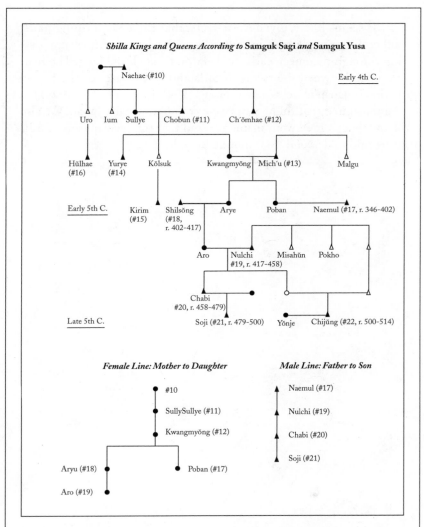

Figure G.6 Kinship chart of Silla royalty. From Nelson 1991b

shows all the relationships that can be extracted from the two texts.
The second chart takes only the queens, to show that the queens'
daughters were the next in line to rule—not the kings' sons. However,
there is a shift at King Naemul, when the rulership begins to pass
from father to son, as seen in the third kinship chart.

It seems likely, given these facts, that there were ruling pairs, rather than a single ruler, in early Silla, with heredity of rulership passing through the queen early on, later on through the king. The relationship between the rulers of Silla and early states of the Kofun period in Japan is well known (Hong 1994). Piggott (1997, 1999) has demonstrated that ruling pairs were common in early Japan. We also know that women were shamans—and that the early queens of Silla were said to descend from mountain goddesses.

EIGHT

SHAMANISM IN THE JAPANESE ISLANDS

The original religion of the Japanese was an unorganized worship of the deities and spirits, both of nature and of the dead.

—Anesaki 1980:11

The oldest shamanic figure of which we have any real record [in Japan] is the Shinto miko. This powerful sacral woman—the term 'female shaman' conveys only feebly the probable majesty of her presence—served in shrines throughout the land in the late prehistoric period as the mouthpiece for numina of certain kinds.

—Blacker 1975:104

THE WORLD of ancient Japan included many spirits as well as humans. Artifacts and burials from prehistoric sites, historic records, and presents studies of Shinto all reveal the beliefs in spirits and the rituals on their behalf. Less is known of the early religious specialists, but some indications are woven into the data.

199

Kami

Kami is the Japanese name for spirits. *Kami* appear in the founding myths of Japan and are worshipped in popular festivals at present. The *kami* are believed to reside in Shinto shrines and in nature, especially mountains and rivers. On the whole they are benevolent spirits. The most revered *kami* were the spirit ancestors of the royal family of Yamato. These included Amaterasu, the Sun Goddess, and her brother Susano-o-no-mikoto. There was also a Moon Goddess named Tsukiyomino-mikoto. The legend of the Sun Goddess describes a time when the sun (in the person of Amaterasu) hid from the world. A sacred mirror, hung outside her cave, lured her out of hiding. Mirrors are ceremonial objects in Japan even today and are related to the sun. The symbolic object in the center of many Shinto shrines is a mirror (Harris 2001:24). It is interesting that the disappearance of the sun would be part of an ancient Japanese myth—known and dated volcanic eruptions in Japan deposited thick layers of ash, which would have blotted out the sun for a considerable time.

Ancient written records in Japan date back to the eighth century. *Kojiki* was written in 712, and *Nihon Shoki* in 720. The Yamato kingdom was in the ascendancy when these histories were written, and they were intended to glorify the Yamato ancestors, giving the right to rule to their descendants. The two documents are similar but do not cover the same history exactly—nor do they totally agree. Both do mention shamans and shamanic events as well as supernatural occurrences.

Japanese Archaeology

Archaeology that indicates ritual activities is found in all time periods and throughout the islands of Japan. These include figurines, clay masks, stone rods, and astronomical alignments. Following the Paleolithic period, between the time when pottery appears and the onset of intensive agriculture, the sites are designated Jomon and divided into time periods according to the pottery chronology. The sites discussed are located on Figure 8.1.

Jomon

Jomon describes a long period when pottery was made and used but before intensive agriculture. It is divided into Incipient Jomon (14,500–10,000 BCE), Initial Jomon (10,000–6000 BCE), Early Jomon (6000–5000 BCE),

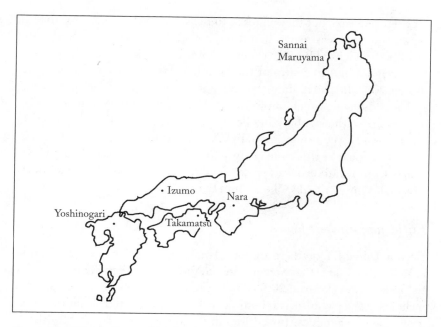

Figure 8.1 Sites in Japan. Map by Andrea Reider

Middle Jomon (5000–4000 BCE), Late Jomon (4000–3000 BCE) and Final Jomon (3000-800 BCE). The periodization was established on the basis of pottery typology, but the radiocarbon dates indicate some overlap of each of these periods (Ikawa-Smith 2000). Jomon is defined by the appearance of pottery, which includes significant ritual, but some ritual is implied even in the Late Paleolithic sites. As Ikawa-Smith (1999:262) emphasizes, there is not one Jomon culture, but a plethora of Jomon cultures that occur sometimes simultaneously in different parts of the archipelago. Jomon begins with the appearance of pottery, which now dates to about 14,500 BCE (calibrated) by AMS dating, and lasts until the beginning of the Yayoi period about 1000 BCE, by the latest reckoning (Ikawa-Smith 1999:82).

The site at which the earliest dated pottery has been found so far is Odai Yamamoto, in Aomori prefecture—far from the first early discoveries from the site of Fukui Cave in Kyushu. The potsherds were fragments of a single deep jar found beneath a sealed layer of volcanic ash, which is dated to 13,000 BCE. Food residues clinging to the sides of some sherds have not yet been analyzed, but they all reach to the same level, so it is clear that the contents were at least partly liquid and boiled. They have been AMS dated to 13,000, which calibrates to about 14,500 BCE (Ikawa-Smith 2002).

Nearly a hundred sites of the Incipient Jomon have been excavated (Kaner 2002:36). Sites show that the pottery was being made in sets even at that early stage, which implies a ritual use of the pottery. Kaner suggests that "some of the symbolizing behaviors associated with changes in the preparation and consumption of food" were already present. Figurines also begin to appear at this time (Ikawa-Smith 2002:333–34). Some incised stones from Kamikuroiwa appear to be representations of female torsos, which also imply ritual (Aikens and Higuchi 1982:107).

Initial and Earliest Jomon

Even in Initial Jomon there are some large sites in Kyushu with indications of sedentism. Plants that were possibly cultivated have been identified in Initial Jomon sites (Pearson 2007).These plants were probably not staples, but included useful plants such as bottle gourd and hemp, as well as various beans, grains, and vegetables. Initial Jomon is characterized by pottery that is increasingly decorated. It mostly consists of open-mouthed jars, which appear to have a communal dining function and perhaps were used for feasting.

Some crude plaques that seem to indicate females are found as early as Earliest Jomon. Female figurines are not found everywhere and not in all time periods, but at some sites more than a hundred of them are found (Nagamine 1986).

Early Jomon

Although pit dwellings are found in substantial villages by Early Jomon, they are often interpreted as nonagricultural settlements, either based on shellfish, fish, acorns, or wild animals—or some combination of these subsistence types. However, it is now known that plants were cultivated. Food plants included perilla, mung bean, and burdock. These were not staple foods, but they were important in the diet.

Personal adornments are widespread. Many take the form of pendants. Earrings shaped like flat split rings were found in Early Jomon burials in the southernmost island of Kyushu. These earrings are similar in shape to the earliest jade carving in northeastern China, from the Xinglongwa period in Inner Mongolia and on the Liaodong peninsula, but whether they represent any kind of interaction is unknown. However, since the Hongshan "pig-dragons" from Liaodong may have been derived from these types of earrings, it raises the question of whether the earrings in Japan might indicate leadership, and/or belong to those with particular relationships with spirits. Lacquer artifacts were also found in Early Jomon sites. Pearson (1992:85) suggests that "Jomon people expanded their spiritual world and adapted to their stable existence with elaborate rituals and magic." While the details of the rituals are beyond the reach of archaeology, it is clear that the Jomon people led a rich ceremonial life.

Middle Jomon

Some of the most striking artifacts in Middle Jomon are the pottery jars with elaborate decorations, especially around the rim (Figure 8.2). These jars are found in sites near a large river in central Japan. The most elaborate of the jars are known as flame pots and crown pots. The rims were extremely fragile, suggesting a thoroughly sedentary population. The very exuberance of the decoration implies ritual purposes, perhaps to call down spirits for a feast. Feasting seems likely, even for this nonagricultural society, for some large storehouses raised on stilts have been found in the same region where the flame pots are

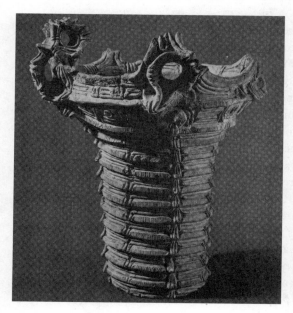

Figure 8.2 Flame design Jomon jar. After Kidder 1965

most prevalent (Kaner 2002:38). Large structures with six posts have been hypothesized to be related to calendrical reckoning (Pearson 2007).

The Middle Jomon is also known for the proliferation of female figurines, but they are not found throughout the Japanese islands. Their distribution is limited to the Kamegoaka culture in the far north of Honshu (see Case Study E). Some of the figurines indicate clothing, elaborate hairdos or headdresses, and painting or tattooing, especially on the face. The figures are rarely complete, and they seem to have been intentionally destroyed. They are often disposed of in what seem to be ritual contexts, such as burial in a pit.

It has been suggested that female skeletons with large numbers of shell bracelets might have been shamans. The bracelets are too small to slip over an adult hand, so they must have been put on children and never removed (Habu 2004). If the bracelets indicate shamans, then children were selected to serve the spirits while still quite young. Perhaps this is an indication that extensive training was involved.

Late and Final Jomon

Many artifacts suggest increasing rituals in Late and Final Jomon. These include stone rods and "swords" said to be phallic, figurines, stone circles, and clay masks.

Clay masks are centered in the Tohoku region. Kidder (1965:63) notes that the Ainu, a nonagricultural people who lived in Hokkaido in historic times, made masks for some of their "shaman-like rituals." The archaeological masks are clearly made to be worn, as they have holes on the sides to tie them on, and holes for eyes.

Personal ornaments include shell bracelets, which seem to belong only to the elite. Ear spools and beads are found in the site as well as in burials. From the large number of beads in various stages of manufacture, it is supposed that this was an area of bead production. During the Final Jomon there was an increase in the quantity and refinement of the finished product.

Communal rituals are implied by stone circles that are found in the Late and Final Jomon. As time went on, the circles became larger and more regular. Some of the ritual included burials, which occur within some of the circles. A vertical stone pillar, interpreted as phallic, may be placed in the center. Stone rods are also believed to imply phalli (Imamura 1996:130). Imamura (1996:116 ff) points out that ritual objects are so prevalent in

Late and Final Jomon that "some think this is indicative of a society ruled by rituals." Earthen burial enclosures have been unearthed in southern Hokkaido. The embankments around these cemeteries can be more than 5 meters high (Ikawa-Smith 1992). There are also rods—said to be phallic musical instruments—which are hollow, turtle-shaped objects, with holes. These also suggest some form of ritual.

Pearson (2007:368) illustrates a "grave of a shamaness" from the Late Jomon site of Karimba in Hokkaido. This shamaness appears to be wearing boots, a belt, a cap, a necklace, and armbands. In the grave are several combs, earrings, a shark's tooth, and additional jewelry, including beads and a curved jewel. Lacquer objects, which take time to make and require great skill, are found in a number of graves attributed to religious specialists (Pearson 2007:369).

Yayoi

The Yayoi period is defined as beginning when rice agriculture became established. Archaeological evidence includes widespread rice padis, wooden tools for cultivating and harvesting rice, and large villages near the rice fields. Imported Chinese and Korean objects also begin to appear, especially artifacts made of metal. Jar burials and polished stone knives are also found on both sides of the Tsushima strait. Barbara Seyock (2004) concludes that a common culture included both southern Korea and Kyushu. This perspective is supported by maps by Mizoguchi (2002) who shows similar fishing equipment in the southern peninsula and islands in the last millennium BCE, if not much earlier.

The Yayoi period contains both ceremonial pottery and increasing numbers of bronze objects. The pottery is similar to hard-fired gray-ware from the peninsula, but soon developed into local forms. Likewise, bronze mirrors, weapons, and bells began to be made in new types. The *dotaku* (bronze bells) are particularly distinctive. They are called bells for their shape, but they do not seem to have been used as musical instruments. They would have made a rattling sound rather than a clear bell tone (Aikens and Higuchi 1982:218). Molds of *dotaku* have been found, showing that they were locally made. They were not found in villages or in burials but in pits, sometimes several bells together. They were decorated with triangles and spirals, which, as noted earlier, may have had a magical or shamanistic meaning. Perhaps these bronze bells of the Yayoi period were related to shamanism (Imamura 1996:133).

One trait that is sometimes attributed to ritual and the marking of special people is tattooing. Figurines and masks sometimes show tattooing around the mouth, a style the Ainu were known to practice into the twentieth century. The Yayoi and Kofun periods in southern Japan were surely shamanistic. "North Kyushu, where the buried foreign articles are found, becomes the first major power center in Japan. It was at this time composed of what the Chinese called 'kingdoms,' a collection of tribal groups often led by a shaman who was, at least in many instances, a woman. The existence of the female mediums, it may be said in retrospect, paved the way of the general acceptance of Japan's supreme deity as a female personification of the Sun Goddess" (Piggott 1997:78).

The Tatetsuki burial mound, found in the Kibi region, is the largest Late Yayoi burial mound, and it is thought to be a stage leading to the construction of key-hole shaped tumuli from the Kofun period. The central mound had projections on two sides. It is 80 meters long and about 4 meters high, with a moat that adds about 20 meters to its length. Five megalithic granite stones weighing about two tons each stand 3 meters high on top of the mound, while the rest of the surface was covered with pebbles. Stone walls surround the entire construction. The leader or chief was buried in a central wooden burial chamber, with a thick layer of cinnabar on the bottom of the coffin. Other graves surrounded the central burial. Burial goods included an iron sword and a string of beads, including the curved jewel and twenty-seven cylindrical beads of jasper. A number of artifacts were found in a heap on top of the mound—including clay figurines, clay beads and clay-curved beads, nonutilitarian iron objects, and large ceremonial jars and stands, as well as bowls with pedestals. All objects appear to have been destroyed in a ceremonial fire. The excavators remark that, "it is quite likely that the Tatetsuki mound was dedicated to a chief, who . . . could direct communal labor to the construction of his/her own burial mound" (Kondo 1992:23).

Kofun Period

Kofun means old mounds, and some of the burial mounds of the Kofun period are immense. They are keyhole-shaped, with a round mound where the burial occurred and a flat area out front.

The fourth-century Chohoji-Minamibara tumulus is likewise of interest. It is a keyhole-shaped mound, with possible shamanistic contents, including six bronze mirrors, beads, weapons, and *haniwa* (Sasaki 1992).

The number of mirrors is particularly interesting, perhaps indicating a powerful shaman.

When it was excavated, the Fujinoki tomb from the sixth century caused a stir in both Korea and Japan. The stone sarcophagus lies inside a stone-lined passageway. The similarities of burial objects to those found in Silla tombs were noted avidly by the Korean press. An immense amount of horse trappings was of note, as well as armor and weapons (Kidder 1972:58). The excavation was closed without opening the sarcophagus.

Grave 3 in a cemetery at Yoshitake-Takagi contains many objects that originated on the Korean peninsula. They include a bronze mirror with geometric patterns, two bronze daggers, a bronze halberd, *gokoks*, and cylindrical bead. These objects are said the mark a "shamanistic leader" (Mizoguchi 2002:156).

Early Japanese History

Rulership in Japan seems to have been truly ungendered. Both kings and queens are recorded, often but not always as a ruling pair. Piggott (1999:17) emphasizes women as rulers: "Women ruled frequently in prehistoric, protohistoric, early historical Japan. In the years 592 to 770, women ruled during 97 of the 179 years, including six females who ruled alone." Piggott (1997:19) writes of "co-rulership . . . with a contrapuntal mutuality between sacral and administrative duties. In the fourth through sixth century, tomb mounds contain burials of dual-gender pairs" (Piggot 1997:22). Some female rulers were buried in their own mound—and these were just as splendid as those of male rulers. The Takematsuzuka tomb near Nara was also a sensation because of its wall paintings. A group of women in brightly colored gowns resemble paintings from Goguryeo tombs. The ritual precinct of Nara was itself the center of a state cult (Nauman 2000).

Pearson (1992:29) emphasizes that "Religion and ritual became important forces for the organization of the state and in the shaping of Japan." These rituals included sacred objects, music, and formalized movements. The fact that singing and dancing were an integral part of ritual is emphasized by the music recorded in the early texts. The legendary Empress Jingu is said to have "assumed the priestly duties herself, and had a koto player to accompany her in the acts." The *Nihon Shoki* relates that Silla sent eighty musicians to the funeral of Emperor Ingyo. They sang and danced as they played their string instruments. Flutes were mentioned in the literature by sixth century. These flutes were bamboo instrument with six holes. Blacker (1975:107) suggests that the bow could be used as a musical instrument because the sound of the bowstring was used to call the *kami*. The catalpa bow was one of the instruments used in sacred dances. Zither music could also summon and soothe the *kami* (Blacker 1975:109).

Shamanism in Present-Day Japan

Shrines

The notion of divine kingship in Japan is based in Shinto, meaning the way of the gods. Shinto shrines date back "at least to Yamato times when religious ideas were forced to serve political ends." Ono (1962) believes that Shinto evolved from shamanism, with both male and female mediums. A five-year project on Shinto and Japanese culture led by Tatsuo Kobayashi came to similar conclusions, based on a detailed study published in three large tomes (Ikawa-Smith, personal communication, 2007).

Shinto shrines preserve material objects, revering the ancient (Harris 2001:12). They also preserve ancient building styles. The shrines, though constructed of wood, are rebuilt every twenty years in precisely the same form, so they have not changed over the centuries.

Japanese shrines are entered by a sacred torii gate (Figure 8.3). The characters used to write the word *torii*, which means "bird perch." These birds were probably not ordinary birds but messengers from the gods. As Montonori Ono (1962:40) notes: "Shrines are served by priests. . . . In very primitive society . . . there were shamans, frequently women, who were thought to possess special occult power which enabled them, by observing the ritualistic requirements for purification, to achieve a position of prestige and respect in the community and to function as mediums for contact with the *kami*. These shamans performed many of the local rites."

Some *kami* are worshipped in shrines, while others are worshipped at annual festivals. Some are worshiped by individual families, some by clans, and some by the whole populace. While most *kami* inhabit shrines, many also inhabit mountains, rivers, springs, and other natural places. The *kami* worshiped at Mt. Fuji is the great grandmother of the first emperor (Ono 1962). The elements of worship at Shinto shrines include purification, offer-

Figure 8.3 Torii gate. Photo by H. S. Nelson

ing, prayer, and a symbolic feast. "There are some instances in ancient writing of white horses, white boar, and white chickens being presented to shrines" (Ono 1962).

The most famous and central Shinto shrine is the shrine of Ise, tended by a High Priestess (Figure 8.4). A princess chose the present location, where the sacred mirror given by the Sun Goddess Amaterasu is enshrined. The Izumo shrine—another important national shrine—is tended by a High Priest said to be descended from eighty-three generations in the same family.

Miko perform ceremonial dances for *kami* wearing a white kimono and a vermillion divided skirt. The miko's hair hangs down her back, tied with a vermillion ribbon. The miko also carries a small baton with bells— similar to objects used by *mudangs* of Korea. Music is made with drums, flutes, and bells.

Kami are worshiped by many kinds of ceremonies. The *kami* are clearly spirits—the Chinese character used for the generic term is pronounced "shen" in Chinese and "shin" in Korean, and means, directly, "spirit" (Ono 1962). The *kami* is also related to animism, a belief that all beings have spirits, including abstract ideas such as production, growth, and fertility. Wind and thunder can also be *kami*, which we have also seen in the Shang oracle

Figure 8.4 Ise shrine. Photo by H. S. Nelson

bone divinations. In addition, the sun, mountains, rivers, trees and rocks, and some animals can house *kami*.

Ancestral spirits are a special class of *kami*. They can be guardian spirits of the land, spirits of certain occupations or skills, or even individual people with special accomplishments.

Even with the presence of shrine priestesses and miko, women in present-day Japan are not allowed to participate in some shrine festivals. However, because some men dress as women for the ceremonies, Kato (1999:120) believes that in the past women did participate in the festivals. Some records that have been retained by families from the sixteenth century include women's names among the participants.

Ryukyu Islands

The Ryukyu islands have several forms of religious practitioners that are shaman-like, but not the same as those in the main islands of Japan. William Lebra (1964:79–85) studied the religious systems of Okinawa, with its hierarchy of hereditary princesses who have both village and national duties, and *yuta*, who perform shamanic functions. Chief priestesses of Okinawa are selected from a particular family. They play an active role in the affairs of state and officiated at national rites (Lebra 1964:111). It was important for the priestess to pray for both the health of the ruler and the prosperity of the country.

The shrine area where the princess stayed was for females only—especially the great room where the *kami* was enshrined, which was taboo to all males. An analogous event was held within villages, "where the senior female of a house performed all rituals on behalf of the family" (Lebra 1964:83).

Another group of women were called *yuta*, who were believed to have been selected by the *kami* because of their "preternatural powers of seeing, hearing, and possession" (Lebra 1964:79). The activities of the *yuta* include spirit possession, curing, exorcism, divination, and prayer. Lebra therefore found that shamanism in the Ryukyu islands was predominantly associated with women.

More than thirty years later, Arne Rokkum (1998) found that the system of ritual princesses was still strong on the islands. His research showed that there was a rule "about a gendered partnership and its reciprocities as relevant for government." The chief priestess and her brother were both involved in the rituals, as "a model relationship is the elementary expression of duality of a sibling pair as ruler of the islands" (Rokkum 1998:38).

Susan Sered's work shows that "Okinawan women are the acknowledged and respected leaders of the publicly supported and publicly funded indigenous religion in which both men and women participate" (Sered 1999:4). Their rituals—both public and private—include drums, dances, and songs. An appropriate segue into the next chapter is Sered's summary of women, religion, and leadership in Okinawa:

> Over the centuries, women's religious preeminence in Okinawa has endured through a range of political structures and political changes: decentralized villages, warring feudal chiefdoms, a centralized monarchy, occupation by a foreign power, and annexation by another foreign power. It has survived extensive culture contact with Buddhist, Shinto, and Christian missionaries. And it has coexisted with Chinese ancestor worship, American cinemas, and Japanese schools. . . . There does not seem to be one unique social or historical backdrop to women's religious leadership in Okinawa." (Sered 1999:5)

Unfortunately there is little to go on archaeologically. The only artifacts that suggest relationships with Japan and Korea are *magatama* found in ancient graves. However, Lebra (1964) notes that such beads are still worn by the village priestesses.

Conclusion

The presence of artifacts used by shamans, as well as textual references to shamans, make it clear that forms of shamanism were everywhere in the peninsula and islands. Differences abound, however. In Okinawa there are shamans who get in touch with sprits, as well as women priests who preside over family rituals. Princesses preside at national ceremonies. On the main islands of Japan, there are also different functionaries in the Shinto shrines, in village rituals, and in fortune telling. Korean shamans deal in issues of health and wealth, consulting the spirits about them. So it seems obvious that women are prominent as shamans and priests in both ancient and modern Korea and Japan.

HANIWA, JAPAN

Haniwa are baked cylinders of clay that were made to place around the outside of noble tombs of the Kofun period in Japan. The earliest examples of *haniwa* were simple, but they quickly evolved into representations of people and artifacts, presumably to be of use to the entombed person in the afterlife. They are fascinating because of the glimpse they afford of the lives of people in the Kofun period.

These figures depict people in various walks of life such as warriors, farmers, singers, and shamans. Other *haniwa* represent horses, boats, houses, dogs, and other objects. The horses wear saddles, stirrups, and other trappings that are similar to those of southern Korea (Figure H.1). The houses show a floor plan covered by an elaborate roof structure (Figure H.2). Granaries and palaces are also found.

Figure H.1 *Haniwa* horse. After Kidder 1965

Figure H.2 *Haniwa* house. After Kidder 1965

The *haniwa* showing shamans are particularly relevant. They are designated as shamans in every book that describes them. They are mostly women, wearing earrings, ankle rings, and necklaces ending in *magatama*. Face paint or perhaps tattooing is indicated on many of them (Kidder 1965:143). They sometimes hold a small bowl (Figure H.3) or wear a sword. Some wear a flat hat (it is sometimes

Figure H.3 *Haniwa* shaman. After Kidder 1965

called a hair-do, but the similarity to the hats on Korean *miruks* suggests that it is likely to be a hat) (Figure H.4). One shaman sits on a stool (Figure H.5). Another female shaman has a jinglebell mirror hanging from her waist and is covered with jewelry, including bracelets, necklaces, and anklets. She also sits on a chair decorated with incised triangles (Kidder 1965:159)

Figure H.4 *Haniwa* shaman. After Kidder 1965

Figure H.5 *Haniwa* shaman. After Kidder 1965

Haniwa instrument players include a drum beater, a woman holding an object similar to a castanet, and a seated figure playing the lyre. Jingle bells appear on shamans' hats, and jingle bell mirrors were used in shaman's ritual. Kidder also notes a *haniwa* of a male shaman with a peaked jingle-bell hat from Fukushima. Another "shaman-like person" wears a crown with serrated edge, and yet another wears a hat with high peak in front marked with triangles.

Besides the *haniwa* horses, small clay horses were sometimes deposited in wells. Horses of clay or iron are found in similar circumstances in the Silla kingdom. Many shrines have a small building housing a life-size model of a horse. But a few horses are found in Yayoi sites, so they are not new in the Kofun period, although they seem to be newly important in Kofun and appear in abundance.

NINE

RETYING THE KNOTS
Leadership, Ideology, Cultural Patterns, Gender, and Shamans in East Asia

A CLOSE LOOK at shamanism in East Asia suggests that some patterns of East Asian archaeology require additional explanation. Issues regarding the role of ideology in the development of leadership, the ways that cultural patterns change (or not) with movements of people and ideas, and assumptions about gender all are intertwined in the attempt to understand ancient East Asia. In this final chapter, I gather these threads into an interpretation of East Asia and shamanism. It is a long way from a finished textile, but some patterns are discernible. To help understand the patterns, I summarize changes in East Asia through time and follow this by a look at spatial relationships—the mosaic of East Asian cultures. Finally, leadership, gender, and shamanism are reexamined in the light of the previous chapters.

Time, Trends, and Gender

A brief recap of shamans as leaders in East Asia puts the gender issue in a larger perspective than simply noting that women leaders might have been obliterated by later historians who wanted to keep women "in their place." While Paleolithic evidence is sparse with regard to shamanism, there is no evidence that only males were leaders. Later periods show that East Asia always has been a mosaic of cultures, even though there are East Asian commonalities as well. For a return to the big picture, it is useful to have a time machine, as follows.

Paleolithic

As previously noted, there is little in East Asian Paleolithic discoveries that shine much light on gender, shamanism, or the development of leadership. But a few glimmers are worth mentioning because of their gender implications. A recently discovered Upper Paleolithic burial near Beijing is that of a woman wearing a necklace. The meaning of such a necklace, whether it indicated status or leadership or something else, can only be teased out within the context of many more discoveries. However, much later necklaces in East Asia, especially those with a curved jewel in the center, were found in rich burials and were presumably worn by leaders and/or by shamans. A male burial with such a necklace would be hailed as the burial of a tribal leader. Should the interpretation be different when it is a female burial?

The early pottery in East Asia—including Japan, northern and southern China, and the Russian Far East—would suggest women's work in many cultures. This is how it is interpreted at the site of Dolni Vestonice in the Czech Republic, which, although not in Asia, is a useful example because religion and ritual can be seen at the site in some detail based on several lines of archaeological evidence (Adovasio et al. 2007). This unusual burial, in which an adult female was weighted down with mammoth shoulder blades, holding bones of arctic fox in her hands, suggests that the woman buried here was a shaman. Her cheek bones indicate a bone disease that would have caused facial distortion. An asymmetrical carved face implies a withered side, and a nude female figurine also suggests a lopsided face. Thus, the two figurines can be conjectured to represent the woman in the burial. If she was a leader and a shaman, what rituals did she perform? The answer lies in a hut on the outskirts of the settlement, where a rudimentary oven and thousands of baked clay fragments of small figurines were found. The figurines were intentionally made to explode in the fire (Soffer 1994). This activity must have been a form of magic used against the frightening world of large beasts and cold weather. But the most interesting "magic" practices are the use of clay to make figurines—and the imprint of textiles left on the clay as it was fired. Thus a glimpse of Upper Paleolithic lives, with magic rituals and the earliest traces of weaving and pottery, suggests gendered tasks—one of which was creating magic.

The unclothed female figurines found at this site deserve comment as well. People may not have worn clothing in the warmth of their lodges. The nudity of Upper Paleolithic female figurines has been taken to indicate "fertility" or sexuality, but it is not necessarily the best interpretation (see Nelson 1990b for discussion and references). Moving closer to East Asia, the female figurines at Mal'ta in Siberia have also been interpreted as shamans (Chard 1974). These people lived in an even colder climate than that of Eastern Europe, and some of the figurines are depicted wearing tailored furs with hoods. The clothing may well have been the work of women, since work with skins is ethnographically known to be women's work around the world, especially in the circumpolar regions (Frink and Weedman 2005).

These examples suggest that women's work often involved transformations, and that such transformations were necessary for adaptation to the Late Pleistocene climate. If women were the inventors and creators of East Asia's clothing and containers to adapt to cold climates, why not also credit women with the invention of pottery, the amazing transformation of soft clay into waterproof and fireproof containers—a transformation that took place in East Asia, from the Russian Far East to southern China to Japan. Making pots could well have been perceived as a transformation with the help of the spirits of fire. Other transformations, such as raw vegetables to edible food, fiber to twine, and osiers to baskets—and later, silk worm cocoons to silk fabric—were also women's work in East Asia. These transformations may have been equally believed to require unseen spirits to help with the processing. The early pottery along the Amur River in Siberia, created at the Pleistocene/Holocene boundary, may be a response to better weather and new kinds of foods to process. In addition, it suggests extra work in processing food and increasing use of vegetables that need to be cooked to become digestible for humans. These transformations may have been an important step in the division of labor by gender because they are time-consuming activities and required specialized knowledge. If the processes were believed to be aided by spirits, why would women involved in these processes not be shamans?

Another possible insight into East Asian adaptations is archaeology in the Arctic, which is beginning to reveal prehistoric women shamans in both Alaska and Siberia. Due to the excellent preservation of perishables in permafrost, the data are easier to interpret than sites limited to stone, bone, shell, and clay. Fitzhugh and Crowell (1988) describe the tomb of a shaman in Siberia dating between 1700 and 1300 BCE, one in which a young woman wears anthropomorphic figures made of mammoth bone attached to her apron. In Chukotka, near the Bering Strait, an older woman shaman was unearthed. She was interred in an elaborate tomb made of stone, wood, and whalebone, and she was accompanied by many artifacts used by women in daily life—as well as objects related to healing and dancing. The woman's face was covered by a death mask, a trait found in some ethnic groups in northeastern China, probably Tungus people. In the Sakha republic of northeastern Siberia, there are bone ornaments of bird-headed persons, like those on local shaman's drums. Thus, these examples show that shamans are found throughout the ancient Arctic—and many of them are women.

Neolithic

The distribution of artifacts in male and female graves suggests to many Chinese archaeologists that the division of labor by gender began as early as the sixth millennium BCE. Indeed, if those who attribute the invention of pottery, weaving, and tailoring to women are correct, the gendered division of labor arose even earlier. Evidence for males as planters and women as textile creators and food processors is said to be present in the Peiligang culture of north central Henan province, where grinding equipment is "never in the same grave with stone axes, sickles, or spades" (Zhang 2005). Spindle whorls and needles were placed only in female burials, thus documenting the processing of food and creation of clothing as women's transformations. Of course it is important to be reserved with such attributions—the division of labor by gender is rarely absolute—but the artifacts may mark a general trend. If these burials indicate a gendered division of labor, then it becomes possible to interpret the bone needles in jade turtle-shaped boxes at Jiahu as belonging to women shamans. Thus women shamans had costly artifacts and elite status—suggesting leadership.

The social structure of Neolithic China as it might be reflected in burials has been widely discussed. One particularly intriguing idea is that cultural elements from the Shandong region were introduced into the Central Plains in the Late Neolithic by females, understood as wives who had come from Dawenkou sites to Dahecun, a site near Zhengzhou (Shao 2005). Female burials include eastern pottery shapes such as *ding* cooking vessels and *dou* serving platters. This suggests that women as marriage partners were cementing the links between regions much earlier than the Shang and Zhou periods.

At Sanlihe, not only gender but age differentiation is evident. Elderly women were given special burial treatment, including thin pottery vessels, jade, and turquoise (Underhill 2002:192). One interpretation could be based on rank: these women lived to old age because they were privileged with enough food and perhaps servants to wait on them throughout their lives. Another interpretation could be based on gendered health: those who managed to live to a great age implied greater wisdom, which afforded them status. A third possibility is that these women were shamans and/or leaders. In any case, the privilege is marked both by gender and age. Old men are not given the same treatment in death at this site.

Another example of Late Neolithic gender distinction occurs in the placement of the bodies by sex at Dadianzi, Inner Mongolia, about 1600 BCE. Women were buried facing east, away from the site, while men faced toward the site. This form of placement is not a status marker. Burials of women and men displayed ranking in the depth of burials and the amount and kind of burial goods. It is possible that the direction of the body indicated that women married into the village from elsewhere. Of the bodies that were preserved well enough to be sexed, the number of males (297) and females (286) is approximately the same. Slightly more women than men reached old age, which suggests equal nutrition and equal hardships (or lack of them) (Wu 2004).

At sites of the Xinglongwa culture, crude female statues less than a meter high foreshadow both the life-sized statue of the Goddess Temple at Niuheliang and the smaller figures at the ritual site of Dongshanzui. Whether spirits of ancestors or spirits of nature, these statues were gendered female. Glimpses of other woman-centered cultures in Northeastern China occur between the time of Xinglongwa and Hongshan. At the site of Xinle in Shenyang, Liaoning province, a wooden staff with a complicated bird design was preserved. It was found in the larger of two Early Neolithic houses at the site and was interpreted as the symbol of leadership of the woman who lived in the larger house. While fanciful, this is an interesting interpretation of a unique discovery. The Early Neolithic site of Chahai, also in Liaoning province, produced the longest dragon sculpture so far found in China. It is likely to be associated with rain, possibly the activities of women shamans who were so closely associated with attracting rain in later cultures.

Xia and Shang

A fascinating example of a royal woman who served the spirits, in addition to many other activities, is Lady Hao, one of Wu Ding's wives (see Case Study D). Everyone who encounters her, either in the oracle bone inscriptions or in the splendor of her burial offerings, is impressed with her accomplishments. Keightley (1999c:25) summarized what Lady Hao's life indicates for elite women of her time:

> Inscriptions and archaeological finds, such as the richly furnished tomb of the royal consort Fu [Lady] Hao . . . show that women wielded considerable power in the Shang—some of them even commanded armies. They may also have influenced the succession. In general, the throne passed from brother to brother, but at certain points it shifted to the next generation, at times that may have been determined by the status of the candidates' mother. This may have occurred when the king's wife was deemed of higher status than the next brother (the heir), in which case the succession would pass to her son by the king. The succeeding Zhou state used primogeniture and denied such importance to women—Zhou propaganda denounced the Shang kings for being female-dominated.

The possible influences of elder women did not escape Keightley's (1999c:31) attention, as well as the potential power of wives who brought their own entourage to the Shang court. He also notes an unenviable selection of males over females in royal graves—that of sacrificial victim. The preponderance of male sacrifices even extended to female graves. Human victims were buried on ramps or pits in large number in royal burials, but even nonroyal graves could include human sacrifice. An exception to the preponderance of male sacrifices is M1, a nonroyal burial at Wuguancun in Anyang in which the ratio was twenty-four women to seventeen men. Some of the sacrificed victims were accompanied by grave goods of their own. Many of the men were buried in wooden coffins, and five who occupied the eastern ledge of the main tomb were accompanied by bronze vessels and jades. The male and female at the center of each ledge had the largest coffins and the largest numbers of grave goods. Presumably some human sacrifices constituted an honor of sorts.

Shang oracle bones have preserved the names of three women shamans. They were Lady Yang, Lady Fang, and Lady Fan. Later legends memorialized two of them as Wu (Shaman) Yang and Wu Fan, but little is known of their actual lives, and their tombs have not been discovered.

Warring States and Later

It is said that after the Zhou dynasty, the female shamans—with a few striking exceptions—were forced to go underground with their spirit contacts. But considerable evidence shows that in some of the states of the Late Eastern Zhou, the art of shamanism was alive and well. One was the state of Chu, which is generally agreed to have included practicing shamans, both women and men. Shamans, leaders, and gods could all be female in this environment, a situation that may have been shocking to Confucianists, but the tradition persisted.

Women's influence and even power remained in China throughout the dynasties. The many rules attributed to minor males, whose mothers were the de facto rulers, are examples. And women continued to be knowledgeable about many things. Superstitious rulers turned to women to tell the future—for example female astrologers in the court of the second emperor of Later Chao (AD 334–349) (Paper 1995:fn20). In order to end a drought in AD 773, the mayor of the capital city constructed an earthen dragon and personally performed a contradance with the *wuxi*, female and male shamans. Not only did the famous Empress Wu rule over the brilliant Tang dynasty of the eighth and ninth centuries, but a woman of the Jin dynasty (1115–1234) ruled seven hundred tribes in Manchuria state and was both a shaman and a famous khan. She developed trade routes across the Sea of Japan, Kamchatka, and the Aleutians.

Korean Peninsula

The presence of women as shamans is undisputable in Korea from early historic periods until the present. At least one queen of the Silla "kingdom" is known to have been buried with the trappings of leadership, including a crown with shamanistic symbols (see Case Study G). Women continued to share in inheritance and have their say in the family through the Koryo dynasty. It was only with the Yi dynasty—which banished Buddhism from the cities and adopted Confucian principles—that women began to lose status in Korea (Deuchler 1992). Female shamans appear regularly in the histories of the dynasties up to the Yi dynasty (1392 to 1910) (Kim Chong-Sun 1977). Current Korean shamans are colorful and forceful. They may be considered lower class, but most make a good living and have autonomy. And these shamans have access to people and ideas that few lower class men are likely to have.

Japanese Islands

On the main islands of Japan, ritual is evident as early as 13,000 BCE. Increasingly complex objects with likely ritual uses, such as artifacts made of lacquer and pottery, are found throughout the Jomon period (Pearson 2007). Women shamans were noted as leaders by Chinese visitors during the Yayoi period and appear in the early histories. The Kofun period included reigning queens as well as kings. Women could be ruling queens or rule in conjunction with a brother or husband. During the Kofun period women leaders are ubiquitous.

Women were and still are ritual and secular leaders in Okinawa. Their system has remained in spite of invaders, trade, and other religious systems. The sturdiness of the belief system on the island should be admired.

Context and the Cultural Mosaic of East Asia

Although nearly all scholars acknowledge that East Asia was (and is) a mosaic of cultures that relocated and changed through time, there is a tendency to use the current nationalist boundaries of nation-states when discussing archaeology, especially in East Asia. This practice subtly distorts the appreciation of similarities, as well as differences across modern borders. This is not new insight. Waley (1955) wrote of the six different ethnic groups of ancient China. Regionalism was noted in the only previous book which synthesizes East Asian archaeology (Barnes 1993). William Watson (1991) noted differences in burial orientations, stone tool shapes, and other traits, especially between eastern groups and those along the Yellow River. Increasingly, the variety of cultures within and across nations of East Asia is specifically mentioned. Chang (1986) produced a map with circles around the regional Neolithic cultures, with arrows between them to show influences of various kinds. Underhill and Habu (2005:121) discuss regional variation in the archaeology in both China and Japan. Allan (2007) notes that regional cultures in the Shang period differed locally but were unified by the beliefs of the elite. Falkenhausen (2006:20) likewise acknowledges considerable variation in China in the Age of Confucius, while he perceives lineages as creating social cohesion.

The point is not merely that diversity existed. The diversity revealed by archaeological sites calls for an explanation. Often that explanation is related to class differentiation. Allan (2007) suggests that the common culture of the Shang, seen in religious practices, is that of the elite, while the nonelite had different practices. Liu (2003) describes and discusses the Neolithic in China and finds that the elite may have developed from artisans in materials with spiritual value, and that trade throughout the region could have solidified the value of particular objects and materials. Falkenhausen (2006) makes a similar point about the social system of the Zhou. His view is that the lineage and clan system serve the elite, and because of clan exogamy the elite are tied together beyond political divisions. Daughters and wives are the social glue that keeps the system functioning. But these analyses show that it is not gender that creates the cultural mosaic or differentiates status—it is class. Thus, in various ways, the elite culture ties diverse peoples together through shared beliefs, trade, and intermarriage of the ruling elite.

The archaeological data to study shamanism mostly is found in elite graves, and contemporary texts—those written on oracle bones and bronze—are by and for the rulers. We know far less about the daily lives of farmers and weavers. Especially with the intermittent and haphazard nature of archaeological discoveries, and the biases of texts, there is value in examining the individual strands of the historical knot or the larger patterns. In the case of China, ranked lineages are highly relevant, while gender is less so. In Korea and Japan, women were more likely to be religious leaders than men were. Archaeologically, a similar diversity can be observed in the Neolithic. Sites said to be shamanistic lack any discernible pattern. This is especially noticeable when discoveries interpreted as shamans are examined. The spectacular Puyang burial, with its tiger and dragon made of shells, is unique. So are burials at Taosi—one medium-sized with a copper bell at the waist, and another elite burial containing musical instruments and fine pottery. Jade turtle shells and real turtle shells, one containing a jade plaque, are also not widely found. It would seem necessary to be cautious about generalizing each bit of possible shamanism to all of East Asia. Cultural differences among regions seem to be the rule—as seen in pottery styles, burial complexes, and so on—and this observation extends to evidence of shamanism as well.

Is shamanism part of the cultural mosaic? While shamanism is marked by colorful artifacts and unusual patterns, the interpretation of archaeological discoveries as evidence of shamanism is often uncritical. The data gathered together here suggest that forms of shamanism have existed through time in East Asia, but the particulars differ by both time and place. Belief in a world of spirits and the ability of humans to manipulate the spirits was widespread. It is the thread upon which East Asian shamanisms hang, but each region seems to have maintained its own paraphernalia of shamanism and its own rituals. Shamanisms are not static, but have been modified—and even have disappeared (and perhaps reappeared) in some areas.

The data are not conclusive in terms of leadership deriving from shamans—many shamans practiced in East Asia, but there is no reason to believe that shamanism drove all East Asian cultures. Animism was prevalent throughout ancient East Asia, but only sometimes did the belief in spirits allow shamans to become leaders of larger polities. This pattern occurred in several places, but was not ubiquitous.

But East Asia also has a larger context. It did not develop without outside contact through Central Asia, and probably other directions as well, as has been seen in chapter 5. It is clear that influences from the west began as early as the Middle Neolithic, if not before. Neolithic evidence points to two avenues of contact. One is a northern corridor, through the grasslands of Central Asia. The other, well known from later times, is the famed Silk Road, around the Taklamakan basin and through the Gansu corridor.

The Qijia culture of Gansu province shows multiple borrowings from the west, including horses and donkeys (Fitzgerald-Huber 1995:38). Metal objects are also earlier in Inner Mongolia and the Gansu corridor than in the rest of China. Piggott (1996:90) reports that iron is found in western China by the tenth century BCE, and the presence of Caucasian mummies at that time is established. Scapulimancy is found earliest in these regions as well. Mirrors also are derived from the west (Juliano 1985; Linduff 1996, 1997; Rubinson 1985, 2002) sometimes with magical and shamanistic meanings (Davis-Kimball 2002). Recall that Lady Hao of the Shang had mirrors in her grave, along with jades that could have been used in shamanistic rites. She is mentioned in the oracle bones as one who prepares the bones for use, and to judge from her burial goods, she certainly was well regarded.

The northern corridor was in use at the dawn of the Bronze Age, if not well before. Horses are found in the Longshan culture in Shandong, along with early writing. Horses were also present in Inner Mongolia and Liaoning province earlier than they appear in the Yellow River basin. Realistic, life-sized statues found at Niuheliang appear without local precedent and have no counterpart in China. These objects and ideas influenced the rest of China gradually. Some of these are found in the territory of the Dongyi, the Eastern Barbarians described in ancient Chinese texts (Keightley 1986).

Shamans were typical of Yue coastal culture of the north. Chinese recorded the Yueshi as barbarians (Cohen 2001), but the Yueshi nevertheless influenced the culture of the plains and may have been more "cultured" than the central groups (Keightley 1986). The question of whether the Shang were related to the Yueshi was cogently discussed by David Cohen and deserves further study as more sites are excavated. Keightley (1986), comparing both archaeology and texts, came to the conclusion that a relationship between Shang and the Yueshi was likely. There are strong advocates for the connections between Shang and Chu. This scenario would suggest a heritage of shamanism from the east coast Shandong area, derived ultimately from Inner Mongolia and Liaoning. The connection among Dadianzi, Yueshi, and Erlitou includes similar painted designs (Fitzgerald-Huber 1995:22). The Shang themselves may have been related to the Dong Yi, but another way to understand the sudden appearance of horse-drawn chariots along with writing on oracle bones at the time of King Wu Ding is to attribute the horses and religious writing to one of Wu Ding's wives from far away. The most likely candidate is Lady Hao, whose burial includes Northern Bronzes. This is an ancient debate that will continue, but it is important in thinking about the Shang as shaman leaders. Perhaps King Wu Ding did not have shamanism in his tradition—but Lady Hao did.

Influences from the west (and vice versa) continued through time. By the Zhou dynasty, influences from the west are more obvious than those from the east, but of course the Zhou themselves first appear in the western side of the Central Plain. Especially in Late Zhou, the Warring States period, variability in the states was visible in their artifacts. The Zhongshan state, with its shamanistic symbolism, can be seen to have a number of stylistic patterns related to the "steppe silk road" (Wu 2004:7). While this is far from the beginning of the use of the steppe corridor as cultural exchange and trade, it indicates increased activity and interaction during the Warring States period. This trade could explain all the traits of shamanism in the

Late Shang that are discussed by Chang and others, without implicating Wu Ding himself as a shaman.

In Korea and Japan, successors of early shamans built upon the leadership of small polities to become leaders of larger polities and eventually states, with the power to conduct long-distance trade, organize artisans, garner the most costly and desirable possessions, wage war, and claim additional political and economic powers. Shamans were able to accomplish the integration of larger polities by basing the right to rulership on a claim of access to several kinds of spirits—especially ancestors and nature powers, whose benevolence was believed to be required for human life and society to continue and prosper. Furthermore, those endowed with the knowledge and ability to reach the spirits were credited with the ability to affect the future. They accomplished this feat by discovering the intent of the spirits through séance and divination, as well as making the proper sacrifices to produce the desired outcome. The well being of the community—and eventually the continuation of the state itself—depended on the knowledge of shaman leaders.

This stage of shaman rulers was followed by the bureaucratization of ritual; but even under that circumstance shamans continued to perform important activities for society and to hold the popular imagination. The Zhou dynasty created rules for shamanic events and put the *wu* in charge of ceremonies. But in spite of attempts by bureaucratic states to suppress shamanism by incorporating and taming it, forms of shamanism have survived in Korea (Howard 1998b; Kendall 1985), Taiwan (Rudolf 2006), central Japan (Blacker 1975), and Okinawa (Lebra 1964; Rokkum 1998, 2006; Sered 1999). The "non-Chinese" rulers of the Chu state in the late Warring States period continued to function as shamans (Cook and Major 1999), and folk religions in China often retain shamanistic elements (Paper 1995:140). Both elite and popular religion found the ecstatic experience important (Paper 1995:81), perhaps as evidence of the ability to contact the multiple dangerous powers. Even Daoism in China, which often seems staid and more philosophical than religious, has permitted some shamanistic branches (Ching 1997:xiv; Major 1999:138). Shamanism has remained potent in many East Asian states.

Other Gender Issues

Female Deities

Peggy Sanday (1977) argues that origin myths and deities describe the gender template of a culture. In this light, it is interesting to consider the female deities of East Asia. Some Chinese deities are not anthropomorphized, especially those of the sky, but East Asian deities that are specifically female are particularly worshipped (Stutley 2002:13). Humphrey and Onon (1996) describe shrines with female figures in them among the Daur of Manchuria. In Central Asia, where shamanism may have first been practiced, it seems that belief in a female divinity was commonplace, as well as a god of the sky. We are told that this deity was beloved and benign. Images of these deities could still be found in shrines in Manchuria into the twentieth century at least (Humphrey and Onon 1996). Even when the Manchu ruled China as the Qing dynasty, the culture retained some of its matrifocal aspects (Paper 1995:234). In Korea, pairs of village guardians made of wood or stone were inscribed "Earth Grandmother" and "Sky Grandfather," and both are necessary for protection from wandering spirits.

Although the earliest evidence of the goddess Nuwa in art and literature is found in the Chu and Han periods, she was attributed to much earlier times. We have seen that as a Creator, she amassed the earth, created heaven, and patched the sky. Chen Meng-jia, who was the first to point out female aspects in early China, believed that Nuwa was a deified shamaness, one who possibly could be identified with a woman called E on the oracle bones (Paper 1995:156).

A mountain known as Wu Shan, Shaman Mountain, was ruled by a goddess who controlled the rain. In one tradition this goddess was the daughter of the Fire God, Yan Di (Paper 1995:142). Paper suggests that Wu Shan was named for the shamanesses who practiced there and was also identified with the goddess. Schafer (1973) finds evidence from Tang dynasty poetry of early goddesses worshipped in China.

Present-Day Shamanism in East Asia

As has been demonstrated in chapters 7 and 8, present-day shamans in East Asia are preponderantly women. Shamanism exists in South Korea alongside Christianity and Buddhism and the Confucian tendencies of the elite. Nevertheless, the *mudang* continue to flourish, patronized by businessmen and housewives. The blessings from the spirits they can reach are valued highly (Kendall 1996).

Likewise, the shrine princesses of Okinawa have maintained their position in society, despite foreign influences of many kinds—and the senior woman in each lineage is the spiritual leader. While Shinto in Japan has the status of being a state-sponsored religion, it nevertheless could have disappeared under a number of imported beliefs—Buddhism, Confucianism, and Christianity. Instead, Shinto worships the Sun Goddess as the principal divinity and features shrine princesses—and even the *miko* dance at the shrine with their hair awhirl. The belief that women have better access to the spirit world therefore is strong. It seems that the farther from China, the more the ancient female shamanism flourishes still.

Conclusion

The problem that this exploration of shamanism in ancient East Asia intended to solve was whether leadership of larger units could and did develop from shamanism. The archaeological—and to some extent textual—data from East Asia show that in some cases leadership could and did arise from shamanism. Shamans were leaders—and as polities grew, shamans used their ability to reach spirits to gain credibility for mobilizing people on behalf of the polity in various ways.

But the question of shamanism is closely tied to the question of gender. The stature of women in the Ryukyu islands, their continuation in local and larger governments, and their perceived efficacy in reaching nonhuman powers is notable. It is likely that the Okinawan culture shows the most continuity with the shamanism of the past. The power of women has persisted there despite a variety of outside influences. The persistence suggests that the system works well for its participants. Okinawa can also be seen as a model for including shamanism and a balance between men and women, rather than a relationship of dominance.

Women in Japan and Korea seem to be unequal to men in the present, although women as spiritual leaders still exist in both regions. However, it seems clear that women were known to have been leaders in the formation of the state in both Korea and Japan. These developing states were probably offshoots of Tungus shamanism, or at least influenced by it. Later Manchu shamanism featured women, and with the advent of the Qing dynasty, the Manchu never quite assimilated to Chinese culture. For example, Manchu women never did bind their feet, but they wore a kind of clog shoe that simulated the walk of bound feet. The Mongols, who also ruled China as the Yuan dynasty and extracted tribute from Korea had shamans who were sometimes leaders and sometimes advisors to leaders. In fact, Mongol *katuns*—queens—sometimes ruled vast territories (Davis-Kimball 2003).

The only conclusion that can be drawn from these findings is that shamans were indeed leaders in many parts of East Asia while states were being formed. At that time, women were often shamans—and they were often leaders. Men may have achieved and maintained control in China through the simple device of the lineage system (Falkenhausen 2006), which, being patrilineal, crowded women out of legitimate power in human affairs. In China, ancestor worship replaced shamanism as the spiritual center of the culture, transferring power to the male lineage. Perhaps lineages eventually deprived women of power even in the world of the spirits in central China. But elsewhere in East Asia, women retained their connections with the spirits—and with power.

References

Adovasio, J. M., Olga Soffer, and Jake Page
    2007 *The Invisible Sex: Uncovering the True Roles of Women in Prehistory.*
        New York: Harper Collins Publishers, Inc.
Aikens, C. Melvin, and Takayasu Higuchi
    1982 *Prehistory of Japan.* New York: Academic Press.
Aikens, C. Melvin, and Irina Zhuschchikovskaya
    In press Korea to California: Millennial Continuities between Asia and
        America along the North Pacific Coast. *Asian Perspectives.*
Aldhouse-Green, Miranda, and Stephen Aldhouse-Green
    2005 *The Quest for the Shaman.* London: Thames & Hudson.
Allan, Sarah
    1991 *The Shape of the Turtle: Art and Cosmos in Early China.* Albany:
        SUNY Press.
    1993 Art and Meaning. In *The Problem of Meaning in Early Chinese Ritual
        Bronzes.* Edited by R. Whitfield. Pp.9–33. London: School of
        Oriental and African Studies.
    1997 *The Way of Water and Sprouts of Virtue.* Albany: SUNY Press.
    1999 Chinese Bronzes through Western Eyes. In *Exploring China's Past.*
        Edited by Roderick Whitfield and Wang Tao. Pp. 63–76. Lon-
        don: Saffron.

2007 Erlitou and the Formation of Chinese Civilization: Toward a New Paradigm. *Journal of Asian Studies* 66:461–96.

Allard, Francis, and Diimaajav Erdenbaatar
2005 Khirigsuurs, Ritual and Mobility in the Bronze Age of Mongolia. *Antiquity* 79:547–63.

Ames, Roger T.
1983 *The Art of Rulership.* Honolulu: University of Hawaii Press.

An Ho-sang
1974 *The Ancient History of the Korean Dong-I Race.* Seoul: Institute of Baedal Culture.

Andaya, Barbara W. (editor).
2000 *Other Pasts: Women, Gender, and History in Early Modern Southeast Asia.* Honolulu: Center for Southeast Asian Studies, University of Hawaii.

Anesaki, Masaharu
1980 *History of Japanese Religion.* Tokyo: Charles E. Tuttle.

Arwill-Nordbladh, Elisabeth
2003 A Reigning Queen, or the Wife of a King—Only? Gender Politics in the Scandinavian Viking Age. In *Ancient Queens, Archaeological Explorations.* Edited by S. M. Nelson. Pp.19–40. Walnut Creek: AltaMira Press.

Atkinson, Jane Monig
1992 Shamanisms Today. *Annual Review of Anthropology* 21:307–30.

Bagley, Robert
1980 The Beginnings of the Bronze Age: The Erlitou Culture Period. In *The Great Bronze Age of China.* Edited by J. Rawson. Pp 69–73. New York: The Metropolitan Museum of Art.
1999 The Archaeology of the Shang Dynasty. In *The Cambridge History of Ancient China.* Edited by M. Loewe and E. L. Shaughnessy. Pp. 124–231. Cambridge: Cambridge University Press.

Bagley, Robert (editor).
2001 *Ancient Sichuan: Treasures from a Lost Civilization.* Princeton: Princeton University Press.

Baines, John, and Norman Yoffee
1998 Order, Legitimacy and Wealth, Setting the Terms. In *Order, Legitimacy and Wealth in Ancient States.* Edited by J. Richards and M. Van Buren. Pp. 13–17. Cambridge: Cambridge University Press.

Balzer, Marjorie Mandelstam (editor)
1990 *Shamanism: Soviet Studies of Traditional Religion in Siberia and Central Asia.* London: M.E. Sharpe.

1997 *Shamanic Worlds, Ritual and Lore of Siberia and Central Asia.* London: North Castle Books.

Barnes, Gina L.
  1988 *Prehistoric Yamato.* Ann Arbor: The University of Michigan, Center for Japanese Studies.
  1993 *China, Korea and Japan, The Rise of Civilization in East Asia.* London: Thames and Hudson.
  2007 *Women in the Nihon Shoki: Mates, Mothers, Mystics, Militarists, Maids, Manufacturers, Monarchs, Messengers and Managers.* Durham East Asian Papers 20. Durham: Department of East Asian Studies, Durham University.

Barnes, Gina L., and Guo Dashun
  1996 The Ritual Landscape of 'Boar Mountain Basin': The Niuheliang Site Complex in Northeast China. *World Archaeology* 28(2):209–19.

Bartz, Patricia M.
  1972 *South Korea.* Oxford: Clavendon Press.

Basilov, Vladimir N.
  1997 Chosen by the Spirits. In *Shamanic Worlds, Ritual and Lore of Siberia and Central Asia.* Edited by M. Balzer. Pp. 3–48. London: North Castle Books.

Bell, Karen
  2003 Ancient Queens of the Valley of Mexico. In *Ancient Queens.* Edited by S. M. Nelson. Pp. 137–50. Walnut Creek: AltaMira Press.

Best, Jonathan
  2006 *A History of the Early Korean Kingdom of Paekche.* Cambridge: Harvard University Asia Center.

Blacker, Carmen
  1975 *The Catalpa Bow: A Study of Shamanistic Practices in Japan.* London: George Allen & Unwin Ltd.

Blakeley, Barry B.
  1999 The Geography of Chu. In *Defining Chu, Image and Reality in Ancient China.* Edited by C.A. Cook and J. S. Major. Pp. 9–20. Honolulu: University of Hawaii Press.

Blanton, R. E., G. M. Feinman, S. A. Kowalewski, and P. N. Peregrine
  1996 A Dual Processual Theory for the Evolution of Mesoamerican Cultures. *Journal of Field Archaeology* 6:369–90.

Boltz, William
  1986 Early Chinese Writing. *World Archaeology* 17(3):420–36.
  1999 Language and Writing. In *The Cambridge History of Ancient China.* Edited by M. Loewe and E. L. Shaughnessy. Pp. 74–127. Cambridge: Cambridge University Press.

Bowers, Robert D., Robert H. Tykot, Rheta Lanehart, Anne P. Underhill, Feng-shi Luan, and Hui Fang.
2006 Phytolith Analysis of Pottery from Liangchenzhen, Shandong Province, China. Poster at Society for American Aechaeology Annual Meeting, Puerto Rico.
Bray, Tamara L. (editor)
2003 *The Archaeology and Politics of Food and Feasting in Early States and Empires.* New York: Kluwer Academic/Plenum Publishers.
Bronson, Bennett
2000 Order, Legitimacy and Wealth in Ancient China. In *Order, Legitimacy and Wealth in Ancient States.* Edited by J. Richards and M. Van Buren. Pp. 120–27. Cambridge: Cambridge University Press.
Bunker, Emma C.
1997 *Ancient Bronzes of the Eastern Eurasian Steppes.* New York: Harry N. Abrams, Inc.
Chang, K. C.
1980 *Shang Civilization.* New Haven: Yale University Press.
1983 *Art, Myth and Ritual: The Path to Political Authority in Ancient China.* Cambridge, MA: Harvard University Press.
1986a *Studies in Shang Archaeology.* New Haven: Yale University Press.
1986b *The Archaeology of Ancient China*, 4th edition. New Haven: Yale University Press.
1989 Ancient China and Its Anthropological Significance. In *Archaeological Thought in America.* Edited by C.C. Lamberg-Karlovsky. Pp. 155–66. Cambridge: Cambridge University Press.
1994a Ritual and Power. In *Cradles of Civilization: China.* Edited by R. E. Murowchick. Pp. 60–69. Norman: University of Oklahoma Press.
1994b Shang Shamans. In *The Power of Culture.* Edited by W.J. Peterson, A.H. Plaks, and Y. Yu. Pp. 10–36. Hong Kong: Chinese University Press.
1999 China on the Eve of the Historical Period. In *The Cambridge History of Ancient China.* Edited by M. Loewe and E. L. Shaughnessy. Pp. 37–73. Cambridge: Cambridge University Press.
2005 The Rise of Kings and the Formation of City-States. In *The Formation of Chinese Civilization; An Archaeological Perspective.* Edited by K. C. Chang and P. Xu. Pp. 125–40. New Haven: Yale University Press.
Chang, K. C., and P. Xu (editors)
2005 *Formation of Chinese Civilization.* New Haven, Yale University Press.

Chard, Chester
    1974 *Northeast Asia in Prehistory*. Madison: The University of Wisconsin Press.
Chatley, Herbert
    1938 Ancient Chinese Astronomy. *The Asiatic Review* 34:140–46.
Chen Cheng-yih
    1996 *Early Chinese Work in Natural Science*. Hong Kong: Hong Kong University Press.
Chen Meng-jia
    1936 Myth and Shamanism of the Shang Dynasty. *Yanjing Xuebao* 20:485–576.
Chen Xiandan
    1999 The Sacrificial Pits at Sanxingdui: Their Nature and Date. In *Exploring China's Past*. Edited by Roderick Whitfield and Wang Tao. Pp. 165–71. London: Saffron.
Childe, V. Gordon
    1942 *What Happened in History*. Harmondworth: Penguin.
Childs-Johnson, Elizabeth
    1988 Dragons, Masks, Axes and Blades from Four Newly Documented Jade-Producing Cultures of Ancient China. *Orientations* (April):30–37.
    1989 The Shang Bird: Intermediary to the Supernatural. *Orientations* 20(1):53–61.
    1991 Jades of the Hongshan Culture: The Dragon and Fertility Cult Worship. *Arts Asiatique* 46: 82–95.
    1995 Ghost Head Mask and Metamorphic Shang Imagery. *Early China* 20:79–92.
    1998 Metamorphic Imagery in Early Chinese Art. *Kaikodo Journal* 6:30–52.
Ching, Julia
    1997 *Mysticism and Kingship in China*. Cambridge: Cambridge University Press.
Choe, Jing-won
    1989 Shinam-ni Site II. Seoul: Report of the Research of Antiquities, Vol. 21. Seoul: National Museum of Korea.
Chung, Jing-won
    1989 *Shinamni Site II*. Report of the Research of Antiquities, Vol. 21. Seoul:National Museum of Korea.
Claessen, Henri, and Jarich G. Oosten (editors)
    1996 *Ideology and the Formation of Early States*. Leiden: E. J. Brill.

Cohen, David
    2001 *The Yueshi Culture, the Dong Yi, and the Archaeology of Ethnicity in Early Bronze Age China*. Ph.D. Dissertation, Harvard University.
Connelly, Joan B.
    2007 *Portrait of a Priestess: Women and Ritual in Ancient Greece*. Princeton; Princeton University Press.
Cook, Constance A., and Barry B. Blakely
    1999 Introduction, in *Defining Chu, Image and Reality in Ancient China*, C. A. Cook and J. S. Major, eds. Pp.1–5. Honolulu: University of Hawaii Press.
Cook, Constance A., and John S. Major (editors)
    1999 *Defining Chu, Image and Reality in Ancient China*. Honolulu: University of Hawaii Press.
Covell, Alan, and Jon Carter Covell
    1984 *Japan's Hidden History*. Seoul: Hollym.
Crawford, Gary W.
    1992 Prehistoric Plant Domestication in East Asia. In *The Origins of Agriculture, an International Perspective*. Edited by C. W. Cowan and P. J. Watson. Pp. 7–38. Washington, DC: Smithsonian Institution Press.
    2006 East Asian Plant Domestication. In *Archaeology of Asia*. Edited by M. T. Stark. Pp. 77–95. Malden, MA: Blackwell Publishing.
Cullen, Christopher
    1996 *Astronomy and Mathematics in Ancient China: The* Zhoubisuanjing. Cambridge: Cambridge University Press.
Da Gen
    1988 China's Oldest Dragon Figure. *China Reconstructs* (July 1988):46.
Davis-Kimball, Jeannine
    2002 *Warrior Women*. New York: Warner Books, Inc.
    2003 Katuns: The Mongolian Queens of the Genghis Khanite. In *Ancient Queens*. Edited by S. M. Nelson. Pp. 151–73. Walnut Creek: AltaMira Press.
Debaine-Francfort, Corinne
    1995 *Du Neolithique a l'Age du Bronze en China du Nord-ouest*. Paris:University of Paris.
DeGroot, J. J. M.
    1910 *Religious Systems of China*, Vol. 6. Leiden: E. J. Brill.
Derevianko, Anatoly P., and Andrei V. Taborov
    2006 Paleolithic in the Primorye (Maritime) Province. In *Archaeology of the Russian Far East*. Edited by S. M. Nelson, A. P. Derevianko, Y. V. Kuzmin, and R. L. Bland. Pp.41–54. Oxford: British Archaeological Reports.

Deuchler, Martina
    1992 *The Confucian Transformation of Korea*. Cambridge, MA: Council on
        East Asian Studies, Harvard University.
Devlet, Ekaterina
    2001 Rock Art and the Material Culture of Siberia and Central Asia. In
        The Archaeology of Shamanism. Edited by N. Price. Pp.43–55.
        London: Routledge.
DeWoskin, Kenneth J. (translator)
    1983 *Doctors, Diviners, and Magicians of Ancient China*. New York: Colum-
        bia University Press.
Di Cosmo, Nicola
    1999 The Northern Frontier in Pre-Imperial China. In *The Cambridge
        History of Ancient China*. Edited by M. Loewe and E. L. Shaugh-
        nessy. Pp. 885–966. Cambridge: Cambridge University Press.
Dietler, Michael, and Brian Hayden (editors)
    2001 *Feasts, Archaeological and Ethnographic Perspectives on Food, Politics,
        and Power*. Washington, D.C.: Smithsonian Press.
Dyakonova, Vera P.
    2001 Female Shamans of the Turkic-Speaking Peoples of Southern
        Siberia. In *Shamanhood Symbolism and Epic*. Edited by J. Pentika-
        nen. Pp. 63–87. Budapest: Académai Kiad?.
Earle, Timothy
    1997 *How Chiefs Come to Power*. Palo Alto: Stanford University Press.
Eberhard, Wolfram
    1950 *A History of China*. London: Routledge & Kegan Paul.
    1968 *The Local Cultures of South and East China*. Leiden: E. J. Brill.
Eckert, Carter, Kibaek Yi, Young Lew, Michael Robinson, and E. W. Wagner
    1990 *Korea Old and New*. Cambridge, MA: Korea Institute, Harvard Uni-
        versity Press.
Egami, Namio
    1964 The Formation of the People and the Origin of the State in Japan.
        Memoirs of the Toyo Bunko 23:35–70.
    1973 *The Beginnings of Japanese Art*. New York: Weatherhill/Heibonsha.
Eliade, Mircea
    1964 *Shamanism, Archaic Techniques of Ecstasy*. Translated by W. R. Trask.
        Princeton: Princeton University Press.
Ellwood, Robert S.
    1973 *The Feast of Kingship: Accession Ceremonies in Japan*. Tokyo: Sophia
        University.
Elvin, Mark
    2004 *The Retreat of the Elephants: An Environmental History of China*. New
        Haven: Yale University Press.

Fagan, Brian
   2007 *Ancient Lives.* Upper Saddle River, NJ: Pearson Prentice Hall.
Falkenhausen, Lothar von
   1993 *Suspended Music: Chime Bells in the Culture of Bronze Age China.*
      Berkeley: University of California Press.
   1995 Reflections on the Political Role of Spirit Mediums in Early
      China: The Wu Officials in the Shou Li. *Early China*
      20:279–300.
   2006 *Chinese Society in the Age of Confucius: The Archaeological Evidence.*
      Los Angeles: Cotsen Institute of Archaeology, University of Cal-
      ifornia at Los Angeles.
Fang Dianchun, and Wei Fan
   1986 Brief Report on the Excavation of the Goddess Temple and Stone
      Graves of the Hongshan Culture at Niuheliang. *Liaohai Wenwu
      Xuegan* 1986(8):1–17.
Federova, Natalia
   2001 Shamans, Heroes, and Ancestors in the Bronze Castings of West-
      ern Siberia. In *The Archaeology of Shamanism.* Edited by N. Price.
      Pp. 56–64. London: Routledge.
Feinman, Gary and Joyce Marcus (editors)
   1998 *Archaic States.* Santa Fe: SAR Press.
Feng Shi
   2001 *Archaeoastronomy in China.* Beijing: Chinese Academy of Social
      Science.
Firth, Raymond
   1967 *The Work of the Gods in Tikopia.* London: Athlone.
Fitzgerald-Huber, Louisa F.
   1995 Qijia and Erlitou: The Question of Contacts with Distant Cultures.
      Early China 20:17–68.
   1999 Tombs of the Lower Xiajiadian Culture at Dadianzi, Aohanqi, Inner
      Mongolia. In *The Golden Age of Chinese Archaeology.* X. Yang. Pp.
      150–61. New Haven: Yale University Press.
Fitzhugh, William W., Jamstranjav Bayarsaikan, and Peter K. Marsh (editors)
   2005 *The Deer Stone Project.* Washington, D.C.: Arctic Studies Center,
      Smithsonian Institution.
Fitzhugh, William W., and Aron Crowell (editors)
   1988 *Crossroads of Continents: Cultures of Siberia and Alaska.* Washington,
      D.C.: Smithsonian Press.
Flad, Rowan
   2002 Ritual or Structure? Analysis of Burial Elaboration at Dadianzi,
      Inner Mongolia. *Journal of East Asian Archaeology* 3(3–4):23–51.

Flannery, Kent V.
  1972 Cultural Evolution of Civilizations. *Annual Review of Ecological Systematics* 3:399–426.
Frink, Lisa, and Kathryn Weedman (editors)
  2005 *Gender and Hide Production.* Walnut Creek: AltaMira Press.
Fung, Christopher
  1994 The Beginnings of Settled Life. In *China: Ancient Culture, Modern Land.* Edited by R. E. Murowchick. Pp. 51–59. Norman: University of Oklahoma Press.
  2000 The Drinks Are on Us: Ritual, Social Status, and Practice in Dawenko Burials, North China. *Journal of East Asian Archaeology* 21(2):67–92.
Gailey, Christine Ward
  1987 Culture Wars: Resistance to State Formation. In *Power Relations and State Formation.* Edited by T. Patterson and C. Gailey. Pp 35–56. Washington, D.C.: American Anthropological Association.
Gale, Esson M.
  1931 *Discourses on Salt and Iron: A Debate on State Control of Commerce and Industry in Ancient China.* Sinica Leidensis, Vol. 2. Leiden: E. J. Brill.
Gao Qiang and Yun-keun Lee
  1993 Biological Perspective on Yangshao Kinship. *Journal of Anthropological Archaeology* 12:266–98.
Gardiner, Kenneth Herbert James
  1969 *The Early History of Korea.* Honolulu: University of Hawaii Press.
Ge Yan and Katheryn Linduff
  1990 Sanxingdui: a New Bronze Age Site in Southwest China. *Antiquity* 64:505–13.
Glavatskaya, Elena
  2001 The Russian State and Shamanhood: The Brief History of Confrontation. In *Shamanhood, Symbol and Epic.* Edited by J. Pentikainen. Pp 237–48. Budapest: Adacemiai Kiado.
Gorman, Michael S. F.
  1999 *The Quest for Kibi and the True Origins of Japan.* Bangkok: Orchid Press.
Grayson, James H.
  1976 Some Structural Patterns of the Royal Family of Ancient Korea. *Korea Journal* 6(6):27–32.
Gryaznov, Mikhail P.
  1969 *The Ancient Civilization of Southern Siberia.* Translated by James Hogarth. New York: Cowles Book Company, Inc.

Guo Dashun
1995a Hongshan and Related Cultures. In *The Archaeology of Northeast China*. Edited by S. M. Nelson. Pp. 21–64. London: Routledge.
1995b Lower Xiajiadian Culture. In *The Archaeology of Northeast China*. Edited by S. M. Nelson. Pp. 147–81. London: Routledge.
1995c "Northern Type" Bronze Artifacts Unearthed in the Liaoning Region. In *The Archaeology of Northeast China*. Edited by S. M. Nelson. Pp. 182–205. London: Routledge.
1997 Understanding the Ritual Burials of the Hongshan Culture through Jade. In *Chinese Jades*. Edited by R. E. Scott. London: Percival David Foundation.
1999 An Archaeological Investigation of the Wudi. In *Exploring China's Past*. Edited by Roderick Whitfield and Wang Tao. Pp. 45–48. London: Saffron.

Guo Dashun and Ma Sha
1985 Neolithic Cultures of the Liao River Valley and Vicinity. *Kaogu Xuebao* (4):417–44.

Guo Dashun and Zhang Keju
1984 Brief Report on the Excavation of Hongshan Buildings at Dongshanzui in Kazuo County, Liaoning Province. *Wenwu* 1984(110):1–11.

Habu, Junko
2004 *Ancient Jomon of Japan*. Cambridge: Cambridge University Press.

Hamada, Ryosaku
1928 *P'i-Tzu-Wo, Prehistoric Sites by the River Pi-liu-ho, South Manchuria*. Tokyo: Archaeological Orientalis, Vol. 1.

Harris, Victor
2001 *Shinto: The Sacred Art of Ancient Japan*. London: The British Museum Press.

Hays-Gilpin, Kelley
2004 *Ambiguous Images: Gender and Rock Art*. Walnut Creek: AltaMira Press.

Henry, Celia M.
2005 Chinese Beverage Is Ancient History. *Chemical and Engineering News*. January 3:32–33.

Henze, Carl
1962 Die Shamanen Kronen zur Han Zeit in Korea. *Ostasiatische Zeitschrift*. Neu Folge IX, Heft 5.

Hinsch, Brit
2004 Prehistoric Images of Women from the North China Region: The Origins of Chinese Goddess Worship? *Journal of Chinese Religions* (32).

Ho Ping-ti
  1975 *The Cradle of the East*. Chicago: University of Chicago Press.
Hogarth, Hyun-key Kim
  1998 'Trance' and 'Possession Trance' in the Perspective of Korean Shamanism. In *Korean Shamanism: Revivals, Survivals, and Change*. Edited by K. Howard. Pp. 45–54. Seoul: Seoul Press.
Holcombe, Charles
  2001 *The Genesis of East Asia: 221 B.C –A.D. 907*. Honolulu: University of Hawaii Press.
Höllman, Thomas O.
  1986 *Jinan, Die Chu Hauptstadt Ying im China der Sp?teren Zhou-zeit*. Mınchen: Verlag C. H. Beck.
Holt, James
  1948 Some Points of Interest from Han Sung Su's Studies on Megalithic Cultures of Korea. *American Anthropologist* 50:573–74.
Hong, Wontack
  1994 *Paekche of Korea and the Origin of and Yamato Japan*. Seoul: Kudara International.
Howard, Keith
  1998a Korean Shamanism Today. In *Korean Shamanism: Revivals, Survivals, and Change*. Edited by K. Howard. Pp. 1–14. Seoul: Seoul Press.
  1998b Preserving the Spirits? Ritual, State Sponsorship, and Performance. In *Korean Shamanism: Revivals, Survivals, and Change*. Edited by K. Howard. Pp. 91–112. Seoul: Seoul Press.
Hsu, Cho-yun
  1986 *The Origin and Diversity of Axial Age Civilizations*. Edited by S. N. Eisenstadt. Pp. 451-68. Albany: SUNY Press.
Huang, Jinsen
  1984 Changes of Sea Level since the Late Pleistocene in China. In *The Evolution of the East Asian Environment*. Edited by E. O. Whyte. Pp. 309–19. Hong Kong: Centre for East Asian Studies, University of Hong Kong.
Huang, Tsui-Mei
  1992 Liangzhu Late Neolithic Jade-yielding Culture in Southeastern Coastal China. *Antiquity* 66:75–83.
Hudson, Mark J.
  1999 *Ruins of Identity, Ethnogenesis in the Japanese Islands*. Honolulu: University of Hawaii Press.
Hudson, Mark, and Gina Barnes
  1991 Yoshinogari, a Yayoi Settlement in Northern Kyushu. *Monumenta Nipponica* 46(2)211–35.

Humphrey, Caroline
1994 Shamanic Practices and the State in Northern Asia: Views from the Center and Periphery. In *Shamanism, History and the State*. Edited by N. Thomas and C. Humphrey. Pp. 191–228. Ann Arbor: University of Michigan Press.

Humphrey, Caroline, and Urunge Onon
1996 *Shamans and Elders: Experience, Knowledge and Power among Daur Mongols*. Oxford: Clarendon Press.

Hwang Yong-hun
1974 A Study of Prehistoric Cup-marks in Korea. *Journal of Regional Development* 5:21–40.

IACASS (Institute of Archaeology, Chinese Academy of Social Sciences)
1996 *Dadianzi*. Beijing: Science Press.

Ikawa-Smith, Fumiko
1986 Late Pleistocene and Early Holocene Technologies. In *Windows on the Japanese Past*. Edited by R. Pearson. Ann Arbor: Center for Japanese Studies, University of Michigan.
1988 Kamegoaka Social Networks. Paper delivered at the annual meeting of the Society for American Archaeology, Phoenix, Arizona.
1992 Kanjodori; Communal Networks of the Late Jomon in Hokkaido. In *Pacific Northeast Asia in Prehistory*. Edited by M. Aikens and S. N. Rhee. Pp. 83–90. Pullman: Washington State University Press.
1999 The Archeology of East Asia and the Population History of the Japanese Archipelago: A Discussion. *Interdisciplinary Perspectives on the Origins of the Japanese*. Edited by K. Omoto. Pp. 257–64. Kyoto: International Research Center for Japanese Studies.
2000 Younger Dryas Radiocarbon Calibration and the Beginning of Pottery Use in Eastern Asia. Paper delivered at the annual meeting of the Society for American Archaeology, Montreal, Canada.
2002 Gender in Japanese Prehistory. In *In Pursuit of Gender*. Edited by S. M. Nelson and M. Rosen-Ayalon. Pp 323–54. Walnut Creek: AltaMira Press.
2004 Introduction: 'The Scandal,' the Aftermath, and Regaining Legitimacy. In *Recent Paleolithic Studies in Japan*. Tokyo: Japanese Archaeological Association.

Ilyon
1972 *Samguk Yusa*. Translated by Tae-Hung Ha and Grafton Mintz. Seoul: Yonsei University Press.

Im, Hyo-jae, and Kwon Hak-su
1984 *Osanni Site: A Neolithic Village Site on the East Coast*. Seoul: Seoul National University.

Imamura, Keiji
  1996 *Prehistoric Japan: New Perspectives on Insular East Asia*. Honolulu: University of Hawaii Press.
IMT (Inner Mongolian Team, Institute of Archaeology, Chinese Academy of Social Sciences)
  1964 Excavation Report of Fuhegoumen Site, Balin Left Banner. *Kaogu* 1964(1):1–5.
Insoll, Timothy
  2004 *Archaeology, Ritual, Religion*. London: Routledge.
James, Jean M.
  1993. Is It Really a Dragon? Some Remarks on the Xishuipo Burial. *Archives of Asian Art* 66:100–101.
Janelli, Roger A. and Dawnhee Yim Janelli
  1982 *Ancestor Worship and Korean Society*. Stanford: Stanford University Press.
Jensen, Lionel M.
  1997 *Manufacturing Confucianism*. Durham: Duke University Press
Joyce, Rosemary A.
  2000 *Gender and Power in Prehispanic Mesoamerica*. Austin: University of Texas Press.
Juliano, Annette
  1985 Possible Origins of the Chinese Mirror. *Source Notes in the History of Art* 4(2/3):36–50.
Kaner, Simon
  2002 Contexts for Jomon Pottery. *Orientations* (February 1):35–40.
Kang, Bong-won
  2005 An Examination of an Intermediate Sociopolitical Evolutionary Type between Chiefdom and State. *Arctic Anthropology* 42(2):22–35.
Kaogu Xuebao [*Chinese Journal of Archaeology*]
  1978–1990 Beijing: Chung-kuo she hui k'o hsueh yuan K'ao ku yen chiu so.
Karlgren, Bernard
  1946 Legends and Cults of Ancient China. *Bulletin of the Museum of Far Eastern Antiquities* 18:119–365.
Kato, Mieko
  1999 Women's Associations and Religious Expression in the Medieval Japanese Village. In *Women and Class in Japanese History*. Edited by H. Tonomura, A. Walthall, and W. Haruko. Pp. 119–34. Ann Arbor: Center for Japanese Studies, University of Michigan.
Kayamoto Kamejiro
  1961 On the Excavation of the Tomb of Wangkeng, Lelang. *Misul Charyo* 4:17–30.
Kehoe, Alice
  2000 *Shamans and Religion*. Prospect Heights, IL: Waveland Press.

2002 Theaters of Power. In *The Dynamics of Power*. Edited by M. O'Donovan. Pp. 259–72. Carbondale: Center for Archaeological Investigations, Southern Illinois University.

Keightley, David

1978 *Sources of Shang History: The Oracle Bone Inscriptions of Bronze Age China*. Berkeley: University of California Press.

1982 Akatsuka Kiyoshi and the Culture of Early China. *Harvard Journal of Asiatic Studies* 42:299–301.

1983 The Late Shang State: When, Where, and What? In *The Origins of Chinese Civilization*. Edited by D. N. Keightley. Pp. 523–64. Berkeley: University of California Press.

1984 Late Shang Divination: The Magico-Religious Legacy. *Explorations in Early Chinese Cosmology*. Edited by H. Rosemont Jr. Pp.11–34. JAAR Thematic Studies. Chico, CA: Scholar's Press.

1986 The Eastern Yi: Archaeological and Textual Evidence. Paper delivered at Association for Asian Studies Annual Meeting, Chicago.

1994 Sacred Characters. In *China: Ancient Culture, Modern Land*. Edited by R. E. Murowchick. Pp. 70–79. Norman: University of Oklahoma Press.

1998 Shamanism, Death, and the Ancestors: Religious Mediation in Neolithic and Shang China. *Asiatische Studies* 52(3):763–831.

1999a Theology and the Writing of History: Truth and the Ancestors in the Wu Ding Divination Records. *Journal of East Asian Archaeology* 1(1–4):207–30.

1999b The Shang: China's First Historical Dynasty. In *The Cambridge History of Ancient China*. Edited by N. Loewe and E. Shaughnessy. Pp. 232–91. Cambridge: Cambridge University Press.

1999c At the Beginning: The Status of Women in Neolithic and Shang China. *Nan Nu* 1(1):1–63.

1999d The Environment of Ancient China. In *The Cambridge History of Ancient China*. Edited by M. Loewe and E. L. Shaughnessy. Pp. 30–36. Cambridge: Cambridge University Press.

2000 *The Ancestral Landscape: Time, Space and Community in Late Shang China*. Berkeley: Institute of East Asian Studies.

2005 Marks and Labels: Early Writing in Neolithic and Shang China. In *Archaeology of Asia*. Edited by M. T. Stark. Pp.177–201.

Kendall, Laurel

1985 *Shamans, Housewives, and Other Restless Spirits*. Honolulu: University of Hawaii Press.

1998 The Shaman's Journey: Real and Ideal in a Living Folk Tradition. In *Korean Shamanism: Revivals, Survivals, and Change*. Edited by K. Howard. Pp. 91–112. Seoul: Seoul Press.

1996 Korean Shamans and the Spirits of Capitalism. *American Anthropologist* 98(3):512–27.

Kessler, Adam T. (editor)

1994 *Empires beyond the Great Wall.* Los Angeles: Natural History Museum of Los Angeles County.

Kidder, J. Edward, Jr.

1965 *The Birth of Japanese Art.* London: George Allen & Unwin, Ltd.

1966 *Japan before Buddhism.* London: Thames and Hudson.

1972 The Fujinoki Tomb and Its Grave Goods. *Monumenta Nipponica* 42(1):57–87.

Kim Byong-mo

1981 A New Interpretation of Megalithic Monuments in Korea. In *Megalithic Cultures in Asia.* Edited by B. M. Kim. Pp. 164–89. Seoul: Hanyang University Press.

1997 *Gold Crowns Decoded.* Seoul: Purun Yoksa.

Kim Chae-Kuei and Lee Un-chang

1975 *A Report on the Excavation of Tombs at Hwangnam dong, Kyongju.* Yongnam University Museum Monograph No. 1.

Kim Chong-Sun

1977 The Kolpum System; Basis of Silla Stratification. *Journal of Korean Studies* 1(2):43–69.

Kim, Janice C. H.

1998 Processes of Feminine Power: Shamans in Central Korea. In *Korean Shamanism.* Edited by K. Howard. Pp. 113–32. Seoul: Royal Asiatic Society, Korea Branch.

Kim Jong-hak

1977 Excavation Report on Yeanni Tombs. *Hanguk Kogo Hakbo* 2:2–18.

1978 *The Prehistory of Korea.* Translated by R. and K. Pearsons. Honolulu: University of Hawaii Press.

Kim Seong-Nae

1998 Problems in Defining Shaman Types and Local Variations. In *Korean Shamanism: Revivals, Survivals, and Change.* Edited by K. Howard. Pp. 33–44. Seoul: Seoul Press.

Kim Shin-kyu

1966 A Study of Prehistoric Mammals in Korea. *Kogo Minsok* 1966(2):4–7.

Kim Tae-gon

1998 What Is Korean Shamanism? In *Korean Shamanism: Revivals, Survivals, and Change.* Edited by K. Howard. Pp. 15–32. Seoul: Seoul Press.

Kim Won-yong

1976 The Six Villages of Saro and Kyongju Tombs. *Yoksa Hakbo* 70:1–14.

1983 *Recent Archaeological Discoveries in the Republic of Korea.* Paris: UNESCO.

1986 *Art and Archaeology of Ancient Korea.* Seoul: Taekwang Publishing Company.

Kim Won-yong and Richard Pearson
1977 Three Royal Tombs: New Discoveries in Korean Archaeology. *Archaeology* 30(5):302–13.

Kim Yang-chung (editor)
1977 *Women of Korea: A History from Ancient Times to 1995.* Seoul: Ehwa Press.

Knecht, Peter
2003 Aspects of Shamanism: An Introduction. In *Shamans in Asia.* Edited by C. Chilson and P. Knecht. Pp. 1–30. London: Routledge

Kohl, Phillip L.
1981 *The Bronze Age Civilization of Central Asia.* Armonk, NY: M.E. Sharpe.

Kondo Yoshiro
1992 *Tatetsuki Mound of Yayoi Period.* Okayama: Project Committee for Tatetsuki Publication.

Krupp, E. C.
1983 *Echoes of the Ancient Skies.* New York: New American Library.
1997 *Skywatchers, Shamans and Kings.* New York: John Wiley and Sons.

Lebra, William P.
1964 The Okinawan Shaman. In *Ryukuan Culture and Society.* Edited by A. H. Smith. Pp. 93–98. Honolulu: University of Hawaii Press.

Lee Kidong
2004 The Indigenous Religions of Silla: Their Diveristy and Durability. *Korean Studies* 28:49–74.

Lee Yong-jo
1986 Paleolithic Culture in Korea—Especially the Turubong and Suyonggae Sites. In *Special Exhibition of Korean Paleolithic Culture.* Pp. 96–101. Daejeon: Chungbuk National Museum.

Lee Yun Keun and Naicheng Zhu
2002 Social Integration of Religion and Ritual in Prehistoric China. *Antiquity* 76:715–23.

Lei Congyun
1996 Neolithic Sites of Religious Significance. In *Mysteries of Ancient China.* Edited by J. Rawson. Pp. 219–24. New York: Georges Brazillier.

Lerner, Gerda
1986 *The Creation of Patriarchy.* New York: Oxford University Press.

Lewis, Mark Edward
    2000 Continuity and Change. In *China, Empire and Civilization*. Edited by
        E. L. Shaughnessy. Pp.24–43. Oxford: Oxford University Press.
Li Chi
    1977 *Anyang*. Seattle: University of Washington Press.
Li Feng
    2006 *Landscape and Power in Early China*. Cambridge: Cambridge University Press.
Li, Xinwei
    2003 *Development of Social Complexity in the Liaoxi Area, Northeast China*.
        Dissertation, La Trobe University, Bundoora, Victoria, Australia.
Li, Xueqin, Garmon Harbottle, Juzhong Zhang, and Changsui Wang
    2003 The Earliest Writing? Sign Use in the Seventh Millennium BC at
        Jiaihu, Henan Province, China. *Antiquity* 77:31–44.
Linduff, Katheryn
    1995 Zhukaigou, Steppe Culture and the Rise of Chinese Civilization.
        Antiquity 69:133–45.
    1996 Art and Identity: The Chinese and Their "Significant Others" in the
        Shang. In *Culture Contact, History, and Ethnicity in Inner Asia*.
        Edited by M. Gervers and W. Schlep. Pp. 12–48. Toronto:
        Toronto Studies in Central and Inner Asia.
    1997 An Archaeological Overview. In *Ancient Bronzes of the Eastern
        Eurasian Steppes*. Edited by E. Bunker. Pp. 18–112. New York:
        The Arthur M. Sackler Foundation.
    2002 Women's Lives Memorialized in Burial in Ancient China at Anyang.
        In *In Pursuit of Gender: Worldwide Archaeological Perspectives*.
        Edited by S. M. Nelson and M. Rosen-Ayalon. Pp. 257–87. Walnut Creek: AltaMira Press.
    2003 Many Wives, One Queens in Shang China. In *Ancient Queens:
        Archaeological Explorations*. Edited by S. M. Nelson. Pp. pp.
        59–75. Walnut Creek: AltaMira Press.
Linduff, Katheryn M., Han Rubin, and Sun Shuyun
    2000 *The Beginnings of Metallurgy in China*. Lewiston: Edwin Mellen Press.
Linnekin, Joyce
    1990 *Sacred Queens and Women of Consequence*. Ann Arbor: University of Michigan Press.
Liu, Li
    2000 Ancestor Worship: An Archaeological Investigation of Ritual Activities in Neolithic North China. *Journal of East Asian Archaeology* 2(1–2):129–64.

2003 "The Products of Minds as well as Hands": Production of Prestige Goods in the Neolithic and Early State Periods of China. *Asian Perspectives* 42(1):1–40.

2004 *The Chinese Neolithic, Trajectories to Early States.* Cambridge: Cambridge University Press.

Liu, Li, and Xingcan Chen

2003 *State Formation in Early China.* London: Duckworth.

2006 Sociopolitical Change from Neolithic to Bronze Age China. In *Archaeology of Asia.* Edited by M. T. Stark. Pp. 147–76. Malden, MA: Blackwell Publishing.

Lu Liancheng and Yan Wenming

2005 Society during the Three Dynasties. In *The Formation of Chinese Civilization: An Archaeological Perspective.* Edited by K. C. Chang and Pingfang Xu. Pp. 141–202. New Haven: Yale University Press.

Ma Cheng-yuan

1980 The Splendor of Ancient Chinese Bronzes. In *The Great Bronze Age of China.* Edited by Wen Fong. Pp. 1–19. New York: Alfred A. Knopf, Inc.

MacNeish, Richard S., and Jane G. Libby (editors)

1995 *Origins of Rice Agriculture.* Publications in Anthropology No. 13. El Paso: University of Texas at El Paso.

Major, John

1978 Research Priorities in the Study of Chu Religion. *History of Religions* 17(3/4):226–43.

1984 The Five Phases, Magic Squares, and Schematic Cosmography. In *Explorations in Early Chinese Cosmography.* Edited by H. Rosemont. JAAR Thematic Studies 50/2:133–66.

1999 Characteristics of Late Chu Religion. In *Defining Chu Image and Reality in Ancient China.* Edited by C.A. Cook and J. S. Major. Pp. 121–44, 167–69.

Marshack, Alexander

1972 *The Roots of Civilization.* New York: McGraw-Hill.

Maspero, Henri

1978 *China in Antiquity.* Translated by F. A. Kierman Jr. Boston: University of Massachusetts Press.

McCafferty, Geoffrey G., and Sharisse D. McCafferty

2003 Questioning a Queen? A Gender-Informed Evaluation of Monte Albans's Tomb 7. In *Ancient Queens: Archaeological Explorations.* Edited by S. M. Nelson. Pp. 41–58. Walnut Creek: AltaMira Press.

McCune, Evelyn
     1962 *The Arts of Korea*. Rutland, VT: Charles E. Tuttle Co.
Merrifield, Ralph
     1987 *The Archaeology of Ritual and Magic*. London: B.T. Bedsford, Ltd.
Mikami, Tsugio
     1961 *The Dolmens and Stone Cists in Manchuria and Korea*. Tokyo:
          Yoshikawa Kobunkan.
Miller, Roy Andrew
     1971 *Japanese and the Other Altaic Languages*. Chicago: University of
          Chicago Press.
     1980 *Origins of the Japanese Language*. Seattle: University of Washington
          Press.
Mizoguchi, Koji
     2002 *An Archaeological History of Japan, 30,000 B.C. to A.D. 700*. Philadel-
          phia: University of Pennsylvania Press.
Morgan, Lewis Henry
     1887 *Ancient Society*. New York: World.
Mou Yongkang and Wu Ruzuo
     1999 A Discussion on the 'Jade Age.' In *Exploring China's Past*. Edited
          by Roderick Whitfield and Wang Tao. Pp. 41– 44. London:
          Saffron.
Muller, Viana
     1987 Kin Reproduction and Elite Accumulation in the Archaic States of
          Northwest Europe. In *Power Relations and State Formation*.
          Edited by T. Patterson and C. Gailey. Pp 81–97. Washington,
          D.C.: American Anthropological Association.
Munro, Neil Gordon
     1911 *Prehistoric Japan*. Yokohama: no publisher given.
Nagamine Mitsukaza
     1986 Clay Figurines and Jomon Society. In *Windows in the Japanese Past*.
          Edited by R. Pearson. Pp. 255–66. Ann Arbor: Center for Japan-
          ese Studies, University of Michigan.
Naumann, Nelly
     2000 The State Cult of the Nara and Early Heian Periods. In *Shinto in
          History, Ways of the Kami*. Edited by J. Breen and M. Teeuwen.
          pp 47–67. Honolulu: University of Hawaii Press.
Nelson, Sarah Milledge
     1990a The Neolithic of Northeast China and Korea. *Antiquity* 64:234–49.
     1990b Diversity of Upper Paleolithic Figurines and Archaeological
          Mythology. In *Powers of Observation, Alternative Views in Archae-
          ology*. Edited by S. M. Nelson and A. B. Kehoe. Pp. 11-22.

Washington, D.C.: Archaeological Paper No. 2, Archaeology Division, American Anthropology Association.

1991a The Goddess Temple and the Status of Women at Niuheliang, China. In *The Archaeology of Gender*. Edited by D. Walde. Pp. 302–8. Calgary: Archaeological Association of the University of Calgary.

1991b The Statuses of Women in Ko-Shilla: Evidence from Archaeology and Historic Documents. *Korea Journal* 31(2):101–7.

1993a *The Archaeology of Korea*. Cambridge: Cambridge University Press.

1993b Gender Hierarchies and the Queens of Silla. In *Sex and Gender Hierarchies*. Edited by B. Miller. Pp. 297–315. Cambridge: Cambridge University Press.

1994 The Development of Complexity in Prehistoric North China. *Sino-Platonic Papers* 63:1–17.

1995a Ritualized Pigs and the Origins of Complex Society: Hypotheses Regarding the Hongshan Cullture. *Early China* 20:1–16.

1995b Roots of Animism in Korea. In *Korean Cultural Roots*. Edited by H. Kwon. Pp. 19–30. Chicago: North Park College and Seminary.

1996 Ideology and the Formation of an Early State in Northeast China. In *Ideology and the Formation of Early States*. Edited by H. J. M. Claessen and J. G. Oosten. Pp. 153–69. Leiden: Brill.

1998 Pigs in the Hongshan Culture. In *Ancestors for the Pigs: Pigs in Prehistory*. Edited by S. M. Nelson. Pp. 99–107. Philadelphia: MASCA Press.

1999a *Spirit Bird Journey*. Littleton: RKLOG Press

1999b Megalithic Monuments and the Introduction of Rice into Korea. In *The Prehistory of Food, Appetites for Change*. Edited by C. Gosden and J. Hather. Pp 147–65. London: Routledge.

2002a Performing Power in Early China: Examples from the Shang Dynasty and the Hongshan Culture. In *The Dynamics of Power*. Edited by M. O'Donovan. Pp. 151–67. Carbondale: Center for Archaeological Investigations, Southern Illinois University.

2002b Ideology, Power, and Emergent Complex Society in Northeast China. In *In Pursuit of Gender: Worldwide Archaeological Perspectives*. Edited by S. M. Nelson and M. Rosen-Ayalon. Pp. 73–80. Walnut Creek: AltaMira Press.

2003a Feasting the Ancestors in Early China. In *The Archaeology and Politics of Food and Feasting in Early States and Empires*. Edited by T. L. Bray. New York: Kluwer Academic/Plenum Publishers.

2003b The Queens of Silla: Power and Connections to the Spirit World. In *Ancient Queens, Archaeological Explorations*. Edited by S. M. Nelson. Pp. 77–92. Walnut Creek: AltaMira Press.

2003c RKLOG: Archaeologists as Fiction Writers. In *Ancient Muses*. Edited by J. H. Jameson, J. E. Ehrenhard, and C. A. Finn. Pp. 162–68. Tuscaloosa: The University of Alabama Press.

2003d Introduction. In *Ancient Queens, Archaeological Explorations*. Edited by S. M. Nelson. Pp. 1–11. Walnut Creek: AltaMira Press.

2004 *Jade Dragon*. Littleton: RKLOG Press.

2006 Archaeology in the Two Koreas. In *Archaeology of Asia*. Edited by M. Stark. Pp. 37–54. Malden, MA: Blackwell Publishing.

2008 Horses and Gender in Korea: The Legacy of the Steppe on the Edge of East Asia. In *Were All Warriors Male?* Edited by K. Linduff and K. Rubinson. Pp. 111–27. Walnut Creek: AltaMira Press.

In press Cultural and Environmental Change in Coastal Korea. *North Pacific Prehistory*.

Nelson, Sarah M., Hungjen Niu, and Yangjin Pak

2004 Leadership in the Honghsan Culture. Paper delivered at the annual meeting of the Society for American Archaeology, Montreal.

Nelson, Sarah M., R. Matson, R. Roberts, C. Rock, and R. Stencel

2005 Manuscript on file. Archaeoastronomy at Niuheliang.

Nivison, David S.

1995 An Interpretation of the "Shao Gao." *Early China* 20:131–71.

Nivison, David S., and Kevin D. Pang

1990 Astronomical Evidence for the *Bamboo Annals*' Chronicle of Early Xia. *Early China* 15:87–95.

NMK (National Museum of Korea)

1998 *Tracing State Formation Processes in Korea*. Seoul: National Museum of Korea.

2001 *The Ancient Culture of NangNang*. Seoul: The National Museum of Korea

Nowak, M., and S. Durrant

1977 *The Tale of the Nissan Shamaness*. Seattle: University of Washington.

O'Donovan, Maria (editor)

2002 *The Dynamics of Power*. Carbondale: Center for Archaeology, Southern Illinois University.

O'Hara, Albert R.

1971 *The Position of Woman in Early China*. Taipei:Mei Ya Publications.

Okladnikov, Alexei

1981 *Art of the Amur: Ancient Art of the Russian Far East*. Leningrad: Aurora Art Publishers.

Ono, Montonori

1962 *The Kami Way*. Rurland, VT.: C.E. Tuttle.

Pai Hyung Il
    2000 *Constructing "Korean" Origins*. Cambridge: Harvard University Asia
        Center.
Pak, Yangjin
    1999 Contested Ethnicities and Ancient Homelands in Northeast China
        Archaeology: The Case of Koguryo and Puyo. *Antiquity*
        73:613–18.
Pankenier, David W.
    1995 Cosmo-Political Background of Heaven's Mandate. *Early China*
        20:121–76.
    2000 Seeing Stars in the Han Sky. *Early China* 25:185–203.
    2005 Characteristics of Field Allocation (*fenye*) Astrology in Early China.
        In *Current Studies in Archaeoastronomy*. Edited by J. W. Fountain
        and R. M. Sinclair. Pp. 499–514. Durham: Carolina Academic
        Press.
Paper, Jordan H.
    1995 *The Spirits Are Drunk: Comparative Approaches to Chinese Religion*.
        Albany: SUNY Press.
Parker, E. H.
    1890 On Race Struggles in Korea. *Transactions of the Asiatic Society of
        Japan*. 23:137–228.
Pearson, Richard J. (editor)
    1992 *Ancient Japan*. Washington, D.C.: Smithsonian Institution.
    2007 Debating Jomon Social Complexity. *Asian Perspectives* 46(2):361–88.
Pearson, Richard J., Jong-wook Lee, Wonyoung Koh, and Anne Underhill
    1986 Social Ranking in the Kingdom of Old Silla. *Journal of Anthropolog-
        ical Archaeology* 8:1–50.
Piggott, Joan R.
    1989 Sacred Kingship in Early Izumo. *Monumenta Nipponica* 44(1):45–74.
    1997 *The Emergence of Japanese Kingship*. Palo Alto: Stanford University
        Press.
    1999 Chieftain Pairs and Co-rulers: Female Sovereignty in Early Japan.
        In *Women and Class in Japanese History*. Edited by H. Tonomura,
        A. Walthall, and W. Haruko. Pp. 17–62. Ann Arbor: Center for
        Japanese Studies, University of Michigan.
Piggott, Vincent C.
    1996 Review Essay on *Iron and Steel in Ancient China* by D. B. Wagner.
        Asian Perspectives 35(1):88–97
Pirazzoli t'serstevens, Michele
    1982 *The Han Dynasty*. New York: Rizzoli.

Price, Nancy T.
    1995 The Pivot: Comparative Perspectives from the Four Quarters. *Early China* 20:93–120.
Price, Neil (editor)
    2001 *The Archaeology of Shamanism.* London: Routledge.
Pyburn, K. Anne (editor)
    2004 *Ungendering Civilization.* London: Routledge.
Qian Hao
    1981 The Yin Ruins and the Tomb of Fu Hao. In *Out of China's Earth.* Edited by H, Qian, H. Chen, and S. Ru. Pp.19–28. New York: Harry N. Abrams, Inc.
Rapp, Rayna
    1977 The Search for Origins: Unraveling the Threads of Gender Hierarchy. *Critique of Anthropology* 3(9–10):5–24.
Rawson, Jessica (editor)
    1980 *Ancient China: Art and Archaeology.* New York: Harper & Row, Publishers.
    1996 *Mysteries of Ancient China.* New York: Georges Brazilier.
Reid, Anna
    2002 *The Shaman's Coat: A Native History of Siberia.* New York: Walker and Co.
Rhee, Song Nai
    1992 Secondary State Formation: The Case of Koguryo State. In *Pacific Northeast Asia in Prehistory.* Edited by C. M. Aikens and S. N. Rhee. Pp. 191–96. Pullman: Washington State University Press.
Rhee, Song Nai, C. M. Aikens, S. Choi, and H. Ro
    2007 Korean Contributions to Agriculture, Technology, and State Formation in Japan. *Asian Perspectives* 46(2):404–59.
Rogers, J. Daniel
    2007 The Contingencies of State Formation in Eastern Inner Asia. *Asian Perspectives* 46(2):249–74.
Rohrlich, Ruby
    1980 State Formation in Sumer and the Subjugation of Women. *Feminist Studies* 6(1):76–102.
Rokkum, Arne
    1998 *Goddesses, Priestesses, and Sisters: Mind, Gender and Power in the Monarchic Tradition of the Ryukyus.* Oslo: Scandinavian University Press.
    2006 *Nature, Ritual, and Society in Japan's Rkukyu Islands.* London: Routledge.

Rubinson, Karen S.
  1985 Mirrors on the Fringe, Some Notes. *Source Notes in the History of Art* IV (2/3):46–50.
  2002 Through the Looking Glass: Reflections on Mirrors, Gender, and Use among Nomads. In *In Pursuit of Gender*. Edited by S. Nelson and M. Rosen-Ayalon. Pp. 67–72. Walnut Creek: AltaMira Press.

Rudolph, Michael
  2006 Rituals as Authenticating Practices: Contemporary Rituals of Taiwanese Austronesians. Paper delivered at SEAA Conference, Hong Kong.

Said, Edward
  1978 *Orientalism*. New York: Random House.

Sample, L. L.
  1974 Tongsamdong: A Contribution to Korean Neolithic Culture History. *Arctic Anthropology* 11(2):1–125.

Sanday, Peggy Reeves
  1977 *Female Power and Male Dominance: On the Origins of Sexual Inequality*. Cambridge: Cambridge University Press.

Sasaki, Kenichi
  1992 Chohoji-Minamibara Investigations in the Framework of the Kofun Period Archaeology. In *Chohoji-Minamibara Tumulus*. Edited by H. Tsude and S. Fukunaga. Pp. 173–94. Osaka: Osaka University Studies in Archaeology, No. 2.

Schafer, Edward H.
  1973 *The Divine Woman*. Berkeley: University of California Press.

Schwarz, Benjamin
  1985 *The World of Thought in Ancient China*. Cambridge, MA: Harvard University Press.

Schulz, Edward J.
  2004 An Introduction to the *Samguk Sagi*. *Korean Studies* 28:1–13.

Sered, Susan
  1994 *Priestess, Mother, Sacred Sister: Religions Dominated by Women*. Oxford: Oxford University Press.
  1999 *Women of the Sacred Groves*. Oxford: Oxford University Press.

Service, Elman
  1975 *Origins of the State and Civilization: The Process of Cultural Evolution*. New York: W.W. Norton.

Seyock, Barbara
  2004 *Auf den Spuren der Ostbarbaren*. Tubingen: Bunka, Vol. 8.

Shao Wangping
  2005 The Formation of Civilization: The Interaction Sphere of the Longshan Period. In *The Formation of Chinese Civilization: An Archae-*

ological Perspective. Edited by K. C. Chang and Pingfang Xu. Pp. 85–120. New Haven: Yale University Press.

Shaughnessy, Edward L.

2000 The Harmony of Heaven and Earth. In *China, Empire and Civilization*. Edited by E. L. Shaughnessy. Pp. 120–35. Oxford: Oxford University Press.

Shelach, Gideon

1994 Social Complexity in North China during the Bronze Age. *Asian Perspectives* 33(2):261–92.

1999 *Leadership Strategies, Economic Activity, and Interrregional Interact/ion: Social Complexity in Northeast China*. New York: Kluwer Academic/Plenum Publishers.

2000 The Earliest Neolithic Cultures of Northeast China: Recent Discoveries and New Perspectives on the Beginning of Agriculture. *Journal of World Prehistory* 14(4):363–413.

2002 Apples and Oranges? A Cross-Cultural Comparison of Burial Data from Northeast China. *Journal of East Asian Archaeology* 3:53–90.

2004 Marxist and Post-Marxist Paradigms for the Neolithic. In *Gender and Chinese Archaeology*. Edited by K. M. Linduff and Y. Sun. Pp. 11–28. Walnut Creek: Alta Mira Press.

Shelach, Gideon, and Yuri Pines

2006 Secondary State Formation and the Development of Local Identity: Change and Continuity in the State of Qin (770–221 BC). In *Archaeology of Asia*. Edited by M. T. Stark. Pp. 202–30. Malden, MA: Blackwell Publishing.

Shen, Chen

2002 *Anyang and Sanxingdui*. Toronto: Royal Ontario Museum.

Silverblatt, Irene

1988 Women in States. *Annual Review of Anthropology* 17:427–60.

So, Jenny F.

1993 A Hongshan Jade Pendant in the Freer Gallery of Art. *Orientations* 24:87–92.

1999 Chu Art: Link between the Old and New Cook. In *Defining Chu, Image and Reality in Ancient China*. Edited by C. A. Cook and J. S. Major. Pp. 33–50. Honolulu: University of Hawaii Press.

So, Jenny F., and Emma C. Bunker

1995 *Traders and Raiders on China's Northern Frontier*. Seattle: University of Washington Press.

Soffer, Olga

1994 Ancestral Lifeways in Eurasia—the Middle and Upper Paleolithic Records. In *Origins of Anatomically Modern Humans*. Edited by M. H. Nitecki and D. V. Nitecki. Pp 102–19. New York: Plenum Press.

Sohn, Powkee
  1974 Paleolithic Culture of Korea. *Korea Journal* 14(4):4–11.
  1978 The Early Paleolithic Industries of Sokchong-ni, Korea. In *Early Paleolithic in South and East Asia*. Edited by F. Ikawa-Smith. Pp. 233–45. The Hague: Mouton.
Stark, Miriam (editor)
  2005 *Archaeology of Asia*. London: Blackwell Publishing.
Stutley, Margaret
  2002 *Shamanism, an Introduction*. London: Routledge.
Su, Bingqi
  1986 Liaoxi Gu Wenhua Gucheng Gugou. [Western Liao Ancient Culture as an Ancient State]. *Wenwu* 1986(8):41–44.
  1999 A New Age of Chinese Archaeology. In *Exploring China's Past*. Edited by R. Whitfield and Wang Tao. Pp. 17–25. London: Saffron.
Sun Shuodao
  1986 Niuheliang and the Hongshan Culture. *Liaohai Wenwu Xuegan* 1989(1):53–56.
Sun Shuodao and Guo Dashun
  1986a Discovery and Study of the Goddess Head of the Hongshan Culture from Niuheliang. *Wenwu* 1986(8):7–10.
  1986b Hongshan: A Lost Culture. *China Pictorial* 8: 2–7.
Sun, Xiaochun
  2000 Crossing the Boundaries between Heaven and Man: Astronomy in Ancient China. In *Astronomy across Cultures: The History of Non-Western Astronomy*. Edited by H. Selin. Pp. 423–54. London: Kluwer.
Sun Xiaochun and Jacob Kistemaker
  1997 *The Chinese Sky during the Han: Constellating Stars and Society*. Leiden: Brill
Sun Yan
  2004 Gender Ideology and Mortuary Practice in Northwestern China. In *Gender and Chinese Archaeology*. Edited by K. M. Linduff and Y. Sun. Pp. 29–46. Walnut Creek: AltaMira Press.
  2006 Colonizing China's Northern Frontier: Yan and her Neighbors during the Early Western Zhou Period. *International Journal of Historical Archaeology* 10(2):159–78.
Takiguchi Naoko
  2003 Miyako Theology, Shamans' Interpretations of Traditional Belief. In *Shamans in Asia*. Edited by C. Chilson and P. Knecht. Pp. 120–52. London: Routledge.

Tang Jigen
1999 The Burial Ritual of the Shang Dynasty: A Reconstruction. In *Exploring China's Past*. Edited by R. Whitfield and Wang Tao. Pp. 173–88. London: Saffron.
Tedlock, Barbara
2005 *The Woman in the Shaman's Body*. New York: Bantown Books.
Teng Shu-p'ing
1997 A Theory of the Three Origins of Jade Culture in Ancient China. In *Chinese Jades*. Edited by R. E. Scott. Pp. 9–26. London: Percival David Foundation.
Teubal, Sarina J.
1984 *Sarah the Priestess: The First Matriarch in Genesis*. Athens: Swallow Press.
Thomas, Nicholas
1994 Marginal Powers: Shamanism and Hierarchy in Eastern Oceania. In *Shamanism, History and the State*. Edited by N. Thomas and C. Humphrey. Pp. 15–31. Ann Arbor: University of Michigan Press.
Thomas, Nicholas, and Caroline Humphrey
1994 Introduction. In *Shamanism, History and the State*. Edited by N. Thomas and C. Humphrey. Pp, 1–12. Ann Arbor: University of Michigan Press.
Thorp, Robert L.
1980 Burial Practices of Bronze Age China. In *The Great Bronze Age of China*. Edited by Wen Fong. Pp. 51–64. New York: Metropolitan Museum of Art.
2006 *China in the Early Bronze Age*. Philadelphia: University of Pennsylvania Press.
Tong, Enzheng
2002 Magicians, Magic, and Shamanism in Ancient China. *Journal of East Asian Archaeology* 4(1–4):27–74.
Trocolli, Ruth
2002 Mississippian Chiefs: Women and Men of Power. In *The Dynamics of Power*. Edited by M. O'Donovan. Pp. 168–87. Carbondale: Center for Archaeology, Southern Illinois University.
Troy, Lana
2003 She for Whom All That Is Said and Done: The Egyptian Queen. In *Ancient Queens: Archaeological Explorations*. Edited by S. M. Nelson. Pp. 91–116. Walnut Creek: AltaMira Press.

Tylor, R. B.
 1889 *Primitive Culture: Researches into the Development of Mythology, Philosophy, Religion, Language, Art and Custom.* New York: Holt.
Umehara, Sueji
 1926 Deux Grande Decouvertes Archaeologique en Coree. *Revue des Artes Asiatiques* 3:24–33.
Underhill, Anne P.
 1997 Current Issues in Chinese Neolithic Archaeology. *Journal of World Prehistory* 11(2):103–51.
 2000 An Analysis of Mortuary Ritual at the Dawenkou Site, Shandong, China. *Journal of East Asian Archaeology* 2(1–2):93–128.
 2002 *Craft Production and Social Change in Northern China.* New York: Kluwer Academic/Plenum Publishers.
Underhill, Anne P., and Junko Habu
 2005 Early Communities in East Asia: Economic and Sociopolitical Organization at the Local and Regional Levels. In *Archaeology of Asia.* Edited by M. Stark. Pp. 121–48. Malden, MA: Blackwell Publishing.
Van Deusen, Kira
 2001 *The Flying Tiger, Women Shamans and Story Tellers of the Amur.* Montreal: McGill-Queens University Press.
 2004 *Singing Story, Healing Drum: Shamans and Storytellers of Turkic Siberia.* Montreal; McGill-Queens University Press.
Vogel, Melissa A.
 2003 Sacred Women in Ancient Peru. In *Ancient Queens.* Edited by S. M. Nelson. Pp. 117–36. Walnut Creek: AltaMira Press.
Vostretsov, Yuri
 In press The Zaisanovka-7 Site: Maritime Adaptions of Early Cultures in Primorye. *North Pacific Prehistory* 2.
Wagner, Mayke
 1993 Traces of Prehistoric Population and Desertification Processes in Horqin Grassland. In *Proceedings of the Japan-China International Symposium on the Study of Desertification.* Edited by M. Ichikuni. Pp. 54–66. Tsukuba, Japan.
 2006 *Neolithikum und Fruhe Bronzezeit in Nordchina vor 8000 bis 3500 Jahren.* Mainz: Verlag Philipp von Zabern.
Waley, Arthur
 1955 *The Nine Songs: A Study of Shamanism in Ancient China.* London: Allen and Unwin.

Wang, Ying
    2004 Rank and Power among Court Ladies at Anyang. In *Gender and Chinese Archaeology*. Edited by K. M. Linduff and Y. Sun. Pp. 95–116. Walnut Creek: AltaMira Press.
Watson, William
    1991 *Cultural Frontiers in Ancient East Asia*. Edinburgh: Edinburgh University Press.
Wen Fong
    1980 *The Great Bronze Age of China*. New York: Alfred A. Knopf, Inc.
Wenwu Press, Editorial Committee
    1959 *Archaeology in China* (3 Volumes plus Supplement). Beijing: Wenwu Press.
    1983 *Yuanzhunmiao Yangshao Muti*. Beijing: Wenwu Press.
    1994a *Zhongguo Kaogu Wenwu Zhimei* (10 Volumes) [*Beauty of Chinese Archaeological Artifacts*] Volume 2: Yinxu Dixia Guibao: Hehan Anyang Fuhaomu (The Tomb of Lady Hao in Anyang, Henan). Beijing: Wenwu Press.
    1994b *Zhongguo Kaogu Wenwu Zhimei* (10 Volumes) [*Beauty of Chinese Archaeological Artifacts*] Volume 3: Shangdai Shuren Mibao: Sichuan Guanghan Sanxingdui Yiji (Secret Treasures of the Shang People in Sichuan: The Unknown Guanghan Sanxingdui in Sichuan). Beijing: Wenwu Press.
Wolf, Eric
    1990 Facing Power: Old Insights, New Questions. *American Anthropologist* 92(3):586–90.
Wright, Henry T.
    1977 Recent Research on the Origin of the State. *Annual Review of Anthropology* 6:379–97.
Wu Hung
    1995 *Monumentality in Early Chinese Art and Architecture*. Palo Alto: Stanford University Press.
    1999 The Art and Architecture of the Warring States Period. In *The Cambridge History of Ancient China*. Edited by M. Loewe and E. L. Shaughnessy. Pp. 651–744. Cambridge: Cambridge University Press.
Wu, Jui-man
    2004 The Late Neolithic Cemetery at Dadianzi, Inner Mongolia. In *Gender and Chinese Archaeology*. Edited by K. M. Linduff and Y. Sun. Pp. 47–94. Walnut Creek: AltaMira Press.

Wu, K. C.
1982 *The Chinese Heritage: A New and Provocative View of the Origins of Chinese Society*. New York: Crown Publishers, Inc.

Wu Xiaolong
2004 Exotica in the Funerary Debris in the State of Zhongshan. In *Silk Road Exchange in China*. Edited by K. Linduff. *Sino-Platonic Papers* 142:6–16.

Wylie, Alison
1991 Gender Theory and the Archaeological Record: Why Is There No Archaeology of Gender? In *Engendering Archaeology*. Edited by J. Gero and M. Conkey. Pp. 31–54. Oxford: Basil Blackwell.
2002 *Thinking from Things: Essays in the Philosophy of Archaeology*. Berkeley: University of California Press.

Xu, Jay
2001a Sichuan before the Warring States Period. In *Ancient Sichuan, Treasures from a Lost Civilization*. Edited by R. Bagley. Pp. 21–37. Princeton; Princeton University Press.
2001b Bronze at Sanxingdui. In *Ancient Sichuan, Treasures from a Lost Civilization*. Edited by R. Bagley. Pp 59–152. Princeton: Princeton University Press.

Xu Pingfang
1999 Archaeological Research on the Origins of Chinese Civilization. In *Exploring China's Past*. Edited by Roderick Whitfield and Wang Tao. London: Saffron. Pp. 33–40.

Xu Yu-lin
1995 The Houwa Site and Related Issues. In *The Archaeology of Northeast China*. Edited by S. M. Nelson. Pp. 65–88. London: Routledge.

Xue, Zhiquang
1998 The Environmental Changes in Northern China since the Holocene. *Beifang Ming Wenhua* 19(4):62–67.

Yan Wenming
1992 Origins of Africulture and Animal Husbandry in China. In *Pacific Northeast Asia in Prehistory*. Edited by C. M. Aikens and S. N. Rhee. Pp.113–24. Pullman: Washington State University Press.
1999 Neolithic Settlements in China: Latest Finds and Research. *Journal of East Asian Archaeology* 1(1–4):131–48.
2005 The Beginning of Farming. In *The Formation of Chinese Civilization: An Archaeological Perspective*. Edited by K. C. Cahng and P. Xu. Pp. 27–42. New Haven: Yale University Press.

Yang Jianhua
  2007 On the Function of the "Spoon-shaped Artifacts"—The Army and
    Mobilization on the Northern Frontier during the Shang and
    Zhou Dynasties. Paper at the Women's Archaeology Conference,
    Jilin University, China.
Yang, Xiaoneng
  1988 *Sculpture of Neolithic China*. Hong Kong: Tai Dao Publishing Ltd.
  1999 *The Golden Age of Chinese Archaeology*. Washington, D.C.: National
    Gallery of Art.
  2000 *Reflections of Early China: Décor, Pictographs, and Pictorial Inscriptions*.
    Seattle: University of Washington Press.
Yeh Che-min
  1975 Recent Finds of Ancient Pottery and Porcelain. *China Reconstructs*
    24(2):25.
Yi Ki-baek
  1984 *A New History of Korea*. Translated by E. W. Wagner. Cambridge,
    MA: Harvard University Press.
Yi Kon-mu, Yi Kang-sung, Han Yong-hee, Yi Paek-kyu, and Kim Chae-yol
  1989 Excavation of the Proto-Three Kingdoms Site at Dahori, Vichang-
    gun. *Kaogu Hakchi* 1:5–174.
Yoffee, Norman
  2005 *Myths of the Archaic State*. Cambridge: Cambridge University Press.
Yoon, Dong-suk
  1984 *Metallurgical Study of the Early Iron Age Artifacts Found in Kora*.
    Seoul: Pohang Iron and Steel Co. Ltd.
Zaichikov, V. T.
  1952 *Geography of Korea*. New York: Institute of Pacific Relations.
Zhang Juzhong, Xinghua Xiao, and Yunkun Lee
  2004 The Early Development of Music. Analysis of the Jiahu Bone
    Flutes. *Antiquity* 78:769–78.
Zhang Yachu and Liu Yu
  1981–1982 Some Observations about Milfoil Divination Based on Shang
    and Zhou *bagua* Numerical Symbols. Translated by E. Shaugh-
    nessy. *Early China* 7: 46–54.
Zhang Zhongpei
  1985 The Social Structure Reflected in the Yuanjunmiao Cemetery. *Jour-
    nal of Anthropological Archaeology* 4:19–33.
  2005 The Yangshao Period: Prosperity and the Transformation of Prehis-
    toric Society. In *The Formation of Chinese Civilization: An Archae-
    ological Perspective*. Edited by K. C. Chang and P. Xu. Pp. 43–84.
    New Haven: Yale University Press.

Zhao Dianzing

1996 The Sacrificial Pits at Sanxingdui. In *Mysteries of Ancient China*.
Edited by J. Rawson. Pp 232–39. New York: Georges Brazillier.

Zheng Zhenxiang

1997 The Royal Consort Fu Hao and Her Tomb. In *Mysteries of Ancient
China*. Edited by J. Rawson. Pp. 240–47. New York: George
Braziller, Inc.

Zhuschchikovskaya, Irina

2006 Neolithic of the Primorye. In *Archaeology of the Russian Far East*.
Edited by S. M. Nelson, A. P. Derevianko, Y. V. Kuzmin, and R.
L. Bland. Pp. 101–22. Oxford: British Archaeological Reports.

Znamenski, Andrei A.

2003 *Shamanism in Siberia*. Dordrecht: Kluwer.

Index

White Di (Baidi), 165
Wiman Chosun (state), 35
wind, 25, 154
wine, 159
    ritual and, 69, 70, 135–136, 158
    vessels for, 161, 162
women, 95–99
    burials of, 124–125, 173
    dragons and, 39, 129
    exclusion of, 97–98, 210
    as leaders, 85–86, 173, 207, 230–231
    as shamans, 81, 95–98, 222–224, 229, 231
    as shamans in Korea, 183–184, 187–188, 223–224
    spirits and, 99, 209, 211, 231
    status of, 96, 98, 99, 196, 224
    in texts, 95, 97–99
    as warriors, 95, 222
    See also figurines; gender; Lady Hao (Fu Hao); princesses; queens
wonhua (girls' society), 188
writing, 2, 70, 83, 130–133
    divination and, 113, 130
    early evidence for, 36, 112
    in Korea, 182, 188
    origins of, 32, 93, 131
    See also characters (Chinese); oracle bones; turtle shell
Wu (empress), 223
Wu (family name), 71, 156
wu (shaman), 5, 51, 55–56, 61–62, 146, 151–153, 228
    character for, 62, *62*, 66
    dancing by, 69, 159–160, 223
    as elites, 94
    functions of, 11–12, 51, 68, 153
    medicines and, 135
    Shang, 152, 153, 156
    women as, 5, 9, 51
    See also shamans
Wu Di (Five Emperors), 31, 32, 41
Wu Ding (ruler), 91, 100, 104, 154
    innovation and, 166–167, 227
    See also Lady Hao (Fu Hao)

wuism, 55, 61–62, 191
wushu (art of *wu*), 55

X

xi (ritual), 158
xi (shaman), 9, 62, 51, 152
Xia dynasty, 33, 145–149, 151, 161–162
Xiajiadian culture, 149–150
Xiao Shi (flautist), 114
Xiaotun (Shang cult center), 153
Xibeigang (Shang tomb area), 153, 154
xie (ritual), 158
Xindian (site), 134
Xinglonggou (site), 111
Xinglongwa (site and culture), 111, 125, 137, 221
    sculptures from, 120, 121, 127
Xinjiang (site), 43
Xinkailiu culture, 122
Xinle (site), 128, 221
Xishuipo (burial site), 39, 47–49
Xiwangmu (Queen Mother of the West), 95, 157, 163
Xiyin (site), 134

Y

ya (shape), 128
Yakut (people), 187
Yalu (Amnok) River, 27, 181, 182
Yamatai (Yamaichi), 37, 77–79
Yamato (state), 37, 79, 83, 91, 97, 179, 200
Baekje and, 37, 189
Yan, 165
    See also Liaoning (region)
Yangjiawa (site), 127
Yangshao culture, 112, 129, 131–132, 138
    representations and, 130, 158
Yangtze (Changjiang; Yangzi) River, 25, 26
Yao (emperor), 32, 40–41, 114
Yaodian (Canon of Yao; text), 39, 40
yarrow (milfoil), 62, 134–135

About the Author

SARAH MILLEDGE NELSON is John Evans Distinguished Professor at the University of Denver. Nelson is a specialist in cultural development, the origins of agriculture, and gender in the ancient world. She has done extensive fieldwork in Korea, China, and the American West. Her books include *The Archaeology of Korea*, *The Archaeology of Northeast China*, *Handbook of Gender and Archaeology*, *Ancient Queens*, *In Pursuit of Gender*, and two editions of *Gender in Archaeology*, which was designated a Choice Magazine Outstanding Academic Book. She is also author of several novels about the prehistory of East Asia.